Volume 16, Numbers 2&3

S0-BAN-812

Contents

Special Double Issue: Ethics & Professional Persuasion

Foreword   73

Public Relations Ethics: Contrasting Models from the
Rhetorics of Plato, Aristotle, and Isocrates   78
    Charles W. Marsh

Philosophy Meets the Social Sciences: The Nature of
Humanity in the Public Arena   99
    Lee Wilkins and Clifford Christians

Semantics and Ethics of Propaganda   121
    Jay Black

Responding To Propaganda: An Ethical Enterprise   138
    Stanley B. Cunningham

The TARES Test: Five Principles for Ethical Persuasion   148
    Sherry Baker and David L. Martinson

Better Mousetrap? Of Emerson, Ethics, and
Postmillennium Persuasion   176
    Thomas Cooper and Tom Kelleher

Toward a Professional Responsibility Theory of Public
Relations Ethics   193
    Kathy Fitzpatrick and Candace Gauthier

Communication in the Unfettered Marketplace: Ethical
Interrelationships of Business, Government, and Stakeholders   213
    Robert I. Wakefield and Coleman F. Barney

Cases and Commentaries

Was Microsoft's Ad Unacceptably Deceptive   234

Book Reviews

God Is Not Dead, Nor Doth He Sleep   244
    A review by D. Keith Shurtleff

Unplug the Simplicity Drug   247
    A review by Michael M. Monahan

Ted Koppel: We Hardly Want to Know Ye   250
    A review by Paul Martin Lester

Subscriber Information

Journal of Mass Media Ethics (ISSN 0890–0523) is published quarterly by Lawrence Erlbaum Associates, Inc., 10 Industrial Avenue, Mahwah, NJ 07430–2262. Subscriptions for the 2001 volume are available only on a calendar-year basis.

Printed journal subscription rates are $35.00 for individuals and $295.00 for institutions within the United States and Canada; $65.00 for individuals and $325.00 for institutions outside the United States and Canada. Order printed subscriptions through the Journal Subscription Department, Lawrence Erlbaum Associates, Inc., 10 Industrial Avenue, Mahwah, NJ 07430–2262.

Electronic: Full price print subscribers to Volume 16, 2001 are entitled to receive the electronic version free of charge. Electronic-only subscriptions are also available at a reduced price of $265.50 for institutions and $31.50 for individuals.

Change of Address: Send change-of-address notice to Journal Subscription Department, Lawrence Erlbaum Associates, Inc., 10 Industrial Avenue, Mahwah, NJ 07430–2262.

Claims for missing issues cannot be honored beyond 4 months after mailing date. Duplicate copies cannot be sent to replace issues not delivered due to failure to notify publisher of change of address.

Journal of Mass Media Ethics is abstracted or indexed in *Columbia Journalism Review; COM Abstracts; Communication Abstracts; Communication Institute for Online Scholarships; Comserve/ComIndex; Humanities Index; Humanities Abstracts; Media and Values; Nordicom Finland; Public Affairs Information Service.*

Microform copies of this journal are available through Bell & Howell Information and Learning, P.O. Box 1346, Ann Arbor, MI 48106–1346.

Special requests for permission should be addressed to the Permissions Department, Lawrence Erlbaum Associates, Inc., 10 Industrial Avenue, Mahwah, NJ 07430–2262.

Journal of Mass Media Ethics, *16*(2&3), 73–77
Copyright © 2001, Lawrence Erlbaum Associates, Inc..

Foreword

A major frustration of professionals in media fields is the academics who don't provide definitive answers to the important questions. When a professional queries an expert, and expects a "this is what to do" answer, she or he often finds the response lays out a myriad of alternatives, perhaps without even a hierarchy. If, for the professional, closure and solution are discussion goals, scholars exalt discussion with closure low in priority. And so it is, perhaps in spades, with media ethics, particularly on a topic as prickly as professional persuasion.

Asked about allowable ethical limits of deception in professional persuasion, a group of scholars in Park City, Utah in late 2000 certainly plumbed some depths of that well of alternatives. The articles in this special issue on Persuasion resulted from that colloquium and conference.

This issue combines the second and third 2001 issues of the *Journal of Mass Media Ethics* (*JMME*) into a double-length special issue on the topic of examining the applied media ethics question of professional persuasion.

Participants were invited to reason their way toward a threshold that would define acceptable deception for a professional persuader in pursuit of favorable market and public opinion conditions for a client.

Deception is a highly emotional word, of course, particularly for ethics specialists whose mantra always includes truth telling and for journalists whose creed implies creation of an image that will match the reality one encounters, an ultimate commitment to truth. Deception implies creation of false or distorted images and manipulation of vulnerable audiences for selfish purposes.

This group was not much different; they were concerned about playing fair with audiences and creating a level playing field in which audience members have a fair chance to make their decisions. However, the 12 Fellows, and one conference paper author, were also concerned that professional persuaders (in public relations, advertising, and marketing) have elbow room to work their persuasive magic in the competitive environment fostered by a free enterprise, entrepreneurial society.

Whether the Fellows, either individually or as a group, in the pages that follow, reached that goal is problematic, but the series of articles that resulted in this double issue certainly explores the extremes of moral diagnosis. Certainly the conclusions that were reached ranged from offering relatively little leeway to persuaders to suggesting the public good requires a few-holds-barred approach to the battle for the hearts, support, and wallets of America's citizens and consumers.

Approaches range from the specific advice of ancient Greek philosophers on such crass endeavors as persuasion to a pair of modern-day marketers who point out that in a global economy (fueled by pervasive modern electronic communications) in which it is increasingly apparent that nobody is in charge, we all better get ready to survive in a no-holds-barred world.

Such a world will call on all of us, on both sides of the persuasion fence, to develop sophisticated skills for coping with an information world in which there will be little protection from onrushing wolves in many types of masked clothing, but with one intent.

The intent produces a variety of interpretations, of course, from the wolves ensnare innocent lambs with their honeyed messages to a more egalitarian climate in which the lambs learn to cope and to develop a cooperative relationship with persuaders, for the benefit and prosperity of all.

Articles were produced by pairs of Fellows over a 5-month period. Three subsequent days of discussions among the gathered Fellows yielded the final results you see here. In most cases, the pairs were able to agree and produce a single article between them. In one case, two separate articles resulted from fundamental differences in perspective. One article, the opening one, was presented in a 2-day conference that followed the Fellows' deliberations.

Another group of Fellows will gather late October 2001 in Lexington, Virginia at Washington and Lee University searching for universal ethics and media values in a global community. Lou Hodges is organizer of the colloquium of Fellows and Brian Richardson is organizing the conference that follows.

Both the 2000 colloquium in Park City and the 2001 gathering in Virginia are part of a series for the 1st decade of the new millennium that will involve 10 universities or institutions in exploring a spectrum of applied media ethics topics.

The colloquia are sponsored and funded by the hosting institutions, with assistance from Lawrence Erlbaum Associates, Inc., publishers of *JMME;* by the Brigham Young University Department of Communications; and by *JMME.*

The series, appropriate for the dawning of a new millennium, is aimed at expanding interest and participation in the scrutiny of applied media ethics. Each subsequent colloquium will deal with a different topic under the applied media ethic umbrella.

Persuasion was selected as the initial topic because of its pervasive nature in a democratic society. Democracy implies, on the up side, wide public participation. The down side, in the view of many, is the intense effort by many to engineer outcomes of that participation through both the mass media and through interpersonal channels. Given the relatively broad individual freedoms of a democratic society, it would appear outright lies are about the only restrictions that can be placed on persuasive efforts, and even those are spotty.

Therefore, it seems important to look at some dimensions of a threshold that will inform professional persuaders seeking limits to the act. Charles Marsh, of the University of Kansas, leads this expanded issue with a look at the ancients and the examples they set as they dealt with the conflict between adversarial and symmetrical, lining Plato and Aristotle up as advocacy adherents against Isocrates who favored a more symmetrical rhetoric, and concluding that the symmetrical model clearly produced better results over the centuries. Marsh's article was selected as the best research paper in the conference, which succeeded the colloquium.

Contrast the Marsh position with the bookend article at the end of this issue by Robert Wakefield and Coleman Barney. Wakefield, who is now at Brigham Young University-Hawaii, was a professional public relations counselor at the time the article was written, and Barney, a managing director at Solutions Bank, International, a venture capital firm specializing in designing electronic systems for medium-sized corporations, argue that global conditions are opening up virtually all economies and making the entire world a competitive arena in which society is best served by rigorous competitive rhetoric, and consumers are well advised to exercise due diligence in assessing persuasive messages directed their way.

Society is best served by rigorous competitive rhetoric.

Between these articles are a variety of philosophical points ranging from the practical to the abstract. The articles are generally arranged in that order.

Lee Wilkins (University of Missouri) and Cliff Christians (University of Illinois) remind us that differences between news and persuasion are contrasts between informing and manipulating, but are both members of a family whose provenance springs from the analytical nature of the human being and the nature of the process of symbol analysis. They use political communications—a mix of information and persuasion to propose a few moral requirements for persuasive efforts.

With Wilkins and Christians assigning public relations and advertising to the propaganda domain, it is fitting for the next two authors, Jay Black of the University of South Florida-St. Petersburg, and Stan Cunningham of the University of Windsor, to define and dissect that concept. Black defines and explains propaganda and Cunningham, calling it unethical, concentrates on cataloging responses.

For Black, dogmatism seems to be a dividing line in contributors to the open market place of ideas, hinting that open-minded persuaders will more likely bear in mind the needs of audiences than dogmata who advance their cause, no matter what.

Cunningham, although calling propaganda (and presumably persuasion) unethical, resigns himself to its ubiquity and provides a catalog for consumers and identifies targets to combat the scourge "unfettered criticism" and the free speech of response are the only antidotes to propaganda, Cunningham suggests, accepting an argument that "liberal science" provides the only functional response to the ravages of persuasion.

In contrast to Cunningham's assertion that professional persuasion (propaganda) is unethical and needs to be countered, Tom Cooper (Emerson College) and Tom Kelleher (University of Hawaii at Manoa) see such professional persuasion as desirable, if not necessary, in a modern world, but would impose a series of tests on the persuader. Whereas Cunningham might condemn the persuader, Cooper and Kelleher invite persuaders to join the community by caring for their audiences, suggesting that thresholds are possible.

Sherry Baker of Brigham Young University and David Martinson of Florida International University invite persuaders to direct their efforts into a systematic evaluation that involves five principles. Progression through consideration of those principles, they suggest, will encourage actions that are in the common good, meeting needs of both persuaders (perhaps modified) and persuadees.

Kathy Fitzpatrick of the University of Florida, and Candace Gauthier of the University of North Carolina at Wilmington found existing theories and models inadequate to the demands of a professional and formulated a proposal of their own by applying expectation for professionals to the persuaders with special attention to loyalties and obligations. Their applicable principles are of harms, respect for persons, and distributive justice.

Authors of the final article, Robert Wakefield of Brigham Young University-Hawaii and Coleman Barney, a managing director of Solutions Bank International, argue for assigning moral responsibilities to market segments (investors, employees, customers, the community), as well as to the persuaders in an increasingly global economy in which they declare that nobody is in charge. In that context, they see the interaction of the relevant groups, and profit-oriented economies, as imposing a realistic moral compass on the professional persuader.

The Cases and Commentaries section looks at an advertisement in which Microsoft ran afoul of the Federal Trade Commission. Five commentators add their voices to the persuasion question.

A commonality of virtually all the writings in this issue is a concern for audiences (those who are target, persuadee, or likely to be manipulated by persuasive messages). Writers who propose solutions tend to part company there, however, to split between advocating morality that protects audiences or a morality that enlists audiences as morally culpable participants in the process, who should develop the analytical skills that would help them contend with the myriad of conflicting messages they encounter.

All in all, this issue seems to cover a broad range of views and expressions of opinion that often come close to defining the threshold between morally acceptable and morally outrageous persuasion, but for which that precise line in the sand continues to prove elusive. It should provide grist for virtually any reader's mill.

The usual Book Reviews section offers glimpses at current offerings in and related to the media ethics fields.

The Editors

Journal of Mass Media Ethics, *16*(2&3), 78–98
Copyright © 2001, Lawrence Erlbaum Associates, Inc.

Public Relations Ethics: Contrasting Models from the Rhetorics of Plato, Aristotle, and Isocrates

Charles W. Marsh Jr.
University of Kansas

❑ *As a relatively young profession, public relations seeks a realistic ethics foundation. A continuing debate in public relations has pitted journalistic/objectivity ethics
against the advocacy ethics that may be more appropriate in an adversarial society. As
the journalistic/objectivity influence has waned, the debate has evolved, pitting the
advocacy/adversarial foundation against the two-way symmetrical model of public
relations, which seeks to build consensus and holds that an organization itself, not an
opposing public, sometimes may need to change to build a productive relationship.*

*A similar battle between adversarial advocacy and symmetry occurred during the
emergence of rhetoric in the Athens of the 4th century B.C. Plato and Aristotle favored
adversarial/advocacy rhetoric, whereas Isocrates favored a symmetrical rhetoric. Four
criteria of comparison of those rhetorics are examined: success of the respective
schools, success of the respective graduates, the evaluation of later Roman rhetoricians, and the impact on the future of education. History shows that Isocrates's symmetrical rhetoric clearly was more effective than its adversarial/advocacy rivals.
Recent studies of the two-way symmetrical model concur, indicating that it may well
be the most effective foundation for public relations ethics.*

The significance of a study of rhetoric in Athens is not entirely historical.
However indifferent we may be to Protagoras and Gorgias, we live in a world
of journalists, publicists, advertisers, politicians, diplomats, propagandists,
reformers, educators, salesmen, preachers, lecturers, and popularizers.

—E. L. Hunt (1925/1990, p. 161)

One can hardly get through a single day without being exposed dozens of
times to some form of persuasive discourse, the main concern of rhetoric. It is
not too much to claim that rhetoric is the art that governs those human relationships that are conducted in the medium of spoken and written words.

—Corbett (1984/1990b, p. 164)

Although critics sometimes compare public relations to the oldest profession, it is, in fact, relatively young. The Publicity Bureau, considered the first ancestor of modern public relations agencies, opened in 1900 (Cutlip, 1994). In 1923, Edward Bernays and Doris Fleischman first used the term *public relations* to describe their fledgling business (Bernays, 1965). The earliest incarnation of the modern Public Relations Society of America was the National Association of Publicity Directors, founded in 1936 (Cutlip, 1994).

Compared with journalism and advertising, the relative youth of public relations can be seen in its struggle to define itself. Before offering his own definition of the profession, Harlow (1976) found and studied almost 500 definitions of public relations. Small wonder, then, that public relations also wrestles with professional ethics. The Public Relations Society of America adopted its first Code of Professional Standards in 1950 (Guth & Marsh, 2000). However, neither that code nor the ethics code of the International Association of Business Communicators (IABC), founded in 1970, has stilled a continuing debate over "the development of a specifically public relations ethical philosophy" (McBride, 1989, p. 5).

In this article I review the current debate over foundations for public relations ethics. More important, in hopes of offering a solution, I examine a similar controversy over the emerging art of rhetoric in Athens in the 4th century B.C.

Definition of Terms

Harlow's (1976) near 500 definitions suggest the difficulty of defining public relations. In this article, I use a recent, succinct summary of several definitions: "Public relations is the management of relationships between an organization and its publics" (Guth & Marsh, 2000, p. 10). Hunt and Grunig (1994) identified four models of such management:

- The *press agentry/publicity* model, which focuses on gaining favorable media coverage by fair or foul means.
- The *public information* model, which focuses on the dissemination of objective, accurate information to parties that request it.
- The *two-way asymmetrical* model, which focuses on researching targeted publics to gain compliance from them.
- The *two-way symmetrical* model, defined later in this section.

In 1992, the IABC Research Foundation, after a 7-year study, concluded that the most effective model of public relations—that is, the model that best advanced organizations toward their expressed goals—was two-way symmetrical public relations (J. E. Grunig & Grunig, 1992). The foundation provided this definition for the model:

Two-way symmetrical describes a model of public relations that is based on research and that uses communication to manage conflict and improve understanding with strategic publics...(J. E. Grunig, 1992, p. 18). With the
symmetrical model, both the organization and the publics can be persuaded;
both also may change their behavior. (J. E. Grunig & White, 1992, p. 39)

Unlike the other models of public relations, two-way symmetry seeks
win–win relationships and incorporates the willingness of an organization
to change to nurture an important relationship.

Like the phrase *public relations*, the term *rhetoric* eludes easy definition.
In addressing the significant diversity among different rhetorics, Miller
(1993) declared, "We can start by admitting that the rhetorical tradition is a
fiction, and a rather strained one at that" (p. 27). Therefore, in this article I
define rhetoric broadly. According to Corbett (1990a), rhetoric is "the art or
the discipline that deals with the use of discourse, either spoken or written,
to inform or persuade or motivate an audience, whether that audience is
made up of one person or a group of persons" (p. 3). Such a definition fits
well with the four models of public relations.

Review of Literature

Perhaps the clearest early statement of the continuing debate over
"the development of a specifically public relations ethical philosophy"
(McBride, 1989, p. 5). McBride contrasted public relations' "dominant yet
dysfunctional" (p. 5) adherence to journalistic ethics with Bernays's "alternative ethic ... drawing from more similar professions of paid advocates"(p. 15). Because the journalistic ethic means disregarding the
consequences of communications (p. 10), McBride championed Bernays'
advocacy foundation, which "offers more promise for ethical progress"
(p. 6).

The beginnings of the decline of the journalism/objectivity foundation
can be seen in a Wetherell (1989) study that found that although the jour-
nalism-inspired public information model was the second most-practiced
model (behind, unfortunately, press agentry), it ranked last in order of
preference among practitioners (J. E. Grunig & Grunig, 1992). Despite its
decline, however, the journalism/objectivity foundation persists largely
for two reasons:

• Veneration for Ivy Lee's 1906 Declaration of Principles (Guth &
Marsh, 2000), in which Lee pledged "to supply the press and the public of
the United States prompt and accurate information"(p. 64). Olasky (1987),
among others, noted the irony of the profound impact of the declaration despite Lee's many deviations from even a moderately strict interpretation of
his own words.

- The location of public relations programs within schools of journalism, some of which "have added a course or two to existing sequences in journalism and advertise them as bona fide programs in public relations" (Ehling, 1992, p. 457).

The seminal application of the advocacy foundation is Barney and Black's (1994) "Ethics and Professional Persuasive Communication." Barney and Black (1994) held that persuasive communication functions in an adversarial society that, although it cannot condone untruths, must accept the delivery of selective truths by public relations practitioners:

> An adversarial society assumes that spokespersons with alternative views will emerge to balance the advocate. If that doesn't work, some will argue the journalist or some other consumer advocate, motivated by an objectivity and stewardship ethic, will assure some balance in the public messages.
> The reality is that there is no guarantee in the court of public opinion that adversaries will square off. Yet, just as a lawyer has no obligation to be considerate of the weaknesses of his opponents in court, so the public relations person can clearly claim it is another's obligation to provide countering messages....
> In an adversary society, truth is not so important as the obligation of opposing counsel to create scenarios that conflict with those of their opponents. (pp. 241, 244)

Five years later, Barney and Black (1999) still classified public relations practitioners as "an adversary group" (p. 67) and concluded that "persuasion needs a body of moral discussion that will provide the moral foundation on which realistic persuasion ethics structures can be built" (p. 67).
More recently, Guth and Marsh (2000) rejected the objectivity/advocacy bifurcation and called the conflict a "misleading ethics debate" (p. 167):

> The entire objectivity-versus-advocacy debate seems to be based on a misleading question: Are public relations practitioners objective communicators or are they advocates? What if the answer is "none of the above"? Many practitioners respond to the debate by saying that public relations practitioners are, first and foremost, relationship builders.... Sometimes relationship building calls for delivering unpopular truths, either to a public or to the organization itself. And sometimes relationship building involves being an advocate—even if that means advocating the viewpoint of an important public within your own organization. (pp. 170–171)

Guth and Marsh viewed this neither/nor-both/and approach as being the most consistent with two-way symmetrical public relations (p. 169).
Indeed, an increasing focus on communitarianism within public relations is shifting the debate from journalism/objectivity versus advocacy to

two-way symmetry versus advocacy—or, better said, two-way symmetry versus two-way asymmetry. Kruckeberg and Starck (1988) clearly rejected asymmetry in their communitarian view of public relations:

> Our theory is that public relations is better defined and practiced as the active attempt to restore and maintain a sense of community. Only with this goal as a primary objective can public relations become a full partner in the information and communication milieu that forms the lifeblood of U.S. society and, to a growing extent, the world. (p. xi)

K. A. Leeper (1996) added that businesses' increasing focus on "quality, social responsibility, and stewardship" (p. 163) argued for a communitarian foundation for public relations ethics. Finally, Culbertson and Chen (1997) demonstrated that communitarian public relations is a form of the two-way symmetrical model. Although not directly a communitarian philosophy, Habermas' discourse ethics have been offered as a foundation for public relations ethics (J. E. Grunig & White, 1992; R. Leeper, 1996) and have been shown to be closely linked to the two-way symmetrical model (R. Leeper, 1996).

With the IABC Research Foundation's endorsement of "the idealistic social role" (J. E. Grunig & White, 1992, p. 53) as a foundation for effective public relations, the debate in public relations ethics clearly has shifted from an analysis of the merits of journalistic objectivity to a comparison of the relative merits of advocacy/asymmetry and symmetry.

Baker (1999) offered a five-level schema to "capture, systematize, and analyze patterns of thinking about an ethical justification of professional persuasive communication practices (public relations, advertising, marketing)" (p. 69):

- *Self-interest* model: "Look out for number one.... Professional persuaders may use society for their own benefit, even if it is damaging to the social order" (p. 70). In the argot of public relations, this is an asymmetrical model.
- *Entitlement* model: "If it's legal, it's ethical.... The focus is on rights rather than responsibilities" (p. 70). Again, in public relations, this would be an asymmetrical model. Baker places Barney and Black's (1994) advocacy/adversarial society foundation in this model.
- *Enlightened self-interest* model: "One serves one's self-interest by ethical behavior.... Businesses do well (financially) by doing good (ethically)" (p. 70). This is a symmetrical public relations model.
- *Social responsibility* model: "Focus is on responsibilities rather than rights.... Corporate citizens have a responsibility to the societies in which they operate and from which they profit" (p. 70). In public relations, this is a symmetrical model.

- *Kingdom of ends* model: With this model's name taken from Kant's categorical imperative,

> Individuals and corporations take responsibility to promote and create the kind of world and society in which they themselves would like to live. ...Individuals treat others as they would wish to be treated and as others would wish to be treated. (p. 70)

This, of course, is a symmetrical public relations model.

Baker (1999) concluded with a call for additional research: "One area of inquiry might be to explore if and how the [five] baselines correspond to standard measures of moral reasoning" (p. 79).

Statement of Purpose

Given this uncertainty over ethical foundations—part of what Pearson (1992) called the "confusing and contradictory present" of public relations—in this article I examine a similar debate over the nature of rhetoric in 4th-century B.C. Athens. I particularly examine advocacy/adversarial/asymmetrical rhetoric versus symmetrical/relationship-building rhetoric with the aim of seeing which ethical foundation fared better.

Classical Rhetoric's
Search for an Ethical Foundation

A glib response to public relations' search for a resolution of the advocacy-versus-symmetry debate would be to say that time will tell. But perhaps time already has told. The Athens of Plato, Aristotle, and Isocrates (400–300 B.C.) wrestled with developing an acceptable ethical framework for a new art of discourse called *rhetoric*. The comparison is not farfetched: Public relations scholars have long recognized the debt of public relations to Greek rhetoric. In his history of public relations, Cutlip (1994) held that "persuasive communication is as old as Plato's *Republic*" (p. xi). L. A. Grunig (1992) noted that Aristotle is "often considered the first public relations practitioner" (p. 68). In his college textbook *The Practice of Public Relations*, Seitel (1998) wrote that the ethical quandaries of public relations may well have begun with the practice of Greek rhetoric in the 5th century B.C. (pp. 25–26).

Rhetoric was born and flourished in a relentlessly adversarial society. In the decades just before Isocrates's birth in 436 B.C., the city-states of Greece had united in the Delian League to counter the continual threat from Persia. The internal squabbles and rivalries that undermined the Delian League led to the Peloponnesian War, which paralleled the first third of

Isocrates's life. That war, in turn, led to the reemergence of Persia as a threat, which ended only when Philip of Macedonia, the father of Alexander the Great, united Greece through conquest—defeating even Athens in 338 B.C., the year of Isocrates's death. Within Athens itself, Socrates and his student Plato were refining the truth-seeking method known as *dialectic*, "a rigorous form of argumentative dialogue between experts" (Bizzell & Herzberg, 1990, p. 29). Even philosophical truths, it seemed, required adversarial relationships—which could, indeed, become dangerous. At the conclusion of Plato's dialectical *Gorgias* (trans. 1925/1975), Callicles scarcely disguised his threats that accurately forecast the trial and execution of his opponent, Socrates. Half a century later, Aristotle left Athens for a decade to avoid a similar fate. The search for an ethical foundation for rhetoric thus transpired in a decidedly adversarial society.

In his *Phaedrus*, Plato (trans. 1914/1928) foreshadowed Baker's (1999) analysis of ethical foundations by outlining three models of rhetoric. In his earlier *Gorgias* (trans. 1925/1975), Plato bitterly attacked rhetoric for its immorality, for its being "some device of persuasion which will make one appear to those who do not know to know better than those who know" (459C). In the *Phaedrus* (Plato, trans. 1914/1928), however, Plato offers an ethical framework for an acceptable rhetoric. Ostensibly about lovers, the three speeches in the *Phaedrus* establish, as shown by Weaver (1953), three possible ethical frameworks for rhetoric: "What Plato has succeeded in doing in this dialogue ... is to give us embodiments of the three types of discourse. These are respectively the non-lover, the evil lover, and the noble lover" (p. 6).

- The *non-lover* model: This ironic model is introduced when Socrates repeats a speech by Lysias, who maintains that the best lover is one who does not actually love his partner. Therefore, his actions (the lovers of the dialogue were exclusively male) are disinterested; the relationship is not worth striving for. Weaver (1953) maintained that Plato equates this relationship to "semantically purified speech" that "communicates abstract intelligence without impulsion. It is a simple instrumentality, showing no affection for the object of its symbolizing and incapable of inducing bias in the hearer" (p. 7).

This model corresponds to the public information model of public relations, in which organizations deliver objective information to publics that request it. The organization makes no other attempt at relationship building; thus, the model is often ineffective for public relations. Plato's Socrates is so ashamed of repeating a speech that denies the holiness of human relationships that he covers his head as he speaks the words. Plato clearly rejects the disinterested non-lover model as an ethical foundation for rhetoric.

- The *evil-lover* model: This model encompasses the rhetoric that Plato condemned in the *Gorgias*. The evil lover, Weaver (1953) wrote, creates a relationship in which he seeks superiority:

> He naturally therefore tries to make the beloved inferior to himself in every respect. He is pleased if the beloved has intellectual limitations because they have the effect of making him manageable.... In brief, the lover is not motivated by benevolence toward the beloved, but by selfish appetite.... The speech is on the single theme of exploitation. (pp. 10–11)

The evil lover, Weaver (1953) wrote, creates a relationship in which he seeks superiority.

This is the two-way asymmetrical form of rhetoric, a form that promotes advocacy and selective truth. Weaver concluded, "This is what we shall call base rhetoric because its end is the exploitation which Socrates has been condemning" (p. 11).

- The *noble-lover* model: This, of course, is the model that Plato offers as the framework for an ethical rhetoric. The noble lover strives to improve his beloved. In the words of Plato (trans. 1914/1928), noble lovers "exhibit no jealousy or meanness toward the loved one, but endeavour by every means in their power to lead him to the likeness of the god whom they honor" (253C).

As we shall see, Plato accepted the noble-lover model, with, perhaps, surprising results. Aristotle rejected the noble-lover model in favor of the evil-lover model. Isocrates rejected the solutions of both of his contemporaries, opting instead for a new definition of the noble-lover model.

Three Schools of Athenian Rhetoric

Though a proliferation of sophists in Athens from 500 B.C. to 300 B.C. meant a proliferation of different rhetorics, at the height of rhetorical studies in the 4th century B.C. there were three main schools: that of Isocrates, founded in 393 B.C.; that of Plato, founded in 385 B.C.; and that of Aristotle, founded in 335 B.C. Aristotle earlier taught rhetoric in Plato's Academy (Welch, 1990, p. 127). Isocrates (436–338 B.C.) lived long enough to joust with each of his great competitors. Each, as Clark (1957) noted, taught a profoundly different kind of rhetoric:

From the beginning, there were three characteristic and divergent views on rhetoric. There was the moral philosophical view of Plato.... There was the philosophical scientific view of Aristotle, who tried to see the thing as in itself it really was, who endeavored to devise a theory of rhetoric without moral praise or blame for it. There was, finally, the practical educational view of the rhetoricians from Isocrates to Cicero to Quintilian. (pp. 24–25)

A brief expansion of Clark's assessment will underscore the profound differences among the three rhetorics.

Platonic Rhetoric

As seen in the *Gorgias* and the *Phaedrus*, Plato rejected rhetoric unless it was in the service of absolute truth. Rhetoric, he believed, should be the exclusive province of philosophers who, through dialectic, had discovered divine, ultimate truths that predated creation (Kauffman, 1982/1994). The enlightened few were then to use rhetoric to lead the unenlightened masses toward those truths—much as the wise, experienced, noble lover was to lead his young protégé "to the likeness of the god whom they honor" (Plato, trans. 1914/1928, 253C). Two problems with Platonic rhetoric, however, have impeded its progress over time: the near impossibility of ascertaining absolute truth and the rhetoric's aggressive intolerance of opposing viewpoints.

Plato's insistence on unshakable knowledge of absolute truth as a prerequisite to rhetoric is, in the words of Jaeger (1944), "repulsive to ordinary common sense" (p. 57). Indeed, in the *Gorgias* (Plato, trans. 1925/1975, 503B), Socrates can name no one, past or present, capable of such insights, though Plato surely thought both himself and Socrates to be such worthies. E. L. Hunt (1925/1990) concluded, "The ideal rhetoric sketched in the *Phaedrus* is as far from the possibilities of mankind as [Plato's] Republic was from Athens" (p. 149).

Plato's intolerance of dissent has drawn far more critical fire than his demand for knowledge of absolute truth. Plato is "one of the most dangerous writers in human history, responsible for much of the dogmatism, intolerance, and ideological oppression that has characterized Western history," wrote Kennedy (1994, p. 41). Because the Platonic philosopher had, through dialectic, gained knowledge of absolute truth, dissenting opinions were worse than irrelevant; they were dangerous and were to be quashed. Kauffman (1982/1994) labeled Platonic rhetoric "totalitarian and repressive" (p. 101), and Black (1958/1994) maintained that it is a form of "social control" (p. 98). E. L. Hunt (1925/1990) concluded that although Platonic rhetoric promoted goodness, it was "goodness as Plato conceived it" (p. 133).

Two millennia of critical response, thus, have found Platonic rhetoric to be based on an impossible prerequisite and to be dangerously asymmetrical. Apart from his categorization of the possible moral foundations for rhetoric, Plato's greatest contribution to persuasive discourse may have been forcing Aristotle and Isocrates to define and refine reactionary, real-world rhetorics.

Aristotelian Rhetoric

Aristotle, of course, was Plato's student. He heard his master's ideas on rhetoric, rejected the absolute truth foundation, and became, which may initially be surprising, the greatest proponent of evil-lover rhetoric—in other words, of the asymmetrical, adversarial, selective truth discourse that Barney and Black (1994) offered as a logical foundation for modern public relations. Aristotle's (trans. 1954) rejection of the noble-lover framework is immediately apparent in his definition of rhetoric: "Rhetoric may be defined as the faculty of observing in any given case the available means of persuasion" (1355b). Rhetoric, therefore, is not the tool of absolute truth; it is for persuasion in any given case. Kennedy (1994) explained this amoral rhetoric by comparing it to Aristotle's "dispassionate" analyses of plants and animals (p. 56). For Aristotle, rhetoric was simply another topic for his fertile mind to analyze, organize, and put to use.

> *"Rhetoric may be defined as the faculty of observing in any given case the available means of persuasion" (1355b).*

Aristotle's greatest distance from Platonic rhetoric, and his clearest embrace of the evil-lover model, came in his discussions of using deception to lead an audience to a conclusion that may not be true and may not be socially beneficial. This, indeed, goes beyond selective truth into absolute falsehood. For example, Aristotle (trans. 1954) taught that *ethos*, the belief-inducing character of the speaker, need exist only in the speech—not, necessarily, in reality (1356a). *Logos*, strategic appeals to the audience's intellect, can include "wanton falsification in epideictic [ceremonial]" speeches (Wardy, 1996, p. 80). *Pathos*, strategic appeals to an audience's emotions, also can favor appearance over reality:

The aptness of language is one thing that makes people believe in the truth of your story: their minds draw the false conclusion that you are to be trusted from the fact that others behave as you do when things are as you describe them; and therefore they take your story to be true, whether it is so or not. (Aristotle, trans. 1954, 1408a)

Wardy (1996) labeled this last deception "a rampant instance of Plato's worst nightmare" (p. 79)—of rhetoric in the service not of absolute truth, but of falsehood.

Aristotle's analytical amorality was not lost on Cicero (trans. 1990), who, in *De Oratore*, had Crassus wonder if orators truly are capable "in Aristotelian fashion to speak on both sides about every subject and by means of knowing Aristotle's rules to reel off two speeches on opposites sides on every case" (iii, 21). E. L. Hunt (1925/1990) noted that in *On Sophistical Refutations*, Aristotle classified logical fallacies with the purpose of enabling the rhetorician to better use them (p. 157). Like Kennedy (1994), E. L. Hunt concluded, "Aristotle's was a scientific and not a moral earnestness.... He is concerned with rhetorical effectiveness and not with moral justifiability" (p. 156).

Isocratean Rhetoric

Gwynn (1926/1966) wrote of the "radical contrast between the ideals of Plato and Aristotle, and the ideal expressed by Isocrates" (p. 48). The differences between Isocratean rhetoric and the rhetorics of his great contemporaries are, indeed, striking. Isocrates clearly rejected Plato's non-lover and evil-lover models, but instead of opting for the remaining version of the noble lover, he crafted a new definition of that third category, one that is much more symmetrical than Plato's "uncompromising" (Jaeger, 1944, p. 70) rhetoric. Gillis (1969) maintained that *Against the Sophists*, Isocrates' first articulation of his school's philosophy, "is a declaration of war, nothing less" (p. 321) against rhetoric designed "to win cases, not necessarily to serve the truth" (p. 329). According to Poulakos (1997), Isocratean rhetoric is "a rhetoric of unification" (p. xii); Isocrates "made a concerted effort to dissociate manipulative rhetoric from his educational program" (p. 24).

Isocrates's (trans. 1928–1945/1986–1992) distance from Plato can be seen in his disbelief, as stated in the *Antidosis*, in the possibility of discovering absolute truth:

> For since it is not in the nature of man to attain a science by the possession of which we can know positively what we should do or what we should say, in the next resort I hold that man to be wise who is able by his own powers of conjecture to arrive generally at the best course. (271)

Because Isocratean rhetoricians seek unification and consensus—and because they cannot be certain of a divinely ordained best course of action—they consider the interests and arguments of others in a debate.

Isocrates (trans. 1928–1945/1986–1992) clearly did so in his letter *To the Children of Jason:* "I myself should be ashamed if, while offering counsel to others, I should be negligent of their interests and look to my own advantage" (p. 14). This clearly is not the asymmetrical, totalitarian rhetoric of Plato's noble lover.

Isocrates' distance from Aristotle can best be seen in his concept of ethos. Although Aristotle, again, believed that only the appearance of character created during the speech mattered, Isocrates (trans. 1928–1945/ 1986–1992), in the *Antidosis,* took a much more comprehensive view:

> The man who wishes to persuade people will not be negligent as to the matter of character; no, on the contrary, he will apply himself above all to establish a most honourable name among his fellow-citizens; for who does not know that words carry greater conviction when spoken by men of good repute than when spoken by men who live under a cloud, and that the argument which is made by a man's life is of more weight than that which is furnished by words? Therefore, the stronger a man's desire to persuade his hearers, the more zealously will he strive to be honourable and to have the esteem of his fellow citizens. (278)

Far from being an adversarial evil lover whose sole motivation in studying rhetoric is to find the successful means of persuasion, the Isocratean rhetorician seeks to attain goals by building relationships in which both parties win. As Castle (1961) summarized

> [Isocrates's] aim was to discover a new ideal that would inform the study of rhetoric with moral purpose and at the same time preserve its practical relevance to political action.... For Isocrates rhetoric is a culture of the mind; it is the poetry of the political world, through whose study men are made better men by a humane and general culture (*paideia*). (pp. 56–57)

Castle's (1961) focus on "practical relevance to political action" (p. 56) is important, for Isocrates was not a wishful idealist who believed a deferential decency would triumph in all disputes. Instead, Isocrates reinvented Plato's noble lover, crafting a moral, symmetrical, practical rhetoric for the rough-and-tumble world of Athenian and Greek politics. Kennedy (1963) noted that Isocrates wove morality into the fabric of broader rhetorical strategies:

> Sharp focus on a single argument and especially argument from expediency is apparently characteristic of fifth-century deliberative oratory. Toward the end of the century it began to be abandoned in favor of a synthesis of arguments.... In no Greek orator is moral synthesis of arguments so much developed as in Isocrates. (p. 183)

Isocrates' motivation to infuse rhetoric with morality may have been his realization, born of enlightened self-interest, of the persuasive value of true integrity (Welch, 1990, p. 123). Whatever his motivation, however, the results of his philosophy are clear and dramatic: As Marrou (1956) declared, "In the hands of Isocrates rhetoric is gradually transformed into ethics" (p. 89).

If it still seems that Isocratean morality (and consequently this article) strays too far from the grim realties of persuasion in a volatile, adversarial environment, we must remember that during Isocrates's life Athens constantly battled external enemies and that, internally, bitter litigation was virtually a way of life. Isocrates began his career in rhetoric as a speechwriter for litigants. His *Antidosis*, the clearest statement of his philosophy of rhetoric, begins with a fictionalized response to a real lawsuit that he lost. The word *antagonist*, in fact comes to English from Greek, with its root of *agon*, or *conflict*. Isocrates's great English translator, George Norlin (Isocrates, 1925–1945/1991), consistently lauded his subject's unwavering devotion to morality in rhetoric—yet Norlin also asserted that Isocratean rhetoric effectively functioned in the turbulence of Athenian society: "[Isocrates] was in reality a political pamphleteer, and has been called the first great publicist of all time". By almost all accounts, Isocrates developed a moral, functional rhetoric. However, compared with the competing rhetorics of Plato and Aristotle, how did it fare in what Burke (1969) more recently called "the Wrangle of the Marketplace" (p. 23)?

The Triumph of Isocratean Rhetoric

My challenge now is to compare the relative, respective effectiveness of the rhetorics of Plato, Aristotle, and Isocrates. My questions, in brief, are these: In the adversarial society of 4th-century B.C. Athens, did one of these unique rhetorics outperform the others? And, if so, which: one of the asymmetrical rhetorics of Plato and Aristotle or the symmetrical rhetoric of Isocrates? Although no established criteria for such a comparison exist, it seems logical to compare them by what they have in common:

- A school with, consequently, a reputation.
- Graduates of the schools.
- The evaluation of classical Roman rhetoricians, who could survey the whole of classical Greek rhetoric.
- The possibility of shaping future (post 4th-century B.C.) education.

These four criteria do not, of course, directly measure the success of symmetry versus asymmetry. However, as the scholars cited previously—Gillis (1969), Poulakos (1997), Castle (1961), Kennedy (1963), and Marrou

(1956)—noted, symmetry infuses Isocratean rhetoric; any triumph of Isocratean rhetoric is de facto a triumph of symmetry. However, because we cannot directly measure the success of symmetry or asymmetry per se, we are left to measure what we can: the more concrete embodiments of the competing rhetorical philosophies such as schools, graduates, and the written opinions of Roman rhetoricians and modern historians.

The Schools

Following the lead of Cicero (trans. 1878/1970), who in the *Brutus* pronounced, "[Isocrates's] house stood open to all Greece as the *school of eloquence*" (8), historians have given the laurels in this category to Isocrates. Of the three schools, Clark (1957) wrote

> In Greece of the fourth century B.C. there was a three-cornered quarrel among the leading teachers concerning what it takes to make a successful speaker. From this quarrel Isocrates (436–338 B.C.) came out triumphant.... For forty years Isocrates was the most influential teacher in Athens. (pp. 5, 58)

Ample critical commentary supports Clark's judgment. Freeman (1907) asserted that "Isokrates was [rhetoric's] greatest professor" (p. 161). Gwynn (1926/1966) said that Isocrates reigned "high above other teachers of rhetoric" (p. 48). Isocrates's reputation among students outstripped that of Plato (E. L. Hunt, 1925/1990, p. 147) as well as that of Aristotle (Corbett, 1990b, p. 167).

Venerated as Plato's fabled Academy may be, scholars of higher education generally agree that Isocrates' school was more influential in ancient Athens than the Academy. Marrou (1956), who clearly felt more loyalty to Plato (p. 79), grudgingly conceded

> There is no doubt that Isocrates has one claim to fame at least, and that is as the supreme master of oratorical culture.... On the whole, it was Isocrates, not Plato, who educated fourth-century Greece and subsequently the Hellenistic and Roman worlds. (p. 79)

Significantly, Beck (1964, p. 300) and Gwynn (1926/1966) believed that the success of Isocratean education and rhetoric ultimately persuaded Plato to alter both his philosophy of rhetoric and of an ideal, truth-seeking curriculum. Gwynn (1926/1966)wrote

> In the *Laws,* his last attempt to win Athenian opinion for his social and political theories, Plato outlines a programme of educational studies very different from the earlier programme of the *Republic.* Metaphysics are no longer mentioned; and the study of mathematics is reduced to that elementary acquain-

tance with abstract reasoning which even Isocrates would have considered desirable. This is a direct concession to public opinion, made by the most haughtily aristocratic of all Athenian philosophers: a concession, too, which must have been largely due to the success of the Isocratean programme. (pp. 50–51)

There is, thus, compelling evidence that Isocrates had the most effective, influential, and popular school.

The Graduates

As with the three schools of Athenian rhetoric, the most dramatic assessment of the three teachers' students comes from Cicero (trans. 1878/ 1970): "Then behold Isocrates arose, from whose school, as from the Trojan horse, none but real heroes proceeded" (ii, 22). Cicero's contemporary, Dionysius of Halicarnassus (trans. 1974), agreed: "[Isocrates] became…the teacher of the most eminent men at Athens and in Greece at large, both the best forensic orators, and those who distinguished themselves in politics and public life". In his *Institutio Oratio,* Quintilian (trans. 1920/1980) wrote, "The pupils of Isocrates were eminent in every branch of study" (iii, 1), adding that "it is to the school of Isocrates that we owe the greatest orators" (xii, 10).

Among more recent critics, Jebb (1911) echoed Cicero's praise of Isocrates's students and added an anecdote about a 4th-century B.C. oratorical competition:

> When Mausolus, prince of Caria died in 351 B.C., his widow Artemisia instituted a contest of panegyrical eloquence in honour of his memory. Among all the competitors there was not one—if tradition may be trusted—who had not been the pupil of Isocrates. (p. 877)

Although Aristotle had not yet opened his school at the time of this competition, he certainly was teaching rhetoric in Plato's Academy.

In specific comparisons between the abilities of his students and those of his rivals, Plato and Aristotle, Isocrates again prevails. Jaeger (1944) said that there "was no near rival" to the quality of Isocrates' students; of Plato's students, Jaeger said, "Most of them were characterized by their inability to do any real service to [the state] and exert any real influence upon it" (p. 137). Of Aristotle's students, E. L. Hunt (1925/1990) wrote that Aristotle's school "seems to have been productive of little eloquence" (p. 132). Jebb (as cited in Johnson, 1959) added that "Aristotle's school produced not a single orator of note except Demetrius Phalereus; the school of Isocrates produced a host" (p. 25). (Jebb did attribute Isocrates' success more to his insistence on performance than his actual philosophy of rhetoric.) In short, most scholars, past and present, concur with Freeman (1907): "The pupils of Isokrates became the most eminent politicians and the most eminent prose-writers of the time" (p. 186).

Reputation Among Classical Roman Rhetoricians

We already have seen something of the preference of Rome's greatest rhetoricians—Cicero, Dionysius of Halicarnassus, and Quintilian—for Isocrates. Their praise of him was effusive, and their preference for his rhetoric, as opposed to those of Plato or Aristotle, was pronounced. In *De Oratore*, Cicero (trans. 1878/1970) labeled Isocrates "the father of eloquence" (ii, 3) and "the Master of all rhetoricians" (trans. 1990, ii, 22). In the *Brutus*, Cicero (trans. 1878/1970) wrote that Isocrates "cherished and improved within the walls of an obscure academy, that glory which, in my opinion, no orator has since acquired. He…excelled his predecessors" (8). Dionysius (trans. 1974) praised Isocrates's "unrivalled power to persuade men and states" (9). Quintilian (trans. 1920/1980) called Isocrates "the prince of instructors" (ii, 8), and he assigned a higher rank to no one.

Modern critics agree that Isocrates, not Plato or Aristotle, inspired the central rhetorical theorists of classical Rome. Too (1995) wrote that "Scholars in Antiquity and in the Renaissance regarded Isocrates … as the pre-eminent rhetorician of ancient Athens" (p. 1). Katula and Murphy (1994) asserted that "Isocrates' school is largely responsible for making rhetoric the accepted basis of education in Greece and later in Rome. His is the chief influence on the oratorical style and rhetorical theory of Cicero" (p. 46). Welch (1990) noted Isocrates' primary influence on both Cicero's and Quintilian's characterizations of the ideal, moral orator (p. 123).

This preference of the Romans for Isocrates is significant, for the Romans, like the Greeks, lived in an adversarial society. Cicero's (trans. 1990) *De Oratore* is redolent with references to what one speaker in that work called "our political hurly-burly" (i, 18), a phrase that foreshadows Burke's (1969) modern "Wrangle of the Marketplace" (p. 23). *De Oratore* (Cicero, trans. 1990), in fact, is a sustained argument in which Crassus, Cicero's persona, debated the nature of rhetoric with polite but firm adversaries who literally label him "an antagonist" (i, 20). Even his adversaries agreed, however, that Roman society is exhaustingly competitive. Antonius, for example, confessed to being "overwhelmed by the hunt for office and the business of the Bar" (Cicero, trans. 1990, i, 21). Not as fortunate as Crassus in his adversaries, Cicero was murdered by his rivals for power, and "his hands and head—which had written and spoken so powerfully—were nailed over the rostrum in Rome" (Bizzell &

Herzberg, 1990, p. 196). In such a society, Cicero and Quintilian could not afford ineffective rhetoric. Their clear preference for the symmetrical rhetoric of Isocrates is its most compelling endorsement.

Influence on Consequent Education

Isocrates' school, more than those of Plato and Aristotle, developed a comprehensive, liberal education, the goal being to prepare orators to think clearly in a variety of disciplines and to have historical and literary examples readily at hand. "[Isocrates] preached that the whole man must be brought to bear in the persuasive process" said Corbett (1990a), "and so it behooved the aspiring orator to be broadly trained in the liberal arts and securely grounded in good moral habits" (p. 542). The historical impact of this fusion of liberal studies and rhetoric has been profound and un-equalled. "There is no doubt that since the Renaissance [Isocrates] has ex-ercised a far greater influence on the educational methods of humanism than any other Greek or Roman teacher," said Jaeger (1944, p. 46).

Marrou (1956)—who literally apologized for praising Isocrates over Plato (p. 79)—once again conceded that history has favored the ideals of the practical, symmetrical Isocrates over the philosophical, totalitarian Plato:

> It is to Isocrates more than to any other person that the honour and responsi-bility belong of having inspired in our Western traditional education a pre-dominantly literary tone.... On the level of history, Plato has been defeated: posterity has not accepted his educational ideals. The victor, generally speak-ing, was Isocrates. (pp. 79–80, 194)

Like Marrou (1956), E. L. Hunt (1925/1990) had mixed feelings regard-ing the triumph of practicality over speculative philosophy, but he too ac-corded the victory to Isocrates. "Whether for good or ill, the conception of the aims and purposes of the American liberal college, as set forth by the most distinguished modern educators, is much closer to Isocrates and Protagoras than to Plato" (p. 135). Corbett (1989), however, was not quite so guarded in his praise. "[Isocrates] might very well be canonized as the patron saint of all those, then and now, who espouse the merits of a liberal education" (p. 276).

When the merits of the rhetorics of Plato, Aristotle, and Isocrates are compared using the four touchstones of school influence, quality of graduates, influence on Roman rhetoricians, and impact on history, we see that the rhetoric of Isocrates was, by far, the most successful, power-ful, and influential rhetoric of the adversarial society that was classical Greece.

Conclusion

Isocrates created a moral, symmetrical rhetoric that proved to be more effective, immediately and historically, than its asymmetrical rivals in classical Greece. Were we to cast it as an ethics foundation for modern public relations and place it into Baker's (1999) schema, it would, at worst, be an enlightened self-interest model and, at best, a social responsibility model. Both models rank higher than the entitlement model, in which Baker located the advocacy/adversarial society model as articulated by Barney and Black (1994). As Baker (1999) said, "The structure [of the schema] implies that each successive baseline represents a higher moral ground than the one preceding" (p. 69). One possible—indeed probable—conclusion, therefore, is that an effective, achievable ethics foundation for public relations need not function at the relatively low level of the advocacy/adversarial society model.

Recent studies, in fact, support what Isocrates demonstrated and, 2 millennia later, the IABC Research Foundation posited that two-way symmetrical public relations, with its idealistic social role, is the most effective model of public relations. Deatherage and Hazleton's (1998) survey of the Public Relations Society of America members concluded that practitioners who use two-way symmetry build more productive relationships than those who do not. In summary, public relations need not be adversarial. It need not adopt an ethics of asymmetrical advocacy. It can, instead, function admirably (in the several senses of that verb phrase) by following the foundation of Isocratean rhetoric: "to form a genuine 'we' out of diversity" (Poulakos, 1997, p. 3).

References

Aristotle. (1954). *The rhetoric and the poetics of Aristotle* (W. R. Roberts & I. Bywater, Trans.). New York: The Modern Library.

Baker, S. (1999). Five baselines for justification in persuasion. *Journal of Mass Media Ethics, 14,* 69–81.

Barney, R., & Black, J. (1994). Ethics and professional persuasive communication. *Public Relations Review, 20*(3), 233–249.

Barney, R., & Black, J. (1999). Foreword. *Journal of Mass Media Ethics, 14,* 67–68.

Beck, F.A. (1964). *Greek Education, 450–350 B.C.* New York: Barnes & Noble.

Bernays, E.L. (1965). *Biography of an idea: Memoirs of public relations counsel Edward L. Bernays.* New York: Simon & Schuster.

Bizzell, P., & Herzberg, B. (1990). *The rhetorical tradition: Readings from classical times to the present.* Boston: Bedford.

Black, E. (1994). Plato's view of rhetoric. In E. Schiappa (Ed.), *Landmark essays on classical Greek rhetoric* (pp. 83–99). Davis, CA: Hermagoras. (Reprinted from *The Quarterly Journal of Speech, 44,* 361–374, 1958)

Burke, K. (1969). *A rhetoric of motives.* Berkeley, CA: University of California Press.

Castle, E. B. (1961). *Ancient education and today.* Baltimore: Penguin.

Cicero. (1970). *On oratory and orators* (J. S. Watson, Ed. and Trans.). Carbondale, IL: Southern Illinois University Press. (Original work published 1878)

Cicero. (1990). *Of Oratory* (E. W. Sutton & H. Rackham, Trans.). In P. Bizzell and B. Herzberg (Eds.), *The rhetorical tradition: Readings from classical times to the present* (pp. 200–250). Boston: Bedford.

Clark, D. L. (1957). *Rhetoric in Greco-Roman education.* Morningside Heights, NY: Columbia University Press.

Corbett, E. P. J. (1989). Isocrates' legacy: The humanistic strand in classical rhetoric. In R. J. Connors (Ed.), *Selected essays of Edward P.J. Corbett* (pp. 267–277). Dallas, TX: Southern Methodist University Press.

Corbett, E. P. J. (1990a). *Classical rhetoric for the modern student* (3rd ed.). New York: Oxford University Press.

Corbett, E. P. J. (1990b). Introduction to the Rhetoric and Poetics of Aristotle. In E. P. J. Corbett, J. L. Golden, & G. F. Berquist (Eds.), *Essays on the rhetoric of the western world* (pp. 162–167). Dubuque, IA: Kendall/Hunt. (Reprinted from *The Rhetoric and Poetics of Aristotle*, pp. v–xxvi, by E. P. J. Corbett, Ed., 1984, New York: Random House)

Culbertson, H. M., & Chen, N. (1997). Communitarianism: a foundation for communication symmetry. *Public Relations Quarterly, 42*(2), 36–42.

Cutlip, S. M. (1994). *The unseen power.* Hillsdale, NJ: Lawrence Erlbaum Associates, Inc.

Deatherage, C. P., & Hazleton, V. (1998). Effects of organizational worldviews on the practice of public relations: A test of the theory of public relations excellence. *Journal of Public Relations Research, 10*(1), 57–71.

Dionysius of Halicarnassus. (1974). Isocrates. In *Dionysius of Halicarnassus: The critical essays in two volumes* (S. Usher, Trans.). Cambridge, MA: Harvard University Press.

Ehling, W. P. (1992). Public relations education and professionalism. In J. E. Grunig (Ed.), *Excellence in public relations and communication management* (pp. 439–464). Hillsdale, NJ: Lawrence Erlbaum Associates, Inc.

Freeman, K. J. (1907). *Schools of Hellas: An essay on the practice and theory of ancient Greek education.* London: Macmillan.

Gillis, D. (1969). The ethical base of Isocratean rhetoric. *La Parola del Passato, 24,* 321–348.

Grunig, J. E. (1992). Communication, public relations, and effective organizations: An overview of the book. In J. E. Grunig (Ed.), *Excellence in public relations and communication management* (pp. 1–28). Hillsdale, NJ: Lawrence Erlbaum Associates, Inc.

Grunig, J. E., & Grunig, L. A. (1992). Models of public relations and communication. In J. E. Grunig (Ed.), *Excellence in public relations and communication management* (pp. 285–325). Hillsdale, NJ: Lawrence Erlbaum Associates, Inc.

Grunig, J. E., & White, J. (1992). The effect of worldviews on public relations theory and practice. In J. E. Grunig (Ed.), *Excellence in public relations and communication management* (pp. 31–64). Hillsdale, NJ: Lawrence Erlbaum Associates, Inc.

Grunig, L. A. (1992). Toward the philosophy of public relations. In E. L. Toth & R. L. Heath (Eds.), *Rhetorical and critical approaches to public relations* (pp. 65–91). Hillsdale, NJ: Lawrence Erlbaum Associates, Inc.

Guth, D. W., & Marsh, C. (2000). *Public relations: A values-driven approach*. Boston: Allyn & Bacon.

Gwynn, A. O. (1966). *Roman education from Cicero to Quintilian*. New York: Teachers College Press. (Original work published 1926)

Harlow, R. (1976). Building a public relations definition. *Public Relations Review, 2*(4), 36.

Hunt, E. L. (1990). Plato and Aristotle on rhetoric and rhetoricians. In E. P. J. Corbett, J. L. Golden, & G. F. Berquist (Eds.), *Essays on the rhetoric of the western world* (pp. 129–161). Dubuque, IA: Kendall/Hunt. (Reprinted from *Studies in rhetoric and public speaking in honor of James Albert Winans*, pp. 19–70, by A. M. Drummond, Ed., 1925, New York: Century Company)

Hunt, T., & Grunig, J. E. (1994). *Public relations techniques*. Fort Worth, TX: Harcourt Brace.

Isocrates. (1986–1992). *Isocrates* (G. Norlin, Trans., Vols. 1–2; L. R. Van Hook, Trans., Vol. 3). Cambridge, MA: Harvard University Press. (Original translation published 1928–1945)

Isocrates. (1991). *Isocrates* (G. Norlin, Trans., Vol. 1). Cambridge, MA: Harvard University Press. (Original work published 1928–1945)

Jaeger, W. (1944). *Paideia: The ideals of Greek culture: Vol. 3. The conflict of cultural ideals in the age of Plato* (G. Highet, Trans.). New York: Oxford University Press.

Jebb, R. C. (1911). Isocrates. In *Encyclopedia Britannica* (11th ed., Vol. 14, pp. 876–878). Cambridge, England: Cambridge University Press.

Johnson, R. (1959). Isocrates' methods of teaching. *American Journal of Philology, 80*, 25–36.

Katula, R., & Murphy, J. (1994). The sophists and rhetorical consciousness. In R. Katula & J. Murphy (Eds.), *A synoptic history of classical rhetoric* (pp. 17–50). Davis, CA: Hermagoras.

Kauffman, C. (1994). The axiological foundations of Plato's theory of rhetoric. In E. Schiappa (Ed.), *Landmark essays on classical Greek rhetoric* (pp. 101–116). Davis, CA: Hermagoras. (Reprinted from *Central States Speech Journal, 33*, 353–366, 1982)

Kennedy, G. A. (1963). *The art of persuasion in Greece*. Princeton, NJ: Princeton University Press.

Kennedy, G. A. (1994). *A new history of classical rhetoric*. Princeton, NJ: Princeton University Press.

Kruckeberg, D., & Starck, K. (1988). *Public relations and community: A reconstructed theory*. New York: Praeger.

Leeper, K. A. (1996). Public relations ethics and communitarianism: A preliminary investigation. *Public Relations Review, 22*(2), 163–179.

Leeper. R. (1996). Moral objectivity, Jurgen Habermas's discourse ethics, and public relations. *Public Relations Review, 22*(2), 133–151.

Marrou, H. I. (1956). *A history of education in antiquity* (G. Lamb, Trans.). New York: Sheed and Ward.

McBride, G. (1989). Ethical thought in public relations history. *Journal of Mass Media Ethics, 4*, 5–20.

Miller, T. P. (1993). Reinventing rhetorical traditions. In T. Enos (Ed.), *Learning from the histories of rhetoric: Essays in honor of Winifred Bryan Horner* (pp. 26–41). Carbondale: Southern Illinois University Press.

Olasky, M. N. (1987). *Corporate public relations: A new historical perspective.* Hillsdale, NJ: Lawrence Erlbaum Associates, Inc.

Pearson, R. (1992). Perspectives on public relations history. In E. L. Toth & R. L. Heath (Eds.), *Rhetorical and critical approaches to public relations* (pp. 111–130). Hillsdale, NJ: Lawrence Erlbaum Associates, Inc.

Plato. (1928). Phaedrus. In *Euthyphro, Apology, Crito, Phaedo, Phaedrus* (H. N. Fowler, Trans.). Cambridge, MA: Harvard University Press. (Original work published 1914)

Plato. (1975). Gorgias. In *Lysis, Symposium, Gorgias* (W. R. M. Lamb, Trans.). Cambridge, MA: Harvard University Press. (Original work published 1925)

Poulakos, T. (1997). *Speaking for the polis: Isocrates' rhetorical education.* Columbia: University of South Carolina Press.

Quintilian. (1980). *The institutio oratia of Quintilian* (H. E. Butler, Trans). Cambridge, MA: Harvard University Press. (Original work published 1920)

Seitel, F. (1998). *The practice of public relations* (7th ed.). Upper Saddle River, NJ: Prentice Hall.

Too, Y. L. (1995). *The rhetoric of identity in Isocrates.* Cambridge, England: Cambridge University Press.

Wardy, R. (1996). Mighty is the truth and it shall prevail? In A. O. Rorty (Ed.), *Essays on Aristotle's "Rhetoric"* (pp. 56–87). Berkeley: University of California Press.

Weaver, R. M. (1953). *The ethics of rhetoric.* Chicago: Henry Regnery Company.

Welch, K. E. (1990). *The contemporary reception of classical rhetoric: Appropriations of ancient discourse.* Hillsdale, NJ: Lawrence Erlbaum Associates, Inc.

Wetherell, B. J. (1989). *The effect of gender, masculinity, and feminity on the practice of and preference for the models of public relations.* Unpublished master's thesis, University of Maryland, College Park.

Journal of Mass Media Ethics, *16*(2&3), 99–120
Copyright © 2001, Lawrence Erlbaum Associates, Inc..

Philosophy Meets the Social Sciences: The Nature of Humanity in the Public Arena

Lee Wilkins
University of Missouri

Clifford Christians
University of Illinois

❏ *Using a base of philosophical athropology, this article suggests that an ethical analysis of persuasion must include not just the logic human response, but culture and experience as well. The authors propose potential maxims for ethical behavior in advertising and public relations and applies them to two case studies, political advertising and the Bridgestone/Firestone controversy.*

Communications scholars have generally approached persuasion through epistemology and communications theory.

In the first case, establishing the actual effects of the persuasion process has proved to be impossible. Uncertainties remain over the variables that directly influence behavior, and the explicit degree of influence of advertising and public relations stimuli is unknown. Since the beginnings of the culture of consumption in the 1920s, advertising's critics, and the majority of its practitioners, have alleged its "ability to influence us directly to buy particular products or brands" and "to shape the consumption agenda; however, because of the complex environment in which advertising operates, there is often no clear-cut proof of either the presence or absence of these effects on the thinking and/or behavior of individuals" (Rotzoll, 2001, pp. 128, 151). Even with the more sophisticated methodologies today, controversies will continue if epistemology is our framework for understanding the responsibility of public relations practitioners.

In terms of mainstream communications theory, information and propaganda (news and persuasion) are considered two qualitatively different domains. Historically the purpose of the news media has been to discover truth, to present factual evidence on which the public can base its decisions. Information in the news is considered vital to informed public opinion. The press' function is enlightenment through neutral, value-free knowledge. *Persuasion,* on the other hand, is a conscious attempt to control the popular mind. The defining feature is manipulation; audiences are to be mobilized. Therefore, public relations and advertising are not essentially informational but subsets of propaganda.

However, if one considers both information and propaganda part of the larger world of symbol formation, then insisting on an explicit distinction between the two is untenable. As communication theory takes an interpretive turn, all forms of communication are seen as value laden. For Stuart Hall, all communication is ideological, that is, loaded with the ideas and presuppositions of communicators and the patterns of belief that hold societies together. If communication on every level is persuasive, then working on the ethics of news and the ethics of public relations as two genres is based on a false premise.

> *If communication on every level is persuasive, then working on the ethics of news and the ethics of public relations as two genres is based on a false premise.*

It is our contention that the limitations of these two standard approaches have kept persuasion ethics from maturing as a field. We propose another alternative for coming to grips with public relations and ethics. We replace epistemology and communications theory with philosophical anthropology. This enterprise we understand "broadly as the philosophical examination of human nature ..." (Schacht, 1990, p. 157). It examines "what characteristics (if any) are both common and unique to human beings as such", or, in other words, "what the necessary and sufficient conditions of being a human being are" (Schacht, 1990, p. 157; cf. Ricoeur, 1967; Rasmussen, 1971). However, philosophical anthropology is not narrowly and strictly limited to those questions, nor does it presuppose there is "a human essence of some sort" (Schacht, 1990, p. 158). We propose to start over intellectually with persuasion ethics by grounding it in philosophical reflection on the nature of our humanness.[1]

Rational Being

In classical theory, the moral reasoning process begins with the individual, specifically the autonomous moral actor who is considered culpable for choices made.

This view of human nature centers on the uniqueness of the rational faculties in the human species and places extraordinary emphasis on the human actor's capacity for rational thought. "Since Parmenides, Greek philosophy assumed the identity of being and reason" (Niebuhr, 1941/1964, p. 6). *Nous,* the capacity for thought and reason, is a universal and immortal principle. Plato and Aristotle shared a common rationalism as identifying our essential humanness, and a common dualism of mind and body. "In the thought of Aristotle only the active *nous,* precisely the mind which is not involved in the soul is immortal; and for Plato the immutability of ideas is regarded as proof of the immortality of the spirit (*nous*)" (Niebuhr, 1941/1964, p.7).

The Greeks first established rationalist ethics. Once we acquire confidence in reason, we dare "to disobey divine or traditional regulations" (Landman, 1974, p. 110) and instead follow what our inner voice dictates. Philosophical ethics in this tradition is "based on the common principle" that we ought to "do the good which stands the test of reason" (Landmann, 1974, p. 110).

Descartes, the father of philosophy in modernity, portrayed human subjects as "interiorized mental substances" (Schrag, 1997, p. 4). Human bodies are subject to inspection and the laws of mechanics, but human minds are private, metaphysical, and abiding (Schrag, 1997, pp. 11–13).[2] The essence of the self is *res cogitans,* a thinking substance. *Cogito ergo sum,* genuine knowledge is testable and objectively true. It is as cognitively clean as mathematics, built in linear fashion from a neutral, noncontingent starting point.

Humankind is rational being. "What was called thought in the eighteenth century was no longer the Platonic contemplation of ideas to which a realm of essences organized by form was revealed" (Landmann, 1974, p. 120). Rather thought was understood as analytic calculating "that dissolves the world into a mechanical contraption made of quantitative particles and thus makes it technically masterable" (Landmann, 1974, p. 120).

Descartes described this method of reasoning in *His Rules for the Direction of the Mind* (1964):

> Reduce complex and obscure propositions step by step to simpler ones, and then try to advance by the same gradual process from the … very simplest to the knowledge of all the rest.… We should not examine what follows, but refrain from a useless task (pp. 163, 172).

Descartes contended, in effect, that we can demonstrate the truth only of what we can measure. The realm of spirit was beyond such measurement, a matter of faith and intuition, not truth. The physical became the only legitimate domain of knowledge. Science gained a stronghold on truth and narrow calculation was accepted as the ideology by which modernity ought to live.

"The entire eighteenth century fell under the spell of Cartesian rationalism" and its dominance "is bound up with the successful development of the science of mathematics" (Levi, 1959, p. 34). Descartes expressed his delight "at the certitude" of mathematics (1637/1938, p. 7), and the "guiding spirit" of his entire work was to erect a philosophy of nature and a picture of the human person "on a mathematical foundation" (Levi, 1959, p. 34). The scientific successes of the 17th century in astronomy and physics became the structural model for philosophy. The cosmos was seen to mirror in its mathematical and quantitative character the explicitly rational character of human thought (Levi, 1959, pp. 34–35).[3] Thus, the 18th century carries over Newtonian science and Cartesian mathematics into its conception of human nature as defined by rational choice, that is, by the "fixed quantitative judgment" we call "calculation" (Levi, 1959, p. 35). Rational calculation becomes the foundation of utilitarian ethics, for example.

Scientific knowledge dominated by Descartes' mathematical physics is the optimistic version of 1848 which asserted that human thought moves through the stages of religious speculation, then through metaphysical abstractions, and finally to scientific reasoning (Comte, 1848/1910). Instead of the primitive tools of theology and philosophy, social science should be ordered on statistical precision, on sophisticated procedures of induction and logic.

In the first half of the 20th century, logical positivism emerged out of a marriage between Cambridge and Vienna. One of the sacred texts is the three-volume *Principia Mathematica* by Bertrand Russell and Alfred North Whitehead (1910–1913) in which mathematics is established as formal logic. With Russell declaring that "the method adopted by Descartes is right" (Levi, 1959, p. 349; cf. p. 350), in his rationalism the world contains clear and distinct facts and properties that are true if they correspond to reality. In turn building on Russell and Whitehead's seminal work, Rudolph Carnap (1937a, p. xiii; cf. 1937b, pp. 35, 99) of the University of Vienna developed a mature scientific philosophy in which the logical analysis of the languages of science and not metaphysics is the philosophers' task.[4] In logical empiricism, all normative assertions are scientifically unverifiable, and because they are not factually testable are merely "emotion-laden expressions of moral sentiment" (Levi, 1959, p. 345). As Carnap (1937b) put it, "In logic, there are no morals" (p. 52); falling outside of science, morals are irrational. "Being essentially unverifiable," religious, poetic, and ethical assertions "are meaningless; being meaningless, they cannot possibly be true; being incapable of being true, they cannot pretend to make a rational or logical claim upon human choice" (Levi, 1959, p. 377).[5]

Although not replicating the structure and content of logical positivism, the scientific method applied to communications research reflects its mathematical rationality. The groundbreaking work in information signaling by Claude Shannon and Warren Weaver (1949) explicitly adopts the title *The Mathematical Theory of Communication*. In surveys, laboratory experiments and content analyses, communication research in this tradition defines itself with a positivist temper. Methodologies are preoccupied with operational precision, internal and external validity, independent and dependent variables in experimental design, and statistical inferences.

Being-in-the-World

The essentialist paradigm rooted in linear rationality has had its detractors within the Western tradition since classical Greece. The Greeks identified the interpretive impulse as a pervasive condition of human existence. Their philological curiosity brought the hermeneutical consciousness into focus. They located *ars interpretandi* within philosophical anthropology as a property of human beings. Aristotle found *hermeneia* (interpretation) worthy of a major treatise by that title, and he outlined a formal theory of communication in his *Rhetoric*. And as Gadamer reminded us, in the *Nicomachean Ethics*, interpretation is explicit and irreducible, presumed to differ from intellection. *Hermeneia* (in this case, self-knowledge governing moral action) belongs to the higher and purer operations of the mind, but it is not just theoretical knowledge (*episteme*), nor is it practical skill (*techne*) because it concerns more than utility. Making a moral decision, Aristotle argued, entails doing the right thing in a particular circumstance, and this discernment, the moment of interpretation in the concrete situation, requires that we deliberate within ourselves; yet it cannot be confused with logical analysis. In this manner, Aristotle confirmed an orienting process beyond the senses, yet differing from *episteme*.[6]

This willingness to consider interpretation as a valid way of knowing persisted through the centuries. Vico was a professor of rhetoric at the University of Naples for 42 years (1699–1741). The main product of his study was an expansive work called *New Science* (1725/1948). His *Study Methods of our Time* (1709/1965) is a testimony to his genius also, considered by some scholars the most brilliant defense of the humanities ever written. *New Science* was a detailed account of the history of language and cultural customs. He contended, contra Descartes, that philology ought to preoccupy philosophers because language was the central human activity. Mathematics, in his view, was a form of knowledge appropriate to the natural order.[7]

Like Aristotle's *hermeneia*, Vico (1725/1948, pp. 114–137) protected a domain of the mind that coheres in imaging, not in a rational linear process.

He contended that animal rationale is an overdrawn summary, at best, of classical Greek culture. He reminded us that one must account for the Homeric tradition—the dominance of a mythopoetic oral culture, a culture so strong that Plato in his *Republic* seeks to drive it from the city. He stressed the poetic imagination that was far from abstract and rational, but rather felt and experienced. Greek literature includes such dramatists as Aeschylus, Sophocles, Euripedes, and the comic Aristophanes. Vico was at pains to demonstrate that there have always been the alternative voices who recognize an intuitive knowing that transcends the linguistic realm and is broader in scope than rationality alone.

Vico (1725/1948) was fascinated with the human power to give imagistic form to experience—*fantasia* he labeled it (see Verene, 1981). He placed the image over the concept, the mythopoetic over the fact, and language over logic. He redefined science, not as an examination of external events, but as the power of imagination to create reality and give us an inside perspective on it. His highly original theory of imaginative universals was rooted in his conviction that grasping the whole is the flower of wisdom, and it remains an ideal of humanists until now.

Hegel's successor at Berlin, Wilhelm Dilthey, illustrated the ongoing concern in the 19th century for a wholistic understanding of our humanness. He considered *New Science* "one of the greatest triumphs of modern thought" (Dilthey, 1966, vol. 14/2, p. 698) and believed with Vico that understanding (*Verstehen*) was the illuminating and inescapable issue. Dilthey put *Verstehen* into the framework of lived experience (*Erlebnis*). *Erlebnis* becomes the ultimate basis and givenness of knowledge. *Erlebnis* is not an epiphenomenon for him, but an irreplaceable, inexhaustible, and immediate grasp of meaning that underlies reflexive thought.

For Dilthey (1958), lived experience is an ever-flowing stream. The relations of life are historical in nature. Our forms of consciousness and expression are determined by history, he argued: "Life contains as the first categorical definition, fundamental to all others, being in time (*Zeitlichkeit*)" (vol. VI, p. 192). He defined the problem of understanding as recovering a consciousness of our historicality (*Geschichtlichkeit*). Human experience he saw as intrinsically temporal and therefore our understanding of experience must also be commensurately temporal.

While broadening our definition of human beings beyond rational being, the concept of essential human nature prevailed. Insisting on moral discernment beyond the rational faculty, and emphasizing *fantasia* and *verstehen*, did not in themselves deny the notion of essence that is central to the tradition of rational being. Existentialism, whose central figure is Martin Heidegger, contradicted essentialism per se. From his early classic *Being and Time* (Heidegger, 1927/1962) through his last major book in 1958 (*What Is Philosophy*), the presupposition and preoccupation of philosophical inquiry was Being. As a student and later successor of Husserl at the University of Freiburg, he pursued his existentialist agenda through a phenomenological method.

In Heidegger's existentialism, human beingness can be properly known only in its concreteness. Heidegger (1927/1962) called human being *Dasein* (literally meaning "therebeing") to indicate that intentional existence distinguished people from all other entities. The human species actualizes the presence of Being, and Being can show itself only through humanity. Humans alone are the beings to whom all things in the world can reveal themselves as meaningful. Phenomena disclose their is-ness through the human opening. Human beings are "the clearing of Being." Humans are in the peculiar position of raising the problem of Being through their unique self-consciousness. Human beingness is not a static substance, but a situated existent receiving and expressing the significance of things. There is no subject–object dichotomy; "the disclosure of things and the one to whom they are disclosed are co-original" (Hood, 1972, p. 353).

Rather than homo faber (humans as tool makers to meet basic needs such as food and shelter), humans build a world as a struggle to overpower death. Heidegger's being is defined by mortality. "We now call mortals mortal—not because their earthly life comes to an end, but because they are capable of death as death.... Rational living beings must first become mortals" (Heidegger, 1971, p. 179). "Being can only presence itself through death" (Fry, 1993, p. 88).

Cultural Being

We contend that philosophical anthropology be taken seriously, but within it are major disputes over the necessary and sufficient conditions of being human. Therefore, we offer a contemporary definition of Homo sapiens as a cultural being. In this view, "we are language-using and culture-incorporating creatures whose forms of experience, conduct, and interaction take shape in linguistically and culturally-structured environments, and are conditioned by the meanings they bear" (Schacht, 1990, p. 173). This philosophy of humanness is not trapped in the essence–existence dispute. It provides a framework and orientation for public relations policy and practice. Empirical social science gives a description for public relations professionals that resonates with their personal observations of everyday life, but it does not yield normative guidelines for the ways public relations ought to be practiced.

The symbolic motif is nurtured in the 19th century by Frederick Schleiermacher's *Hermeneutik* (1805–1833), August Schleicher's *Comparative Grammar* (1848), Jacob Burckhardt's *Civilization of the Renaissance in Italy* (1860), and George Simmel's *Problems of Philosophy of History* (1892).

It also establishes definitive form in an intellectual trajectory from Ferdinand De Saussure's *Course in General Linguistics* (1916) to Ernst Cassirer's four-volume *Philosophy of Symbolic Forms* (1923–1929/1953–1957/1996). For Cassirer, symbolization is not merely the hallmark of human cognition; our representational capacity defines us anthropologically. Cassirer (1944) titled his summary monograph, *An Essay on Man*. He identified our unique capacity to generate symbolic structures as a radical alternative both to the *animale rationale* of classical Greece and Descartes' modernity, and to the biological being of evolutionary naturalism. Arguing that the issues are fundamentally anthropological rather than epistemological per se, Cassirer's creative being is carved out against a reductionism of intellectus and disciplined thinking on one hand, and a naturalistic neurophysiology and biochemistry on the other.[8]

In this shift from rational being to cultural being, reason is reoriented and redefined, but it does not disappear. Charles Taylor (1985), in fact, on the question of reason saw a "displacement of its center of gravity" but not a major leap "between the traditional formulation of the nature of man" and that "twentieth century thought and sensibility" (p. 217) where language is central to our humanness. The shift takes place within the "thought/language complex, where the intersection is defined by thinking, words, reasoning, and reasoned account" (Taylor, 1985, p. 217). Language is not a vehicle of private meaning and subjectivism, but belongs to a community where it is nurtured in reflection as well as action. Reason is not the domain of my innermost being isolated from communications, as Locke argued, nor is it a separate faculty. However, as humans create worlds through language, this creation itself is permeated by thinking, ideas, analysis, and generalization.

Animale symbolicum contradicts at its roots the stimulus–response model in which stimuli are presumed to impact inert receptacles. Cassirer (1944) collapsed the hoary differences among human symbolic systems. Music, art, philosophical essays, mathematics, religious language, and Bacon's scientific method are placed on a level playing floor. James Carey (1988) called communication as a symbolic process the ritual view—rituals being ceremonies or sacraments in which we define meaning and purpose; they are events of celebration (graduation, weddings, birthdays) and not merely exchanges of information.

Symbol is the critical concept. What atom is to physical science and cell to biology, symbol becomes for communications. Cultures are interconnections of symbolic forms—those fundamental units of meaning expressed in words, gestures, and graphics. Realities called *cultures* are inherited and built from symbols that shape our action, identity, thoughts, and sentiment. Communication, therefore, is the creative process of building and reaffirming through symbols, and culture signifies the constructions that result. Although not identical to that which they symbolize, symbols participate in their meaning and power; they share the significance of that to which they point. In addition, they illuminate their referents so as to make them transparent; they permit us to express levels of reality that otherwise remain hidden.

Because the symbolic realm is considered intrinsic to the human species, this tradition proves particularly significant for communications study. Humans alone of living creatures possess the creative mind, the irrevocable ability to reconstruct, to interpret. From this perspective, communication is the symbolic process expressing human creativity and grounding cultural formation. This definition operates with an integrated but cone-shaped paradigm of ever-broadening categories: symbol, communicative capacity, human species, and culture. Culture is the womb in which symbols are born and communication is the connective tissue in culture building; yet symbols precede culture. Symbol is the basic unit that carries meaning, thus anchors the communicative capacity, which in turn is central to our humanity, and humans are the culture builders. Communication is the catalytic agent, the driving force in cultural formation, and its most explicit expressions are symbolic creations (communications phenomena) such as the dramatic arts, discourse, literature, and electronic entertainment.

Culture is the result of human communicative ability. It is the distinctive and immediate human environment, the human heritage in time and place, built from the material order by men and women's creative effort. Culture is a set of practices, a mode of activity, and a process of creative imagination by which humans construct their environment. As we reduce spatial luxuriance by maps, so we impose organization in all areas to serve human purposes. As the alphabet organizes the complex world of sound into its phonemic parts—into a finite code—so humans find specific forms to endow their existence with order, to preserve what they consider the most important.

The cultural paradigm is decisively value centered. Values, signification, and meaning are the culturalists' stock-in-trade. Presuppositionlessness is considered a myth. If cultures are sets of symbols that orient life and provide it significance, then cultural patterns are inherently normative; they constitute the human kingdom by organizing reality and by indicating what we ought to do and avoid. Assuming that culture is the container of our symbolic capacity, the constituent parts of such containers are a society's values. As ordering relations, values direct the ends of societal practice and provide implicit standards for selecting courses of action. Our concern then is to articulate the appropriate use of language, the ends communication should serve, and the motives it should manifest.

With standards recognized as inherent in the concept of symbolic environments, we can begin putting content into the normative, asking what authentic social existence involves. Communities are knit together linguistically, but because the lingual is not neutral but value laden, our social bonds are moral claims.

Framework for Advertising and Public Relations

Our goal in this article was to begin the process of putting philosophical conceptions of human beings to work as a foundation for public relations ethics. We argue for a cultural definition as escaping the reductionistic and static view of humans as rational beings while bringing our humanness decisively into the public arena. We advocate an integrated view of the human as whole beings—body, mind, and spirit—who create and maintain through language the value-centered world we call culture. By applying that integrated view to persuasion, we suggest it is possible to evaluate in a different way assertions about the way culture-based selves operate. We use it to address the nature of accountability and autonomy, and to orient our thinking about such issues as veracity and role that are the core of many of the professional conundrums that arise in advertising and public relations. This attempt to outline a defensible view of the human based on philosophical anthropology is intended to provide practitioners with evocative ideas with which to assess and invigorate their work. It suggests the implications for humanistic social sciences most adequate for public relations research. In other words, it seeks to make the intellectual contributions of the ivory tower useful in the professional workplace, and in turn aid the academy in understanding the nature of humanity more productively.

Our social bonds are
moral claims.

Dynamic cultural beings bring something to the message, not merely in an individual sense but the capacity to interpret reality that is grounded in shared myths, shared images, and the power to critique. Individual humans have both cognitive and behavioral connections to culture, to other individuals within the culture, and to society that we suggest both precedes and empowers the actualization of self.[9] Specifically, we argue that our robust concept of humanness embedded in culture as a more vital description of 21st-century humanity, means that activities based on caveat emptor lack moral suasion. We suggest instead a moral model of persuasion based on the notion of empowerment for multiple stakeholders. This foundation of empowerment at once allows advertising and public relations practitioners to retain loyalty to their employers and clients, to acknowledge that even autonomous moral actors have moments of greater and lesser autonomy rooted in culture as well as in self, and that community by necessity plays a crucial role in interpreting reality.

In Paulo Freire's (1973) terms, our aim in persuasion is critical consciousness ("conscientization"). The question is how we can empower people to fill their own political space. For Freire, communication is dialogue and culture creation, with human linguistic relations a priori. Thus critical consciousness must always be nurtured dialogically, that is, dialogue is the only morally acceptable instrument of critical consciousness. When we gain our voice and pronounce our own word and project our own destiny, we demonstrate a critical consciousness. Through speaking a true word out of reflection and action, we build a new culture in the interstices and open spaces within the status quo and contrary to the power elite.

Potential Maxims for Ethical Behavior in Persuasion

If our definition of humanity as creator of culture with rational dimensions is accepted, then the following guidelines are appropriate when the issue under discussion is persuasion.

1. Clients and the public need information that gives them "a good reason to adopt a course of action.… A reason to act is a non-arbitrary, thought-satisfying determination supporting one course of action over another" (Koehn, 1998, p. 106).

• In contemporary American democratic society, a single persuasive message exists in an ecology of other messages, many of them persuasive. Social science findings suggest that people do navigate between and among messages, and that they are capable of evaluation. The problem in such a society is when a single message dominates discussion of any particular issue, particularly for lengthy periods of time.

2. Rather than only proffering expert opinion, persuasion should foster ongoing discussion among people so they can explore what opinions are sound and which practical knowledge is superior (Koehn, 1998, p. 113). The aim is critical consciousness.

3. To foster "community of the best sort—an ethically reflective community—requires identification with, total commitment to, immersion in, and ongoing interaction with the community" (Koehn, 1998, p. 119).

• A logical extension of this guideline is that persuasive communication that erodes trust among members of the community or between community members and essential institutions should be considered morally blameworthy. In this sense, selling a product and espousing a particular point of view should not trump essential social connection. Critical consciousness can and does distinguish between the criticism necessary to promote needed change and the sort of cynical communication that makes no distinction between means and ends.

4. Because we are not isolated individuals but cultural beings who create organizations and social structures, we must know the historical background and underlying issues. The question is not merely the personal decisions of executives but enabling individual assessment of institutions and policies.

5. As cultural beings we are situated in such cultural contexts as race, gender, class, and religion. Persuasive discourse must reflect with authenticity those multiple voices and identities.

Having developed these general guidelines, the next step is application.

Application I: The Case for Political Persuasion

Media ethicists have long suggested that political persuasion represents a "special case" through which to examine the ethical issues underlying the persuasive process (Seib, 1995; Denton, 1991). Critical theory, extending at least to the work of Marcuse, makes similarly powerful assertions; political persuasion, because it has the capacity to influence the lives of both individuals and the societies in which they live, represents an important test for any discussion of the ethics of persuasion.

Furthermore, social science has spent a great deal of time investigating at least some of the effects of political persuasion—on both individuals and on institutions and political community. Both schools of thought acknowledge, based on very distinct world views, that people do acquire knowledge based on political communication, including advertising and propaganda, but that the knowledge acquisition is neither universal nor uniform. Political communication can influence both action and belief (cultural) systems; furthermore, action may contradict belief systems. Political communication, then, is part of a communication environment in which the human being exists. It helps people to understand and participate in political culture, it provides part of the necessary impetus to promote and provoke political change, and it can be a stabilizing force within political community—in both a positive and negative sense. Political communication is thus a contributor to human political behavior—it is part of the environment in which the organism functions (Davies, 1964).

For this case study, we consider one small, but important, element of the environment of political communication: political advertising. We base our analysis on the findings of social science research about the impact of political advertising on individuals and larger social institutions. In addition, we imbed our analysis in a robust democratic system; we acknowledge that significant alterations in political culture would have an impact on our discussion.

As the work of Jamieson (2000) and others indicates, political advertising occurs within a media ecology of political messages, some of them news based and others of them more overtly persuasive. This is a system that is open to at least imperfect correction from a multitude of sources—political journalists, opposing candidates, supporters of various candidates, third and fourth political parties, and so forth. We agree with Thomas Jefferson that democracy, although messy and imperfect, does represent the best-to-date effort at human self-governance. Democracy is not a rational process, at least in the sense that Descartes would have acknowledged, but it does represent a robust intersection of narrative, culture, rationality, and emotion where the sort of dynamic human being we have outlined can and does function. It is a reflective equilibrium of sorts, not necessarily lodged only within individuals but lodged within a culture as a whole, where various forces balance one another but where change is sometimes necessary and possible.

In addition, political theorists as well as contemporary social scientists do acknowledge that politics is about community. Political persuasion about politics must respect the power of community, in both a negative and positive sense, as well as the autonomy of the political individual. In such a polity, the oft-stated rationale of persuasion—let the buyer beware—is a distinctly insufficient rationale to justify the content of political persuasion. Instead, we believe a better aphorism in terms of political persuasion in a democratic society is persuasion that allows the "buyer" or citizen to "buy in" to a process that requires and responds—albeit imperfectly—to thoughtful critique. Political persuasion that fundamentally distances the recipient from political community serves no one; it carries within it the seeds of destruction of polity itself.

With the foregoing as background, we posit the following specific maxims for ethical evaluation of political communication.

1. A political ad is ethical when it presents needed information.

Needed information is not always policy based. Recent work indicates that one form of political advertising—the candidate biography—is not only approved of by voters but serves the necessary political function of introducing a candidate, or aspects of a candidate, to the voters. Biographical ads tend to make cultural connections; they allow the voters to decide whether a candidate shares their history and perhaps a world view.

Thus, advertising that accurately recounts the candidate's life history—birth, education, job history, family, and geographic connections—provides voters with important cultural as well as policy information. Vice

President Al Gore's ads emphasizing his life history, particularly his disagreement with his father over the Viet Nam war, would be an example of ethical advertising of this sort.

Biographical ads attempt to place the candidate in a political context, they are open to outside correction, and they provide the voters with reason to consider their sponsor as a possible elected official. In fact, recent work on political advertising indicates that about one third of all political ads fall into the "biographical category" (Benoit, 2000); Jamieson (2000) and her colleagues have discovered that voters find them worthwhile.

In our view, a more troubling kind of advertising—the political image ad perhaps best captured in former President Ronald Reagan's "morning in America" ad campaign—would only marginally meet this test. This series of ads provoked an emotional response without providing much information. As such, they were models of highly produced political vagueness. They call on culture, an important component of politics, but blunt reflection. And, because many of the "claims" in such ads are couched in their visual content—content that, as many scholars have noted, is designed to bypass some of the brain's more logic-based cognitive structures—they appear to attempt to substitute emotion for reason.

2. A political ad is ethical when it provides a logical and/or emotional reason to vote for a particular candidate providing that appeal allows for counterargument and reflection.

Our inclusion of emotion in this maxim is deliberate. People can be appropriately emotionally moved by political choices. Some of those emotional responses are what the Greeks would have categorized as base, for example fear of the outsider that the infamous Willie Horton ad came to epitomize. But other emotions arise from connection. Political ads that focus on issues surrounding education or the provision of various services and entitlements for the elderly rightly stir those who are concerned with immediate and social connections.

Counterargument and reflection can, of course, be promoted in a variety of ways. Furthermore, our base emotions, although they can be intransigent, can also be modified through the collection of additional information and reflection. Recent scholarly work indicates that one of the most common methods to encourage reflection is the "contrast" ad where the stances of candidates on specific public policy issues are compared. Such contrast ads have several virtues: They are information rich, within the ad itself there is a call for reflective comparison, and voters do not perceive them as a political "turn off" (Jamieson, 2000, p. 77). In short, for one candidate to subject an opponent's policy stance to comparison is the stuff of political debate as the founders probably intended it.

Similarly, ads that employ subliminal messages (the now well-known "bureaucRATS" ad recently pulled by the George W. Bush campaign) that distort an opponents' record (by the misleading use of graphics or editing the candidate's words or votes out of context), or that emerge at a time in the campaign (the last 24–48 hr) when corrective response is logistically impossible, all would fail to meet this test.

So, too, would negative or attack political advertising that does not employ comparison or that attempts to campaign against the system without providing reasons. Some negative political advertising employs other questionable techniques, among them deception, ridicule, invidious comparison, hate mongering, and so forth. But most important, voters find them a political turnoff; they eat away at the connections that are the core of the democratic electoral process. Also, recent research indicates that voters are fairly savvy about negative ads and that they dislike them (Jamieson, 2000). In addition, the dislike often backfires on the campaign individual voters believe promulgated the negative ads.

Although negative advertising is subject to correction, it often takes that correction some time to permeate political discourse. What cannot be corrected, however, is the increasing load of cynicism that negative political advertising contributes to the cultural understanding of politics.

These two maxims, of course, do not cover all the various forms of political advertising that will be created in the next century. However, we suggest that they fall within the general guidelines for persuasion that we propose and that they can be applied broadly in a democratic society. At least as important, they do not appear to contradict the emerging body of social science research on how voters actually react to political ads. In sum, we suggest that they attempt to apply theory to practice in such a way as to reaffirm the core of each—one important test of the usefulness of theory in examined life.

Application II:
Firestone and the Corporate Narrative

Most crises tell a story of sorts, and the unfolding events surrounding the Bridgestone/Firestone© controversy seem to represent one part soap opera and one part cautionary tale. It is to the insight that narrative provides that we now turn.

First, because we have characterized human beings as culture-creating entities, it is important to understand the corporate history of Bridgestone/Firestone. One of America's oldest industrial enterprises, Firestone was almost driven into bankruptcy in the early 1970s for stonewalling a tire recall effort by the U.S. government. Business historians suggest Firestone never financially recovered from the battle that led, in turn, to its acquisition by a Japanese firm—Bridgestone—in 1988.

In the larger industrial world, the 1970s also provided two additional illustrations of the potential role of public relations in a crisis: the Ford Pinto®, where profit outweighed human life to the detriment of the corporation's reputation and bottom line, and the Johnson & Johnson© Tylenol® crisis, where prompt public communication about a life threatening act of sabotage saved lives and left the corporation financially healthy less than 2 years later. Public relations practitioners working for Bridgestone/Firestone should have known their own corporate history, and as professionals, they should also have understood two of the classic ethics cases of their profession.

Rather than attempt to summarize all the events of the Bridgestone/Firestone crisis, events that are unlikely to be resolved in the near future, we suggest that the events in their totality have provided a narrative on how this particular corporation has dealt with a crisis. Like many cultural narratives, there are some essential lessons in this understanding of the interweaving of persuasion and corporation. Among them are these three:

• Most coporations that produce products that can have an impact on human life and health are, fundamentally, in the safety business. This is particularly true in a postindustrial culture where "normal accidents" (Perrow, 1928/1984) are to be expected, but where both government and consumers have taken some actions to minimize those consequences. In the Pinto case, Ford did not understand that it was in the safety business; in the Tylenol case, Johnson & Johnson did. Bridgestone/Firestone had its own corporate history that could have informed it of the same thing.

• When normal accidents take on a pattern, to develop a critical consciousness of what is at issue the public needs information that provides good reasons to act. Action, in this case, may include seeking more information, taking particular steps to avoid risk, or continuing as before but with better information and deeper understanding.

This need for complete and continuing communication is the basic lesson of the Johnson & Johnson case. Although current news accounts have not yet documented the internal communications at Bridgestone/Firestone, it does appear that certain portions of the corporation, for example that portion of the company that dealt with warranty problems, was not "talking" to engineering about the pattern of tire problems that began to emerge in 1997. Ford, which recalled cars outside the United States, also wasn't talking to Firestone about the problems it was finding or to the U.S. government. Although there is no legal requirement for Ford to report its recall domestically, prudence—and willingness to acknowledge the multiple voices involved—might have suggested such a course of action. Perhaps just as importantly, when a Houston television journalist began reporting on the story in February 2000, not only did Bridgestone/Firestone deny any problems, the corporate attorneys wrote letters to the television station that could have been interpreted as threatening litigation. Reflective communities are less able to flourish when major stakeholders demand silence; the corporation should have understood that the news story would fall into an ecology of messages, including persuasive messages from Bridgestone/Firestone, that would have helped individuals develop reasons for courses of actions. Furthermore, such individual activity could have functioned as part of a feedback loop to Bridgestone/Firestone, providing at least some support for what is obviously an economic gamble.

> *Reflective communities are less able to flourish when major stakeholders demand silence.*

Bridgestone/Firestone's initial reaction to the journalistic reports employed the corporation's "old" narrative. However, the corporation did demonstrate that it had learned from past events; a voluntary recall was eventually instituted. Whether it occurred soon enough to preserve the corporation's reputation and financial health is yet to be determined.

- Finally, both corporations are involved in the substitution of expert opinion for practical wisdom, at least in their Congressional testimony. Engineering, particularly the technical engineering that produces sports utility vehicles and the tires they move on, is subject to the sort of debate that characterizes cutting edge science as opposed to textbook science. Only years more testing will determine whether the Ford Explorer® has a design flaw that can't be corrected by underinflating tires or whether the tires themselves, the result of complex engineering, are fundamentally flawed or flawed when underinflated and driven at high speeds in hot climates. But, while the experts debate, practical wisdom would suggest that there is something problematic in the combination. Such an evaluation is not strictly rational, at least in the terms of the scientific evidence that is currently in hand, but it makes common sense. Although litigation is a looming presence, both corporations could have done much to foster community by doing less blaming of one another and more cooperation to correct whatever problems do exist.

This recounting cannot "solve" the Bridgestone/Firestone tire case, at least in terms of the public relations professionals involved. It does, however, demonstrate how understanding the narrative of a crisis can spur ethical action. Firestone, unwittingly or not, violated all the guidelines we have suggested for ethical persuasive activity. Although we do not know how much actual access public relations practitioners had to corporate decision making, we suggest that had the people in charge at Bridgestone/ Firestone understood the impact of the narrative they were creating, their own narrative history, and their connection to community by being in the "safety" business, perhaps the corporation would have responded differently internally. Externally, consumer trust, corporate health, and lives might be saved.

Conclusion

When we set out to write this article, we realized that we had taken on an "impossible" task. No brief recital of philosophical debate can deal with the profound questions that surround the nature of humanity, particularly humanity that makes ethical choices. But we do believe it is important for the findings of social science to speak to philosophical understanding. No single theory from either discipline will adequately answer all questions; what we have tried to do instead is to provide a different way of thinking through the questions that the persuasive enterprise raises. We have not dismissed rationality but attempted to place it on equal footing with other human intellectual efforts, those that spring as much from poetry as they do from deduction. Our work draws almost equally from ancient and contemporary theory. We have made some controversial assertions. However, we suggest that continued application of this alternate view to the problems of persuasion may help make those problems more tractable to those working in applied ethics, both in the academy and in the larger community.

Notes

1. The status and character of philosophical anthropology are controversial. "It is not always included in the ranks of classical philosophical disciplines: metaphysics, epistemology, logic, ethics.... Metaphysics considers it not sufficiently general and fundamental; individual sciences consider it too much so" (Landman, 1974, p. 9). For Marx, it "fails to recognize the essentially historical and changing nature of man" (Landmann, 1974, p. 11).

   Yet, Landmann (1974) concluded correctly, "it survives as a school of philosophy.... In its substantive origins, it dates back to Greek philosophy. In the Renaissance and the Age of Goethe it reached new peaks" (p. 9). And it "was reestablished in the 1920s by Helmut Plessner and Max Scheler" (p. 9).

   For Richard Schacht (1990), philosophical anthropology has received little attention in Anglo-American philosophy, because of the influence of positivistic thought and the fact that the philosophy of mind filled in its intellectual space (p. 155). On the European continent it "may have been eclipsed by existential philosophy, and may have been criticized by European philosophers as diverse as Heidegger, Althusser and Foucault; but it has persisted as a philosophical enterprise, and remains an area of serious philosophical inquiry" (Schacht, 1990, p. 155). It has been "part of the European philosophical landscape for the past century and a half, emerging as a main interest and focus of post-Hegelian philosophers from Feurbach and Marx to Nietzsche and Dilthey" (Schacht, 1990, p. 155; see Schacht, 1975; Gehlen, 1988).

2. The Oxford philosopher Gilbert Ryle (1949) rejected Descartes on the ground that his dualism of mind and matter was a category mistake that confused the discourse concerning minds with the logic of discourse pertaining to physical bodies.

3. Between the rationalistic, scientific philosophy of the 17th and 18th centuries, and the mature positivism of Russell and Carnap, are two explicit paths not developed here: (a) Hume's shift in causal inference from the necessary connection of things to the connection of ideas in the mind, and (b) the discovery of non-Euclidean geometry in the first half of the 19th century (cf. Levi, 1959, p. 334).

4. As Hempel has pointed out, given Carnap's emphasis on the empirical, on factual propositions and on logical syntax, the correspondence theory of verification in Russell becomes a coherence theory of truth in Carnap. For the complexities of their intellectual connections and an extensive bibliography, see Levi (1959), "The Passion for Logic: Bertrand Russell and Rudolph Carnap" (chap. 9, pp. 331–382).

5. Positivism differs from Cartesian rationality in that it accounts for logic and mathematics without appealing to philosophical concepts of ultimate meaning. In developing a universal language of science, positivism eliminated metaphysics, or rather than highlighting its antimetaphysical bias, Levi (1959) correctly argued that it established "a metaphysics founded upon logic" (p. 347).

6. In addition to the work of Aristotle, *hermeneia* and its cognates appear in such familiar ancients as Plutarch, Xenophon, Euripides, Longinus, Epicurus, and Lucretius. One already detects the faint beginning of a theoretical enterprise when Plato uses the phrase *he hermeneutike techne* (the hermeneutical art; *Politicus* 260D). The history of the Hermes mythology (god of language) from the Iliad and Odyssey to the Stoic period illustrates the refinement of Greek thinking on *hermeneia*. For a summary, see Grossberg and Christians (1981, pp. 60–62).

7. For documentation that Vico was not merely anti-Descartes, but was inspired by a living, pre-Enlightenment tradition, see Janik (1983). For stimulating essays on Vico and the Counter Enlightenment generally, see Berlin (1982, pp. 1–24, 80–129).

8. For understanding cultural beings in the context of Enlightenment rationality, see Cassirer (1951). For a systematic treatment of the cultural sciences that emerge from his philosophy of language, see Cassirer (1960, pp. 3–38, 117–158) especially.

9. Taking human selfhood seriously after deconstruction and postmodernity is controversial. The death of the human is a common motif in contemporary literature. Michael Focault (1970), for instance, contended "man is an invention of recent date" and will soon "be erased like a face drawn in the sand at the edge of the sea" (p. 387). This "death of man" motif has taken on "a variety of

formulations, to wit ... the 'death of the author,' the 'deconstruction of the subject,' the 'displacement of the ego,' the 'dissolution of self-identity,' and at times a combination of the above" (Schrag, 1997, p. 2). We follow Schrag (1997) in his argument that contradicting the essentialist rational self and versions of being-in-the-world do not "entail jettisoning every sense of self" (p. 9). Our definition of the human is consistent with Schrag's (1997) effort to construct "a praxis-oriented self, defined by its communicative practices, oriented toward an understanding of itself in its discourse, its action, its being with others, and its experience of transcendence" (p. 9).

References

Benoit, W. (2000). *The spot.* New York: Praeger.

Berlin, I. (1982). *Against the crowd: Essays in the history of ideas.* New York: Penguin.

Carey, J. W. (1988). *Communication as culture.* Boston: Universe Hyman.

Carnap, R. (1937a). *The logical syntax of language.* London: Routledge & Kegan Paul.

Carnap, R. (1937b). *Philosophy and logical synax.* London: Routlendge & Kegan Paul.

Cassirer, E. (1944). *An essay on man: An introduction to the philosophy of human culture.* New Haven, CT: Yale University Press.

Cassirer, E. (1951). *The philosophy of the enlightenment.* Princeton, NJ: Princeton University Press.

Cassirer, E. (1953–1957, 1996). *The philosophy of symbolic forms* (R. Manheim and J. M. Krois, Trans., Vols. 1–4). New Haven, CT: Yale University Press. (Original work published 1923–1929)

Cassirer, E. (1960). *The logic of the humanities* (C. S. Howe, Trans.). New Haven, CT: Yale University Press.

Comte, A. (1910). *A general view of positivism* (J. H. Bridges, Trans.). London: Routledge. (Original work published 1848)

Davies, J. C. (1964). *Human nature in politics.* New York: John Wiley & Sons.

Denton, R. E. (Ed.). (1991). *Ethical dimensions of political communication.* New York: Praeger.

Descartes, R. (1938). *Discourse on method.* Chicago: Open Court Publishing. (Original work published 1637)

Descartes, R. (1964). *Rules for the direction of the mind. In his philosophical essays* (pp. 147–236) (L. J. Lafleur, Trans.). Indianapolis, IN: Bobbs-Merrill.

Dilthey, W. (1914–1982). *Gesammelte shriften.* (19 vols.) Leipzig & Berlin, Germany: Tuebner; Götingen, Germany: Vadenhoeck & Ruprecht.

Foucault, M. (1970). *The Order of things: An archeology of the human sciences.* New York: Random House.

Freire, P. (1973). *Education for critical consciousness.* New York: Seabury Press.

Fry, T. (Ed.). (1993). *RUA TV? Heidegger and the televisual.* Sydney, Australia: Power.

Gehlen, A. (1988). *Man: His nature and place in the world.* (C. McMillan, Trans.). New York: Columbia University Press.

Grossberg, L., & Christians, C. (1981). Hermeneutics and the study of communication. In J. Soloski (Ed.), *Foundations for communication studies* (pp. 57–81). Iowa City: University of Iowa Center for Communication Study.

Heidegger, M. (1958). *What is philosophy?* New York: Twayne Publishers.

Heidegger, M. (1962). *Being and time* (J. Macquarrie & E. Robinson, Trans.). New York: Harper & Row. (Original work published 1927)

Heidegger, M. (1971). *Poetry, language, thought* (A. Hofstadter, Trans.). New York: Harper & Row.

Hood, W. F. (1972). The Aristotelian versus the Heideggerian approach to the problem of technology. In C. Mitcham & R. Mackey (Eds.), *Philosophy and technology: Readings in the philosophical problems of Technology* (pp. 347–363). New York: Free Press.

Jamieson, K. H. (2000). *Everything you think you know about politics … and why you're wrong.* New York: Basic Books.

Janik, L. G. (1983). A renaissance quarrel: The origins of Vico's anti-cartesianism. In G. Tagliacozzo (Ed.), *New Vico studies* (pp. 39–50). Atlantic Highlands, NJ: Humanities.

Koehn, D. (1998). *Rethinking feminist ethics: Care, trust and empathy.* New York: Routledge.

Landmann, M. (1974). *Philosophical anthropology* (D. J. Parent, Trans.). Philadelphia: Westminster Press.

Levi, A. W. (1959). *Philosophy and the modern world.* Bloomington, IN: Indiana University Press.

Niebuhr, R. (1964). *The nature and destiny of man. Vol. 1: Human nature.* New York: Scribner's. (Original work published 1941)

Perrow, C. (1984). *Normal accidents: Living with high risk technologies* (H. Meyerhoff, Trans.). New York: Basic Books. (Original work published 1928)

Rasmussen, D. M. (1971). *Mythic-symbolic language and philosophical anthropology: A constructive interpretation of the thought of Paul Ricoeur.* The Hague, Netherlands: Martinus Nijhoff.

Ricoeur, P. (1967). The antinomy of human reality and the problem of philosophical anthropology. In N. Lawrence and D. O'Connor (Eds.), *Readings in existential phenomenology* (pp. 390–402). Englewood Cliffs, NJ: Prentice Hall.

Rotzoll, K. B. (2001). Persuasion Advertising. In C. Christians, K. B. Rotzoll, & K. B. McKee (Eds.), *Media ethics: Cases and moral reasoning* (6th ed., pp. 127–196). New York: Longman.

Russel, B. & Whitehead, A. N. (1910–1913). *Principia mathematica.* London: Cambridge University Press.

Ryle, G. (1949). *The concept of the mind.* New York: Barnes & Noble.

Schacht, R. (1975). *Existentialism, existenz-philosophy, and philosophical anthropology* (pp. 228–253). Pittsburg, PA: University of Pittsburg Press.

Schacht, R. (1990, Fall). Philosophical anthropology: What, why and how. *Philosophy and Phenomenological Research, 50,* 155–176.

Schrag, C. O. (1997). *The self after postmodernity.* New Haven, CT: Yale University Press.

Seib, C. & Fitzpatrick, K. (1995). *Public relations ethics.* Fort Worth, TX: Harcourt Brace.

Shannon, C. & Weaver, W. (1949). *The mathematical theory of communication.* Urbana, IL: University of Illinois Press.

Taylor, C. (1985). Language and human nature. In *Human nature and language. Philosophical Papers 1* (pp. 215–247). Cambridge, England: Cambridge University Press.

Verene, D. P. (1981). *Vico's science of imagination*. Ithaca, NY: Cornell Universiy Press.

Vico, G. (1948). *The new science of G. Vico* (T. G. Bergin & M. H. Fisch, Trans.). Ithaca, NY: Cornell University Press. (Original work published 1725)

Vico, G. (1965). *On the study methods of our time* (E. Gianturco, Trans.). Indianapolis, IN: Bobbs-Merrill. (Original work published 1709)

Journal of Mass Media Ethics, *16*(2&3), 121–137
Copyright © 2001, Lawrence Erlbaum Associates, Inc.

Semantics and Ethics
of Propaganda

Jay Black
University of South Florida—St. Petersburg

❏ *This article explores shifting definitions of propaganda, because how we define the slippery enterprise determines whether we perceive propaganda to be ethical or unethical. I also consider the social psychology and semantics of propaganda, because our ethics are shaped by and reflect our belief systems, values, and language behaviors. Finally, in the article I redefine propaganda in a way that should inform further studies of the ethics of this pervasive component of modern society.*

Shifting Perspectives on Propaganda

In this portion of the article I offer a brief overview of propaganda's definitional history. Students of ethics should be struck by certain commonalties among most (but certainly not all) of the traditional and a few of the contemporary definitions: a presumption of manipulation and control, if not outright coercion, that dehumanizes the audiences or intended "victims" of propaganda; a power imbalance—rhetorical, political, economic, and so forth—between propagandists and propagandees; and a presumption that principles of science, rhetoric, semantics, and enlightened or open-minded education serve as powerful antidotes to propaganda. More subtle, but perhaps as intriguing, are recent suggestions that propaganda is systemic in a democratic, technological, postindustrial information society and that instruments of mass media (in particular, advertising and public relations, and other tools of persuasion) are every bit as propagandistic as were totalitarian dictatorships of days gone by.

Early Approaches to Propaganda

One implication of the term *propaganda*, when it was first used in the sociological sense by the Roman Catholic Church, was to the spreading of ideas that would not occur naturally, but only via a cultivated or artificial generation. In 1622, the Vatican established the Congregatio de Propaganda Fide, or "Congregation for the Propaganda of Faith," to harmonize the content and teaching of faith in its missions and consolidate its power. As Combs and Nimmo maintained (1993, p. 201), this early form of propaganda was considered by the Church to be a moral endeavor.

Over time the term took on more negative connotations; in a semantic sense, propaganda became value laden, and in an ethical sense, it was seen as immoral. In 1842 W. T. Brande, writing in the *Dictionary of Science, Literature and Art,* called propaganda something "applied to modern political language as a term of reproach to secret associations for the spread of opinions and principles which are viewed by most governments with horror and aversion" (Qualter, 1962, p. 4).

Education aims at independence of judgment. Propaganda offers ready-made opinions for the unthinking herd.

Following World War I, R. J. R. G. Wreford (1923) maintained that propaganda had retained its pejorative connotations as "a hideous word" typical of an age noted for its "etymological bastardy" (Qualter, 1962, p. 7). At that time, the forces of propaganda, public relations, and psychological warfare had become inextricably intertwined in the public's mind. Social scientists and propaganda analysts, strongly influenced by models of behaviorism, tended to depict a gullible public readily manipulated by forces over which it had little control (Institute for Propaganda Analysis, 1937; Lee & Lee, 1988). This depiction offended humanists and progressives who feared propaganda as a threat to democracy and saw public enlightenment through education as the best defense against the inevitability of propaganda. (For a good treatment of this, see Michael Sproule, 1989 and 1997.) In 1929, for instance, Everett Martin wrote that

> Education aims at independence of judgment. Propaganda offers ready-made opinions for the unthinking herd. Education and propaganda are directly opposed both in aim and method. The educator aims at a slow process of development; the propagandist, at quick results. The educator tries to tell people how to think; the propagandist, what to think. The educator strives to develop individual responsibility; the propagandist, mass effects. The educator fails unless he achieves an open mind; the propagandist unless he achieves a closed mind. (p. 145)

In a 1935 book, Leonard Doob drew a further distinction between education and propaganda by saying that

If individuals are controlled through the use of suggestion … then the process may be called propaganda, regardless of whether or not the propagandist intends to exercise the control. On the other hand if individuals are affected in such a way that the same result would be obtained with or without the aid of suggestion, then this process may be called education, regardless of the intention of the educator. (p. 80)

Harold Lasswell (1927) offered the first attempt to systematically define propaganda to assure some degree of validity and reliability in studies of the phenomenon. Propaganda, Lasswell wrote, is "the control of opinion by significant symbols, or, so to speak, more concretely and less accurately, by stories, rumors, reports, pictures, and other forms of social communications" (p. 627).

A year later George Catlin (1936) defined propaganda as the mental instillation by any appropriate means, emotional or intellectual, of certain views. He said the "instillation of views may be animated by no strong sense of moral or political urgency," and that "it may amount to little more than the distribution of information, public acquaintance with which is advantageous to the institution concerned" (pp. 127–128).

The 1930s and 1940s saw propaganda's definitions reflecting social science's struggles between behaviorism (the "stimulus response" model) and a more value neutral stance. At the same time, propaganda was applied to increasingly broad categories of social and political phenomena.

Edgar Henderson (1943) proposed that no definition of propaganda can succeed unless it meets several requirements: (a) it must be objective; (b) it must be psychological, or at least sociopsychological, rather than sociological or axiological; (c) it must include all the cases without being so broad as to become fuzzy; (d) it must differentiate the phenomenon from both similar and related phenomena; and (e) it must throw new light on the phenomenon itself, making possible a new understanding and systematization of known facts concerning the phenomenon and suggesting new problems for investigation (p. 71). Given these criteria, Henderson claimed previous definitions fell short, and proposed that "propaganda is a process which deliberately attempts through persuasion-techniques to secure from the propagandee, before he can deliberate freely, the responses desired by the propagandist" (p. 83).

Doob (1948) defined propaganda as "the attempt to affect the personalities and to control the behavior of individuals toward ends considered unscientific or of doubtful value in a society at a particular time" (p. 240). Doob employed propaganda in a neutral sense "to describe the influence of one person upon other persons when scientific knowledge and survival values are uncertain," indicating that "propaganda is absolutely inevitable and cannot be exorcised by calling it evil-sounding names" (1948, p. 244).

Past Half Century

Following World War II, propaganda was often defined in accordance
with constantly shifting perspectives on political theory and the pro-
cesses/effects and structures/functions of mass communication. Some
scholars, such as Alfred McClung Lee (1952), stubbornly held to earlier
models of humanity-as-victim when defining propaganda as something
that was vivid, emotional, and attempted to override common sense. Increasingly, however, as media and organized persuasion enterprises in and
of themselves were seen to have diminished mind-molding influences,
definitions (and, we presume, fears) of propaganda softened. Many of the
midcentury explorations of propaganda considered the phenomena in
terms of the totality of persuasive characteristics of a culture or society.
More recently, definitions have incorporated concerns about subtle, long-
term but difficult to measure media effects. Also, many modern approaches to the subject have allowed that propaganda need not necessarily
be deliberately and systematically manipulative of consumers-cum-vic-
tims, but may merely be the incidental by-product of our contemporary
technological and/or information society.

Terrence Qualter, in his 1962 book on propaganda and psychological
warfare, called propaganda

> The deliberate attempt by some individual or group to form, control, or alter
> the attitudes of other groups by the use of the instruments of communication,
> with the intention that in any given situation the reaction of those so influ-
> enced will be that desired by the propagandist. (p. 27)

Qualter (1962) argued that the phrase "the deliberate attempt" was the
key to his concept of propaganda, because, as he claimed, he had established "beyond doubt" that anything may be used as propaganda and that
nothing belongs exclusively to propaganda. The significance, he said, was
that any act of promotion can be propaganda "only if and when it becomes
part of a deliberate campaign to induce action through the control of attitudes" (p. 27).

French social philosopher Jacques Ellul (1964, 1965), whose ideas have
significantly informed the propaganda research agenda in recent decades,
held a sophisticated view construing propaganda as a popular euphemism
for the totality of persuasive components of culture. Ellul (1965) saw a
world in which numerous elements of society were oriented toward the
manipulation of individuals and groups, and thereby defined propaganda
as "a set of methods employed by an organized group that wants to bring
about the active or passive participation in its actions of a mass of individuals, psychologically unified through psychological manipulations and in-

corporated in an organization" (p. 61). Propaganda performs an indispensable function in society, according to Ellul (1965):

> Propaganda is the inevitable result of the various components of the techno-logical society, and plays so central a role in the life of that society that no eco-nomic or political development can take place without the influence of its great power. Human Relations in social relationships, advertising or Human Engineering in the economy, propaganda in the strictest sense in the field of politics—the need for psychological influence to spur allegiance and action is everywhere the decisive factor, which progress demands and which the indi-vidual seeks in order to be delivered from his own self. (p. 160)

Although recognizing the significance of the traditional forms of propa-ganda utilized by revolutionaries and the heavy-handed types of propa-ganda employed by despots and totalitarian regimes—"agitation" and "political" propaganda—Ellul (1965) focused more on the culturally per-vasive nature of what he called "sociological" and "integration" propa-ganda. What Ellul (1965) defined as "the penetration of an ideology by means of its sociological context" (p. 63) is particularly germane to a study of mass media persuasion. Advertising, public relations, and the culturally persuasive components of entertainment media are all involved in the "spreading of a certain style of life" (p. 63), and all converge toward the same point.

In a sense sociological propaganda is reversed from political propa-ganda because in political propaganda the ideology is spread through the mass media to get the public to accept some political or economic structure or to participate in some action, whereas in sociological propa-ganda, the existing economic, political, and sociological factors progres-sively allow an ideology to penetrate individuals or masses. Ellul (1965) called the latter a sort of persuasion from within, "essentially diffuse, rarely conveyed by catchwords or expressed intentions" (p. 64). He added that it is instead "based on a general climate, atmosphere that in-fluences people imperceptibly without having the appearance of propa-ganda" (Ellul, 1965, p. 64). The result is that the public adopts new criteria of judgment and choice, adopting them spontaneously, almost as if choosing them via free will—which means that sociological propa-ganda produces "a progressive adaptation to a certain order of things, a certain concept of human relations, which unconsciously molds individ-uals and makes them conform to society" (Ellul, 1965, pp. 63–64). In con-temporary society this is a "long-term propaganda, a self-reproducing propaganda that seeks to obtain stable behavior, to adapt the individual to his everyday life, to reshape his thoughts and behavior in terms of the permanent social setting" (Ellul, 1964, p. 74).

It is significant to point out that those who produce sociological or integration propaganda often do so unconsciously, given how thoroughly (and perhaps blindly) they themselves are invested in the values and belief systems being promulgated. Besides, if one is an unintentional "integration" propagandist merely seeking to maintain the status quo, one's efforts would seem to be prima facie praiseworthy and educational. However, when considering propaganda as a whole, Ellul (1981) concluded that the enterprise was pernicious and immoral—a view shared by many but not all other students of the subject. Ellul (1981) argued that pervasive and potent propaganda that creates a world of fantasy, myth, and delusion is anathema to ethics because (a) the existence of power in the hands of propagandists does not mean it is right for them to use it (the is–ought problem); (b) propaganda destroys a sense of history and continuity and philosophy so necessary for a moral life; and (c) by supplanting the search for truth with imposed truth, propaganda destroys the basis for mutual thoughtful interpersonal communication and thus the essential ingredients of an ethical existence (Combs & Nimmo, 1993, p. 202; Cunningham, 1992; Ellul, 1981, pp. 159–177; Johannesen, 1983, p. 116).

Persuasion researcher George Gordon's (1971) eclectic definition of propaganda suggested that most teachers and most textbooks, except those involved in teaching abstract skills, are inherently propagandistic. (In his chapter on "Education, Indoctrination, and Training," Gordon argued that one failure of the American educational system is that there is not enough propaganda in the lower grades, and too much in graduate schools.)

John C. Merrill and Ralph Lowenstein (1971) published the first mass media textbook in the modern era that seriously analyzed propaganda and its employment in media. The authors Merrill generalized that from the numerous definitions of propaganda they had read they discerned certain recurring themes or statements or core ideas, among them "manipulation," "purposeful management," "preconceived plan," "creation of desires," "reinforcement of biases," "arousal of preexisting attitudes," "irrational appeal," "specific objective," "arousal to action," "predetermined end," "suggestion," and "creation of dispositions" (pp. 221–226). They concluded

> It seems that propaganda is related to an attempt (implies intent) on the part of somebody to manipulate somebody else. By manipulate we mean to control—to control not only the attitudes of others but also their actions. Somebody (or some group)—the propagandist—is predisposed to cause others to think a certain way, so that they may, on some cases, take a certain action. (p. 214)

Notwithstanding the work of Gordon, Merrill, and a few others whose textbooks containing observations about propaganda were published in the 1970s, an honest appraisal of propaganda scholarship shows a void of what Cunningham (2000) called "front-line academic research" between the 1950s and early 1980s. Cunningham (2000) went so far as to call propaganda a "theoretically undeveloped notion" during that period, and lauded the recent Ellulian-motivated resurgence of propaganda scholarship (p. 2). Some of that recent research and commentary (see especially Combs & Nimmo, 1993; Edelstein, 1997; Jowett & O' Donnell, 1999; Pratkanis & Aronson, 1992; Smith, 1989) has painted propaganda with a wider brush that covers the canvas of media, popular culture, and politics, and posits that propaganda need not necessarily be as systematic and purposive as earlier definitions demanded. Indeed, the likelihood of unconscious or accidental propaganda, produced by unwitting agents of the persuasion industry, makes the ethical analysis of contemporary propaganda ever more intriguing.

Consider only a few of the most recent definitions and discussions of propaganda (Cole, 1998). Ted Smith (1989), editor of *Propaganda: A Pluralistic Perspective*, called propaganda "Any conscious and open attempt to influence the beliefs of an individual or group, guided by a predetermined end and characterized by the systematic use of irrational and often unethical techniques of persuasion" (p. 80). Jowett and O' Donnell (1999) recently echoed that perspective, calling propaganda "The deliberate and systematic attempt to shape perceptions, manipulate cognitions, and direct behavior to achieve a response that furthers the desired intent of the propagandist" (p. 279). In Smith's (1989) edited volume Nicholas Burnett (1989) defined propaganda simply as "discourse in the service of ideology" (p. 127).

Pratkanis and Aronson (1992), in *Age of Propaganda: The Everyday Use and Abuse of Persuasion*, used the term *propaganda* to refer to "the mass persuasion techniques that have come to characterize our postindustrial society," and "the communication of a point of view with the ultimate goal of having the recipient of the appeal come to 'voluntarily' accept this position as if it were his or her own" (p. 8).

Media scholar Alex Edelstein, in his 1997 book *Total Propaganda: From Mass Culture to Popular Culture*, said "old propaganda" is traditionally employed by the government or the socially and economically influential members in "a hierarchical mass culture, in which only a few speak to many,"(p. 5) and it is intended for "the control and manipulation of mass cultures" (p. 4). He contrasts this with the "new propaganda" inherent in a broadly participant popular culture "with its b̲ṛ̲uck of First Amendment rights, knowledge, egalitarianism, and access to communication" (p. 5).

Social Psychology of Propaganda

Scholarly analyses of propaganda tend to focus on either the political or semantic/rhetorical nature of the beast. An equally intriguing set of insights has been offered by social psychologists, concerned as they are with the nature of belief and value systems and the various psychological needs that a phenomenon such as propaganda tends to fulfill. Until recently, philosophers have been noticeably absent from the fray.

Throughout the 20th century, various schools of sociology and psychology (and, recently, the hyphenated pairing of the two) have concluded that propaganda is produced and consumed by individuals with particular sociopsychological characteristics. What Ellul (1965) has described as sociological and integration propaganda has been the focus of their attention, as it is ours.

The past half-century's concerns over media propaganda have been based on the often stated assumption that one responsibility of a democratic media system is to encourage an open-minded citizenry—that is, a people who are curious, questioning, unwilling to accept simple pat answers to complex situations, and so forth. Mental freedom, the argument goes, comes when people have the capacity, and exercise the capacity, to weigh numerous sides of controversies (political, personal, economic, etc.) and come to their own rational decisions, relatively free of outside constraints.

Open and Closed Mind

A growing body of research on perception and belief systems seems to be concluding that individuals constantly strive for cognitive balance as they view and communicate about the world, and that individuals will select and rely on information consistent with their basic perceptions. This holds true for mass media practitioners as well as for their audiences. A *Journalism Quarterly* study by Donohew and Palmgreen (1971), for instance, showed that open-minded journalists underwent a great deal of stress when having to report information they weren't inclined to believe or agree with because the open-minded journalists' self-concepts demanded that they fairly evaluate all issues. Closed-minded journalists, on the other hand, underwent much less stress because it was easy for them to make snap decisions consistent with their basic world views—especially because they were inclined to go along with whatever information was given to them by authoritative sources (Donohew & Palmgreen, 1971, pp. 627–39, 666).

Social psychologist Milton Rokeach (1960), in his seminal work *The Open and Closed Mind: Investigations Into the Nature of Belief Systems and Personality Systems*, concluded empirically that the degree to which a person's belief system is open or closed is the extent to which the person can receive, evaluate, and act on relevant information received from the outside on its own intrinsic merits, unencumbered by irrelevant factors in the situation arising from within the person or from the outside (p. 57). To Rokeach (1960), open-minded individuals seek out sources (media and otherwise) that challenge them to think for themselves rather than sources that offer overly simplified answers to complex problems. Open-minded media consumers seek independent and pluralistic media because they value independence and pluralism—even, on occasion, dissonance—in their own cosmology, interpersonal relationships, and political life. Closed-minded or dogmatic media consumers, on the other hand, seek out and relish the opposite kinds of messages, taking comfort in simplified, pat answers (usually relayed by "authoritative sources"), in conformity, in a world in which the good guys and the bad guys are readily identifiable, in which there is a simplistic and direct connection between causes and effects (Rokeach, 1954, 1960, 1964).

Belief Systems and Media Propaganda

One of the dominant themes in media criticism for much of the past half century or so has been the tendency of media to mitigate against open-mindedness. Recent assessments reinforce the 1922 lamentations of Walter Lippmann concerning the stereotypical pictures in the heads of people, the incomplete reflections of political, economic, and social reality from which individuals make choices and public opinion is produced. If people lack time, opportunity, and inclination to become fully acquainted with one another and with their environment, it is only natural for them to act as Rokeach's (1954, 1960, 1964) dogmatic, closed-minded media consumers—prompted and fulfilled by media whose stock in trade is production of such public opinion-molding propaganda.

There is, of course, an argument that people need media to provide them with predigested views because they can't experience all of life firsthand. By definition, media come between realities and media consumers, and we are certainly not arguing for the elimination of those media. (Some have noted that online media and the Internet may appear to eliminate the mediating—and hence propagandistic—function of traditional media, but that argument falls when one considers that a prime reason to use new media is to pander to self-interest and to reinforce preexisting prejudices.)

The logic of Ellul (1965) is compelling in this regard, as he argued that people in a technological society need to be propagandized, to be "integrated into society" via media. As Ellul (1965) saw it, people with such a need get carried along unconsciously on the surface of events, not thinking about them but rather "feeling" them. Modern citizens, Ellul (1965) concluded, therefore condemn themselves to lives of successive moments, discontinuous and fragmented—and the media are largely responsible. The hapless victims of information overload seek out propaganda as a means of ordering the chaos, according to Ellul (1965).

If our nature is to eschew dissonance and move toward a homeostatic mental set, the crazy quilt patterns of information we receive from our mass media would certainly drive us to some superior authority of information or belief that would help us make more sense of our world. Propaganda thus becomes inevitable.

Most of the foregoing emphasizes the propagandee's belief system, showing parallels between dogmatic personality types and the "typical" propagandee. Not much of a case has been made to maintain that propagandists themselves possess the basic characteristics of the dogmatist, but there is much evidence suggesting that communicators who are intentionally and consciously operating as propagandists recognize that one of their basic tasks is to keep the minds of their propagandees closed. The conscious propagandists can operate most successfully by raising themselves above their messages and goals, conducting propaganda campaigns as a master conductor plays with an orchestra. (As Eric Hoffer, 1951, reminded us, Jesus was not a Christian, nor was Marx a Marxist [p. 128].) Unconscious propagandists are another matter; they may have unconsciously absorbed the belief and value system that they propagate in their daily integration or socialization propaganda. Their unexamined propagandistic lives reflect a cognitive system that has slammed shut every bit as tightly as the authorities for whom they blindly "spin" and as the most gullible of their propaganda's recipients.

As Donohew and Palmgreen (1971) implied, it appears to be very difficult and stressful for both media practitioners and media consumers to retain pluralistic orientations. If people are not undergoing any mental stress, it may be that they aren't opening their minds long enough to allow belief discrepant information to enter. This is not to say that stress and strain in and of themselves make for open-minded media behavior. They may just make for confusion and result from confusion. However, if media personnel and audiences never find themselves concerned over contradictory information, facts that don't add up, opinions that don't cause them to stop and think, then they are being closed-minded purveyors and passive receivers of propaganda.

The Semantics of Propaganda

Most of the empirical findings of belief systems researchers are entirely consistent with the body of knowledge referred to as "general semantics," as both study how people perceive the world and how they subsequently communicate their perceptions or misperceptions. Numerous empirical studies of general semantics reinforce many of Alfred

Korzybski's (1948) original statements in *Science and Sanity: An Introduction to Non-Aristotelian Systems and General Semantics,* first published in 1933: that unscientific or Aristotelian assumptions about language and reality result in semantically inadequate or inappropriate behavior. Studies of children and adults trained in general semantics principles have demonstrated that semantic awareness results in such diverse achievements as improved perceptual, speaking, reading, and writing skills, generalized intelligence, and decreased prejudice, dogmatism, and rigidity (Black, 1974). These studies offer substantive refutation to early criticisms of general semantics as an overly generalized and pedantic system of gross assumptions about language behavior. From the studies emerge a series of semantic patterns typifying the semantically sophisticated or unsophisticated individual (many general semanticists refer to "sane" and "un-sane" behaviors, but those terms are fraught with semantic difficulties!). The patterns are highly reflective of Rokeach's (1954, 1960, 1964) typologies of the open-minded or closed-minded individual and of propaganda analysts' descriptions of the nonpropagandistic or propagandistic individual.

Highlighting general semanticists' descriptions of sophisticated (sane) language behavior are such concepts as

1. Awareness that our language is not our reality, but is an inevitably imperfect abstraction of that reality, and that tendencies to equate language and reality (through the use of the verb *to be* as an equal sign) are setting up false-to-fact relations. This is seen in the "intensionalized is-of-identity," and is to be replaced by "extensionalized" analysis and description of reality as we perceive it.

2. Awareness that the use of *to be* to describe something usually reveals more about the observers' projecting their biases than it does about the object described. This is seen as the "intensionalized is-of-predication" and is to be replaced by extensionalized awareness of our projections.

3. Awareness that people and situations have unlimited characteristics, that the world is in a constant process of change, that our perceptions are limited, and that our language cannot say all there is to be said about a person or situation. This is seen in attempts to replace a dogmatic "allness orientation" with a multivalued orientation that recognizes the "etc.," or the fact that there is always more to be seen and observed than we are capable of seeing, observing, and describing.

4. Awareness that a fact is not an inference and an inference is not a value judgment, and subsequent awareness that receivers of our communications need to be told the differences.

5. Awareness that different people will perceive the world differently, and we should accept authority figures', sources', and witnesses' view-

points as being the result of imperfect human perceptual processes and not as absolute truth.

6. Awareness that persons and situations are rarely if ever two valued, that propositions do not have to be either "true" or "false," specified ways of behaving do not have to be either "right" or "wrong," "black" or "white," that continuum-thinking or an infinite-valued orientation is a more valid way to perceive the world than an Aristotelian two-valued orientation (Korzybski, 1948; see also *Etcetera: A Review of General Semantics*, a quarterly published by the International Society for General Semantics, now in its 58th year of publication).

Numerous other semantic formulations exist, but these six can begin to offer a framework for semantic analysis of propaganda. As noted earlier, awareness and conscious application of these formulations have resulted in empirically improved levels of perception, reading, writing, speaking, generalized intelligence, and open-mindedness. Also, as in the case of being open-minded, it can be seen that being semantically sophisticated (sane) is not the easiest way to go through life because it tends to result in a mass of often contradictory perceptions and language behavior that the semantically unsophisticated (un-sane) individual never has to worry about. But such is the responsibility of the ethical, professional communicator, and the fate of the mature media consumer. As the Institute for Propaganda Analysts maintained 60 years ago, being a sophisticated consumer of propaganda, remaining aware of how propaganda is structured, and knowing how to respond to its various truth claims are crucial to the public welfare.

Propaganda Revisited

At this juncture, insights from propaganda analysts, media critics, social psychologists, and semanticists can be amalgamated into reasonably objective insights into the propagandistic nature of contemporary society. The insights can be applied to the producers of propaganda, the contents of propaganda, and the consumers of propaganda.

The emerging picture of propagandists/propaganda/propagandees and their opposites, as uncovered by the preceding discussions, reveals several definite patterns of semantic/belief systems/ethical/and so forth behavior. Note that on one hand the dogmatist (typical of propagandist and propagandee, and revealed in the manifest content of propaganda) seeks psychological closure whether rational or not; appears to be driven by irrational inner forces; has an extreme reliance on authority figures; reflects a narrow time perspective; and displays little sense of discrimination among fact/inference/value judgment. On the other hand, the nondogmatist faces a constant struggle to remain open-minded by evaluating information on its own merits; is governed by self-actualizing forces rather than irrational inner forces; discriminates between and among messages and sources and has tentative reliance on authority figures; recognizes and deals with contradictions, incomplete pictures of reality, and the interrelation of past, present, and future; and moves comfortably and rationally among levels of abstraction (fact, inference, and value judgment).

> *Whereas, creative communication accepts pluralism and displays expectations that its receivers should conduct further investigations of its observations, allegations, and conclusions, propaganda does not appear to do so.*

The preceding typologies help lead us to an original synopsis of propaganda, one meeting the criteria laid down by Henderson in 1943. It is sociopsychological, broad without being fuzzy, differentiates propaganda from similar and related phenomena, and sheds new light on the phenomena. In addition, it describes the characteristics of the propagandists, the propaganda they produce, and the propagandees—something sorely lacking in most other definitions. The synopsis is as follows:

Although it may or may not emanate from individuals or institutions with demonstrably closed minds, the manifest content of propaganda contains characteristics one associates with dogmatism or closed-mindedness; although it may or may not be intended as propaganda, this type of communication seems noncreative and appears to have as its purpose the evaluative narrowing of its receivers. Whereas creative communication accepts pluralism and displays expectations that its receivers should conduct further investigations of its observations, allegations, and conclusions, propaganda does not appear to do so. Rather, propaganda is characterized by at least the following six specific characteristics:

1. A heavy or undue reliance on authority figures and spokespersons, rather than empirical validation, to establish its truths, conclusions, or impressions.

2. The utilization of unverified and perhaps unverifiable abstract nouns, adjectives, adverbs, and physical representations rather than empirical validation to establish its truths, conclusions, or impressions.

3. A finalistic or fixed view of people, institutions, and situations divided into broad, all-inclusive categories of in-groups (friends) and out-groups (enemies), beliefs and disbeliefs, and situations to be accepted or rejected in toto.

4. A reduction of situations into simplistic and readily identifiable cause and effect relations, ignoring multiple causality of events.

5. A time perspective characterized by an overemphasis or underemphasis on the past, present, or future as disconnected periods rather than a demonstrated consciousness of time flow.

6. A greater emphasis on conflict than on cooperation among people, institutions, and situations.

This synopsis encourages a broad-based investigation of public communications behavior along a propaganda–nonpropaganda continuum. Practitioners and observers of media and persuasion could use this definition to assess their own and their media's performance (Black, 1977–1978).

The definition applies to the news and information as well as to entertainment and persuasion functions in the media. Many criticisms of the supposedly objective aspects of media are entirely compatible with the aforementioned standards. Meanwhile, because most people expect the advertisements, public relations programs, editorials, and opinion columns to be nonobjective and persuasive, if not outright biased, they may tend to avoid analyzing such messages for propagandistic content. However, because those persuasive messages can and should be able to meet their basic objectives without being unduly propagandistic, they should be held to the higher standards of nonpropaganda. (For what it's worth, persuasive media that are propagandistic, as defined herein, would seem to be less likely to attract and convince open-minded media consumers than to reinforce the biases of the closed-minded true believers, which raises an intriguing question about persuaders' ethical motives.)

Conclusions

We are not suggesting that the necessity for mediating reality and merchandising ideas, goods, and services inevitably results in propaganda. Far from it. Yet we do suggest that when there is a pattern of behavior on the part of participants in the communications exchange that repeatedly finds them dogmatically jumping to conclusions, making undue use of authority, basing assumptions on faulty premises, and otherwise engaging in inappropriate semantic behavior, then we can say they are engaging in propaganda. They may be doing it unconsciously. They may not be attempting to propagandize, or ever be aware that their efforts can be seen as propagandistic, or know that they are falling victim to propaganda. It may just be that their

view of the world, their belief systems, their personal and institutional loyalties, and their semantic behaviors are propagandistic.

But this doesn't excuse them.

It is sometimes said, among ethicists, that we should never attribute to
malice what can be explained by ignorance. That aphorism certainly applies to propaganda, a phenomenon too many observers have defined as
an inherently immoral enterprise that corrupts all who go near it. If instead
we consider propaganda in less value-laden terms, we are better able to
recognize ways all participants in the communications exchange can proceed intelligently through the swamp, and we can make informed judg-
ments about the ethics of particular aspects of our communications rather
than indicting the entire enterprise.

It is possible to conduct public relations, advertising, and persuasion
campaigns, plus the vast gamut of informational journalism efforts, without being unduly propagandistic.

In a politically competitive democracy and a commercially competitive
free enterprise system, mass communication functions by allowing a competitive arena in which the advocates of all can do battle. What many call *propaganda* therefore becomes part of that open marketplace of ideas; it is not only
inevitable, but may be desirable that there are openly recognizable and competing propagandas in a democratic society, propagandas that challenge all of
us—producers and consumers—to wisely sift and sort through them.

What many call propaganda ...
becomes part of that open
marketplace of ideas.

A fully functioning democratic society needs pluralism in its persuasion
and information, and not the narrow-minded, self-serving propaganda
some communicators inject—wittingly or unwittingly—into their communications and which, it seems, far too many media audience members unconsciously and uncritically consume. Open-mindedness and mass
communications efforts need not be mutually exclusive.

References

Black, J. (1974). *General semantics, belief systems, and propaganda: Interrelationships in
journalism.* Unpublished doctoral dissertation, University of Missouri,
Columbia.

Black, J. (1977–1978). Another perspective on mass media propaganda. *General Semantics Bulletin, 44/45,* 92–104.

Brande, W. T. (1842). Propaganda. *Dictionary of science, literature and art.* London.

Burnett, N. (1989). Ideology and propaganda: Toward an integrative approach. In T. J. Smith III (Ed.), *Propaganda: A pluralistic perspective* (pp. 127–137). New York: Praeger.

Catlin, G. E. G. (1936). Propaganda as a function of democratic government. In H. W. Childs (Ed.), *Propaganda and dictatorship: A collection of papers.* Princeton, NJ: Princeton University Press.

Cole, R. (Ed.). (1998). *The encyclopedia of propaganda.* Armonk, NY: Sharpe.

Combs, J. E., & Nimmo, D. (1993). *The new propaganda: The dictatorship of palaver in contemporary politics.* White Plains, NY: Longman.

Cunningham, S. (1992). Sorting out the ethics of propaganda. *Communication Studies, 43,* 233–245.

Cunningham, S. (2000, October). *Responding to propaganda: An ethical enterprise.* Paper presented at Colloquium 2000 in Applied Media Ethics, Park City, UT.

Donohew, L., & Palmgreen, P. (1971). An investigation of "mechanisms" of information selection. *Journalism Quarterly 48,* 627–639, 666.

Doob, L. W. (1935). *Propaganda, its psychology and technique.* New York: Holt.

Doob, L. W. (1948). *Public opinion and propaganda.* New York: Holt.

Edelstein, A. (1997). *Total propaganda: From mass culture to popular culture.* Mahwah, NJ: Lawrence Erlbaum Associates, Inc.

Ellul, J. (1964). *The technological society.* New York: Vintage.

Ellul, J. (1965). *Propaganda: The formation of men's attitudes.* New York: Knopf.

Ellul, J. (1981). The ethics of propaganda: Propaganda, innocence, and amorality. *Communication, 6,* 159–177.

Gordon, G. N. (1971). *Persuasion: The theory and practice of manipulative communication.* New York: Hastings House.

Henderson, E. H. (1943). Toward a definition of propaganda. *Journal of Social Psychology, 18,* 71–87.

Hoffer, E. (1951). *The true believer.* New York: Harper & Row.

Institute for Propaganda Analysis. (1937, November). How to detect propaganda. *Propaganda Analysis, I,* 1–4.

Johannesen, R. L. (1990). *Ethics in human communication* (3rd ed.). Prospect Heights, IL: Waveland.

Jowett, G. S., & O'Donnell, V. (1999). *Propaganda and persuasion* (3rd ed.). Thousand Oaks, CA: Sage.

Korzybski, A. H. (1948). *Science and sanity: An introduction to non-Aristotelian systems and general semantics* (4th ed.). Lakeville, CT: Non-Aristotelian Library.

Lasswell, H. D. (1927). The theory of political propaganda. *American Political Science Review,* 627.

Lee, A. M. (1952). *How to understand propaganda.* New York: Rinehard & Company.

Lee, A. M., & Lee, E. B. (1988). An influential ghost: The institute for propaganda analysis. *Propaganda Review, 3,* 10–14.

Lippmann, W. (1922). *Public opinion.* New York: Macmillan.

Martin, E. D. (1929). Our invisible masters. *Forum, 81,* 142–145.

Merrill, J. C., & Lowenstein, R. L. (1971). *Media, messages, and men: New perspectives in communication.* New York: McKay.

Pratkanis, A., & Aronson, E. (1992). *Age of propaganda: The everyday use and abuse of persuasion.* New York: Freeman.

Qualter, T. H. (1962). *Propaganda and psychological warfare.* New York: Random House.

Rokeach, M. (1954). The nature and meaning of dogmatism. *Psychological Review, 61,* 194–206.

Rokeach, M. (1960). *The open and closed mind: Investigations into the nature of belief systems and personality systems.* New York: Basic Books.

Rokeach, M. (1964). Images of the consumer's mind on and off Madison Avenue. *Etcetera, 31,* 264–273.

Smith, T. J., III (Ed.). (1989). *Propaganda: A pluralistic perspective.* New York: Praeger.

Sproule, J. M. (1989). Social responses to twentieth-century propaganda. In T. D. Smith (Ed.), *Propaganda: A pluralistic perspective* (pp. 5–22). New York: Praeger.

Sproule, J. M. (1997). *Propaganda and democracy: The American experience of media and mass persuasion.* Cambridge, England: Cambridge University Press.

Wreford, R. J. R. G. (1923). Propaganda, evil and good. *The Nineteenth Century and After, XCII,* 514–24.

Journal of Mass Media Ethics, *16*(2&3), 138–147

Responding To Propaganda: An Ethical Enterprise

Stanley B. Cunningham[1]
University of Windsor

❑ *By virtue of its epistemic deficits, propaganda is very much an unethical phenomenon. Coping effectively with propaganda requires a communicative response that confronts its inherent unethicality with ethically grounded resistance. In this article, I propose two congruent plans of communicative action, each of which rests on an apparent ethical connection: J. Michael Sproule's (1994) reclaiming of classical eloquence, and Jonathan Rauch's (1993) provocative program of "liberal science."*

Toward the end of his article in this issue, Jay Black (2001) identified a number of recurrent motifs that show up in the definitions of propaganda. These include an undue reliance on authority figures and spokespersons; the use of abstract language that does not lend itself to empirical validation; a panoply of simplistic thinking and reductionistic language in representations of people, institutions, and situations; and an inordinate preoccupation with conflict. Although Black opted to consider propaganda in less value-laden terms as an approach that saves us from indicting too much of our overall communication enterprise, I submit that an alternative judgment about the ethics of propaganda also needs to be considered.

I argue, less permissively, that undue reliance on authorities; the practice of applying abstract and unverifiable language; simplistic portrayals of people, institutions, and situations—all these are themselves forms of defective action that work against communication. So the flaws itemized by Black (2001) are neither innocent nor ethically indifferent. Indeed, the trouble with the neutralist approaches to propaganda and mass persuasion, so evident in most social science treatments, is that they tend to hide or to minimize the manifold epistemological deficiencies and unethical aspects of propaganda.

Thanks to the work of theorists such as Ellul (1957, 1962/1973) and Combs and Nimmo (1993), we now understand that propaganda is a far more diversified and complex phenomenon than just uttering lies and the slick manipulation of beliefs and language. These evident sorts of maneuvers, along with their assorted psychological effects, are just the tip of the iceberg. More radical disorders are at work. Propaganda comprises a whole family of epistemic disservices abetted mostly (but not entirely) by the media: It poses as genuine information and knowledge when, in fact, it generates little more than ungrounded belief and tenacious convictions; it prefers credibility, actual belief states, and mere impressions to knowledge; it supplies ersatz assurances and certainties; it skews perceptions; it systematically disregards superior epistemic values such as truth, understanding, and knowledge; and it discourages reasoning and a healthy respect for rigor, evidence, and procedural safeguards. In sum, what really defines propaganda is its utter indifference to superior epistemic values and their safeguards in both the propagandist and the propagandee. Moreover, these epistemic disorders immediately situate the whole propaganda process as an unethical state of affairs.

> *What defines propaganda is its utter indifference to superior epistemic values and their safeguards.*

The case has been argued elsewhere (Cunningham, 1993; Marlin, 1989) that propaganda is not ethically neutral. The truth in what we say, and the virtue of truthfulness in speakers—that is, a firm disposition to utter a true statement—have traditionally been regarded as premier moral qualities. Accordingly, propaganda's widespread mishandling of crucial epistemic values translates into immediate ethical significance. To disregard truth values (honesty or truthfulness, accuracy, reality, canons of evidence, investigative protocols, and safeguards) in situations where they are expected, and to abuse them as in the case of distortion or the misuse of information, is to engage in unethical conduct. To elevate lesser epistemic values such as mere attention, credibility, belief, and ungrounded certainty above the higher imperatives of accuracy, knowledge, and sound reasoning is to unseat that which should prevail in informative and descriptive discourse (cf. Postman, 1985). At the same time, to allow and to tolerate these kinds of inversions works against taking personal responsibility (within the limits of our ability and opportunities) for our own states of understanding and ignorance.

It seems like an exaggeration to claim that propaganda robs us of our freedom and turn us into automatons, yet it certainly sets impediments in our way, thereby inhibiting our capacity to know and to act well. Propaganda, that is, impairs the quality of willingness or voluntariness in our active life such that had we been informed otherwise, we could have, we might have, or would have judged, spoken, or voted otherwise. Moreover, in as much as propaganda practices (e.g., flawed reportage, negative political advertising) directly reduce the quality of democracy, it thereby erodes in manifold ways the primordial ethical values of justice and equity on which democracy rests (Ansolabehere & Iyengar, 1995; A. Carey, 1997).

In sum, propaganda is anything but ethically neutral. Rather, propaganda is very much a determinate social phenomenon such that its deep-structured epistemic and ethical deficits become the constitutive conditions that bring it into existence. This fact, I submit, becomes important in charting ways to deal with propaganda: To cope effectively with propaganda requires a response that confronts its inherent unethicality with ethically informed communication.

Reclaiming the Public Communication Sector

Now, because propaganda is a social phenomenon that poses as communication and exploits communication resources, I believe this points us in the direction we need to take: The most effective way in which to respond to propaganda is to establish a program of appropriate communicative action. I use the word *action* advisedly. It is not just enough to think about and analyze propaganda, to be aware of it, and to lament its ubiquity. Rather, we need to do something about it. We need, that is, to move out of the passive into the active zone; and the active in this case is nothing less than the business of ethically attuned public discourse within what is now regularly called the "age" and the "century of propaganda" (Pratkanis & Aronson, 1991; Wilke, 1998, pp. 1–2).

I have in mind two congruent plans of communicative action each of which rests on an apparent ethical connection: J. Michael Sproule's (1994) reclaiming an ancient rhetorical concept and Jonathan Rauch's (1993) provocative program of liberal science. Sproule (1994) urged a historic conception of eloquence as a necessary antidote to the lifeless and impoverished political propaganda of today. I view Rauch's analysis of liberal science as an elaboration of the argumentative and ethical virtuosity at work in the eloquence enterprise. My argument in this article, as it moves through the arguments of Sproule and Rauch, frames itself as an elaboration in which it becomes increasingly evident that responding to propaganda is necessarily and unavoidably an ethical enterprise.

Responding to Propaganda Through Eloquence

One of the more striking responses to propaganda is that proposed by Sproule (1994) in the concluding chapter of his *Channels of Propaganda* (pp. 327–356) when he urged a return to the classical value of eloquence. Sproule reminded us that the dominant educational remedy taught in U.S.

schools and colleges since the 1940s has been the "critical thinking" approach. Under the early influence of the Institute for Propaganda Analysis (1937–1942) and its bulletins, propaganda analysis usually became synonymous with detecting seven common propaganda devices or fallacies: for example, name calling, glittering generalities, card stacking, and so forth (Sproule, 1997, pp. 129–137). The result, according to Sproule (1994), was that the early analysts neglected the larger social context, including leading corporate propagandists (e.g., private energy companies, governments, lobby and political action groups), self-serving objectives, and the co-optation of major channels. Sproule's (1994) point was that when text-based analysis is too narrowly focused it misses out on the broader, nondiscursive features of manipulation.

Sproule (1994) offered three arguments (pp. 334–335) to bolster his position. First, detecting propaganda through critical thinking and assorted linguistic devices works satisfactorily with well-defined utterances such as speeches, advertisements, and announcements, but it is much less successful when the manipulative intent is extended and "buried in the practices and formulae of journalism, research, education, and entertainment" (p. 334). It is easy to overlook manipulative appeal when it is embedded within press relations practices or the allure of promilitary entertainment such as, say, the film *Top Gun*. Second, fine-tuned text analysis may blind the analysts themselves to the propaganda of social groups and organizations whom they favor or with whom they share an ideology. Groups within the educational sector are just as susceptible to this kind of unwitting complicity. J. W. Carey (1989), for instance, pointed out that in the 1930s when propaganda analysis was not always able to maintain critical detachment, some of the early progressive analysts "used propaganda analysis to propagate another piece of propaganda" (p. 279). Finally, Sproule (1994) argued, linguistic devices analysis may distract us from recognizing the "wider social reality of which these expressions are but a small part" (p. 335). Losing sight of the relation between the part and the whole misleads us, and seriously weakens the investigative enterprise itself. "[P]ropaganda analysis," Sproule (1994) insisted, "requires the scrutiny of the discursive context more than of individual texts" (p. 335). The point is convincingly substantiated by the weight of scholarship (A. Carey, 1997; Herman & Chomsky, 1988; Parenti, 1993).

Although journalism and education assist us as antipropaganda resources, our real challenge is to restore the public sphere by reclaiming participation in political debate and action. To this end, Sproule (1994) advocated the broad enterprise of "revitalizing rhetorical tradition" (p. 339) and "restoring eloquent speechmaking" (p. 339) that, he added, signifies "merging the practitioner and progressivist points of view" (p.

339) that defined so many of the original and earliest responses to propaganda in the 1930s. It marks, that is, a return to the classical idea of eloquence that Sproule (1994) called "a *kind of communication* [italics added] that draws upon great ideas, passionate commitment, and the highest values of a society or culture" (p. 340). A climate of eloquence, Sproule (1994) argued, "*incapacitates propaganda*" (p. 340, italics added) because it encourages speakers or advocates to harness their ideas to the aspirations of citizens; this, in turn, energizes otherwise passive audiences. Eloquence neutralizes propaganda-induced passivity in other ways, too: It "dissolves the power of unsupported conclusions by inculcating an appreciation for reasons," and it "negates the power of visual images by forcing people to think about society as well as to watch fragments of it on TV" (Sproule, 1994, p. 340).

A climate of eloquence, Sproule argued, "incapacitates propaganda" (p. 340).

Sproule's (1994) concept of eloquence stands in stark contrast to what he characterized as the "impoverished," "ghost written" speechmaking of today—"disembodied discourse ... pseudo-eloquence [that] lacks every ingredient of eloquence" (p. 343). Eloquence, on the other hand, is a complex armament of speaking and reasoning skills, passionate commitment, and a dedication to "the highest values of the society rather than lower-level appeals to hate, fear, or self-assertion" (Sproule, 1994, p. 343). Sproule's (1994) spirited advocacy, then, was an invitation to restore the elements of argument, engagement, and accountability to public and political discourse whose eclipse Kathleen Hall Jamieson (1992) lamented, for example, in the 1988 presidential election (pp. 203–236). By contrast, eloquence is a mode of communication that engages the whole person—speaker and listener—through an integration of values, reason, and passion aligned thereto. By virtue of its sensitivity to a range of moral and epistemic values, it constitutes a profoundly moral response to the triviality and expediency that characterizes today's propaganda.

Although he did not single out Cicero, Sproule's (1994) antipropagandist respondent resurrects the Ciceronian ideal of the consummate rhetor in whom wisdom, probity, and rhetorical mastery inform each other. That integration of these value-laden skills is called *eloquence*. In the *De Oratore, Book III* (1960, #55–#56, pp. 43–45), Cicero stressed its alliance with the moral virtues. Indeed, "eloquence is one of the supreme virtues" (*Est enim eloquentia una quaedam de summis virtutibus*, p. 43), and he called it "supreme wisdom" (*summa prudentia, sapientia,* p. 43–45). Nor is Cicero's an isolated testimony. There are later echoes in Seneca and Quintilian, and we can find even earlier statements of this theme in Aristotle's original view of rhetoric as ethically grounded discourse (Johnstone, 1980; Thorp, 1993). The less explicit motif I also underscore here is that the original theorists of rhetoric never labored under the fact-value shibboleth that has dominated social science thinking throughout the 20th century. The ancients would have been puzzled, even appalled by the kind of divisions that we have allowed to intrude between public discourse and moral habitudes. As part of responding to the culture of mass persuasion and propaganda, then, we need to reconsider both the ethical realism and the unabashed moral engagement that lay behind that earlier mind-set.

Responding to Propaganda through "Liberal Science"

In *Kindly Inquisitors: The New Attacks on Free Thought* (1993), Rauch supplied a compelling supplement to Sproule's (1994) concept of eloquence. In the concluding lines of this work, Rauch stated, "What hurts us is not wrong-thinking people but propaganda and ignorance; and unfettered criticism— liberal science—is the cure, not the disease" (p. 162). Rauch's monograph is a thoughtful response to ostensibly well-intentioned attempts to silence offensive speech in the name of compassion and sensitivity for groups, usually minorities. The offending speech in question covers a wide range of hate and racist mongering, gender insults, and gay bashing—virtually any kind of inflammatory epithet and discriminatory utterance.

Rauch's (1993) remarks, then, are directly relevant to the issue of developing an ethical response to propaganda. First, offensive speech has long been recognized as a form of propaganda: "Hate propaganda," after all, is one of its standard categories. Second, offensive speech acts (including degrading language, stereotypes, visuals, and racist history) are forms of symbolic inducement that influence beliefs, feelings, and behavior. Third, in reacting to offensive speech, organizations (including the courts, school boards, and universities) have often formulated policies and engaged in practices that are themselves indistinguishable from propaganda techniques: censorship; regulations and codes that restrict speech freedoms; legislating (in)correct speech usage; inducing climates of uneasiness that inhibit free expression; and the imposition of spurious equivalence (e.g., creationism in science texts, epistemological relativism).

Although freedom of speech is legally assured within our democracy, the central issue for Rauch (1993) was "What should be society's principle for raising and settling differences of opinion"? (p. 5). Rauch understood that the metalegal choice we face is unavoidably epistemological, moral, and political. With a keen historical grasp of legal and philosophical developments, he enumerated (p. 6) five major contenders, four of which constitute serious threats to healthy rationality and its free expression. These four range from the elitism of fundamentalism whose sanctions are based on the authority of its leaders and their brand of scripture, to "Simple Egalitarianism" ("all sincere persons' beliefs have equal claims to respect") to the "Radical Egalitarian Principle" whereby "the beliefs of persons in historically oppressed classes or groups get special consideration" (p. 6). Rauch believed that only the fifth principle, that of liberal science, is acceptable, but in today's society it is increasingly in a state of siege.

The most insidious challenge to free speech, however, is the "humanitarian threat" whose central tenet is "allow no pain to be caused" (Rauch, 1993, p. 122). In point of fact, at the heart of the humanitarian threat there are really two fallacious principles that coalesce: (a) the high-minded principle that speech-generated offenses are inherently wrong, and (b) each individual's sincerely held opinions carry equal weight; and so this credo of political equality graduates into being the criterion of truth, knowledge, science, and teachability. In some quarters (e.g., college campuses), these principles have taken on the status of imperatives such that certain forms of speech are prohibited and subject to severe sanctions (Hentoff, 1993).

In opposition to all this, Rauch (1993) posited liberal science or "unfettered criticism" as the only defensible alternative. Rauch's (1993) choice of principles is backed up by a developed theory of knowledge, undergirded in turn by a profoundly ethical vision of communication. Consider first the epistemology of liberal science. Liberal science is not a body of certitudes, nor is it anything like a mechanical accumulation of facts and apodictic laws. Rather, it is "a society, an ecology" (Rauch, 1994, p. 58) in which "the desire to find error, to find new beliefs which correct the inadequacies of old ones" (p. 65) are ever bit as important as the discovery of truths. Inspired by C. S. Peirce, Rauch (1993) said we are "a community of people looking for each other's mistakes" (p. 63). In such a society, certitude and the satisfaction of personal certainty cede right of way to scepticism, the quest to challenge all opinions and beliefs, thereby nudging some of them closer and closer to a state of truth or knowledge. More than once, Rauch quoted Plato's dictum that "belief without knowledge is an ugly thing, and that there is always an element of blindness in ungrounded opinions" (Plato, 1945, pp. 216–217 [505–506]). Ultimately, it is the dialectic of open discussion that filters out weak and unsupportable opinions, and confirms others as knowledge—subject always, of course, to later revision.

Rauch's (1993) concept of liberal science, then, is an "evolutionary epistemology [in which] hypotheses and ideas evolve as they compete under pressure from criticism, with intellectual diversity providing the raw material for change" (p. 58). Knowledge is not private or privileged glimpses. Rather, it is a social product, a product of what Rauch (1993) called "the knowledge industry" and "the reality industry" (p. 38), names for the community of scholars and critics who sustain the dialectic. Two rules dominate the discourse within this community and provide its "epistemological constitution" (p. 76):

1. No one gets the final say, which means that, in principle, all knowledge is revisable and therefore uncertain.
2. No one has personal authority. This is not an assault on expertise and credentials, but rather the recognition that the method of (in)validating claims should produce the same results when exercised by others, regardless of personal identity or reputations. (Rauch, 1993, pp. 46–50)

The name *liberal science*, then, paraphrases a social philosophy of truth that defines itself not as a body of unchanging truths, nor by mere consensus and agreement, but primarily as "a self-organizing swirl of disagreements" (Rauch, 1993, p. 73). Rauch thought that "it is very good at resolving conflicts" and, in the same breath, gleefully conceded that it is "very good at not resolving conflicts" (p. 73). Its power of dialectic, then, is boundless, the social conversation open ended—even if the language is sometimes offensive, the sentiments painful, and the ideas unwelcome.

Accordingly, liberal science is both an epistemology and an ethic. "Taking seriously the idea that we might be wrong," Rauch (1993) told us, "is … an intellectual style, an attitude or ethic" (p. 45). Elsewhere he called liberal science's dominant principles ("No Final Say", "No Personal Authority") "moral commandments, ethical ideals" (pp. 75–76). As with Kant's categorical imperative, liberal science empowers each of us as an enfranchised participant and critic with the same moral entitlement to question, to seek out the errors in others' speech and, of course, to be wrong (Rauch, 1993, p. 53). To say all that is to say something very different from saying that X's opinion is every bit as valid or defensible as Y's because what has now been added is openness to unflinching review and evaluation of everything we say, and ownership of our own fallibility. It's important, too, to realize that we should not view Rauch's foundational ethical imperatives as infallible truths or content principles that reflexively exempt themselves from review. Rather, these imperatives stand as directives, procedures by virtue of which the enterprise of public discourse is inherently ethical.

In all of this, Rauch (1993) added, we should not even pretend to eliminate bias or prejudice but only to channel it and to hold it in check through the diversity of others' arguments. With obvious resonances to J. S. Mill's

On Liberty and Milton's *Areopagitica,* Rauch even celebrated the presence of bias, prejudice, and "inspired error" in society because it promotes debate: "It is a positive good to have among us some racists and anti-Semites, some Christian-haters and some rabid fundamentalists" (p. 68). Such an inclusive society "pits people's prejudices against each other. Then it sits back and watches knowledge evolve" (p. 68). Even though Rauch's liberal science allows for the insolence of the street fighter, it remains unswervingly committed to its own defining rules of engagement: No speaker or opinion is special, and no belief or principle is infallible.

We should not even pretend to eliminate bias or prejudice but only to channel it and to hold it in check.

Conclusions

Propaganda, with all its protean variety, its lurking interlinear presence, and slick visual appeal demands a special repertoire of communication talents to recognize and respond to it. Confronting it for what it is requires a complex habitude, which combines moral vision, critical reasoning, and communication skills, and a solid base of virtuous attachments. Sproule's (1994) reclaimed concept of eloquence, I argue, nominates the "kind of communication" needed to neutralize the pseudocommunication of propaganda. Rauch's (1993) liberal science, at the same time as it spells out the conversational tenacity needed in public discourse, also magnifies the moral engagement that lies at the heart of eloquence. The result would be a quality of public discourse, a communication ethic, that effectively addresses and exposes the climate of propaganda within which multitudes of symbolic inducements parade as gratifying "communication" to an otherwise unresisting public. In tandem, I argue, Sproule and Rauch supply us with a blueprint for this kind of principled response.

Note

1. Copyright of this article has been retained by the author.

References

Ansolabehere, S., & Iyengar, S. (1995). *Going negative: How political advertisements shrink and polarize the electorate.* New York: Free Press.

Black, J. (2001). Semantics and Ethics of propaganda. *Journal of Mass Media Ethics, 16,* 120–136.

Carey, A. (1997). *Taking the risk out of democracy: Corporate propaganda versus freedom and liberty.* Ed. Andrew Lohrey. Chicago: University of Illinois Press.

Carey, J. W. (1989). Communications and the progressives. *Critical Studies in Mass Communication, 6,* 264–282.

Cicero, M. T. (1960). *De oratore, Book III* (H. Rackham, Trans.). Cambridge, MA: Harvard University Press.

Coombs, J. E. (1993). *The new propaganda: The dictatorship of palaver in contemporary politics.* New York, London: Longman

Cunningham, S. B. (1993). Sorting out the ethics of propaganda. *Communication Studies, 3,* 233–245.

Ellul, J. (1957). Information and propaganda. *Diogenes, 18,* 61–77.

Ellul, J. (1973). *Propaganda: The formation of men's attitudes.* New York: Random House. (Original work published 1962)

Hentoff, N. (1993). Speech codes on campus. In A. Alexander & J. Hanson (Eds.), *Taking sides: Clashing views on controversial issues in mass media and society* (2nd ed., pp. 178–183). Guilford, CT: Dushkin.

Herman, E. S., & Chomsky, N. (1988). *Manufacturing consent: The political economy of the mass media.* New York: Pantheon.

Jamieson, K. H. (1992). *Dirty politics: Deception, distraction and democracy.* New York: Oxford University Press.

Johnstone, C. L. (1980). An Aristotelian trilogy: Ethics, rhetoric, politics, and the search for moral truth. *Philosophy and Rhetoric, 13*(1), 1–24.

Jowett, G. S., & O'Donnell, V. (1992). *Propaganda and persuasion* (2nd ed.). Beverly Hills, CA: Sage.

Marlin, R. R. A. (1989). Propaganda and the ethics of persuasion. *International Journal of Moral and Social Studies, 4,* 37–72.

Parenti, M. (1993). *Inventing reality: The politics of the mass media* (2nd ed.). New York: St. Martin's Press.

Plato. (1945). *The republic of Plato* (F. M. Cornford, Trans.). New York: Oxford University Press.

Postman, N. (1985). *Amusing ourselves to death: Public discourse in the age of show business.* New York: Penguin.

Pratkanis, A., & Aronson, E. (1991). *The age of propaganda: The use and abuse of persuasion.* New York: Freeman.

Rauch, J. (1993). *Kindly inquisitors: The new attacks on free thought.* Chicago: The University of Chicago Press.

Sproule, J. M. (1994). *Channels of propaganda.* Bloomington, IN: EDINFO & ERIC.

Sproule, J. M. (1997). *Propaganda and democracy: The American experience of media and mass persuasion.* Cambridge, England: Cambridge University Press.

Thorp, J. (1993). Aristotle's rehabilitation of rhetoric. *The Canadian Journal of Rhetorical Studies/La Revue Canadienne D'Études Rhétoriques, 3,* 13–30.

Wilke, J. (1998). *Propaganda in the 20th century: Contributions to its history.* Cresskill, NJ: Hampton.

Journal of Mass Media Ethics, *16*(2&3), 148–175
Copyright © 2001, Lawrence Erlbaum Associates, Inc..

The TARES Test: Five Principles for Ethical Persuasion

Sherry Baker
Brigham Young University

David L. Martinson
Florida International University

❏ *Whereas professional persuasion is a means to an immediate and instrumental end (such as increased sales or enhanced corporate image), ethical persuasion must rest on or serve a deeper, morally based final (or relative last) end. Among the moral final ends of journalism, for example, are truth and freedom. There is a very real danger that advertisers and public relations practitioners will play an increasingly dysfunctional role in the communications process if means continue to be confused with ends in professional persuasive communications. Means and ends will continue to be confused unless advertisers and public relations practitioners reach some level of agreement as to the moral end toward which their efforts should be directed.*

In this article we advance a five-part test (the TARES test) that defines this moral end, establishes ethical boundaries that should guide persuasive practices, and serves as a set of action-guiding principles directed toward a moral consequence in professional persuasion. The TARES Test consists of five principles: Truthfulness (of the message), Authenticity (of the persuader), Respect (for the persuadee), Equity (of the persuasive appeal) and Social Responsibility (for the common good). We provide checklists to guide the practitioner in moral reflection and application of TARES Test principles.

Individuals active in some area of professional persuasive mass communication—that is, advertising, public relations, and so forth—frequently have a difficult time defending what it is they do from a societal, common good, and ethical perspective, in their own minds as well as in their conversations with others.

Defenders—apologists—for advertising and public relations, although not denying that ethical considerations have been a problem, also contend that critics often overstate the case. Speaking specifically to the question of societal value, advertisers frequently contend that without advertising the American free enterprise system simply would not exist. In this they echo the rhetoric of U.S. Supreme Court Justice Harry Blackmun in his opinion for the court in the landmark *Virginia Board of Pharmacy v. Virginia Citizens*

Consumer Council (1976) case that afforded commercial advertising limited First Amendment protection. In his opinion in that case Justice Blackmun wrote

> Advertising, however, tasteless and excessive it sometimes may seem, is nonetheless dissemination of information as to who is producing and selling what product, for what reason, and at what price. So long as we preserve a predominately free enterprise economy, the allocation of our resources in large measure will be made through numerous private economic decisions. It is a matter of public interest that those decisions, in the aggregate, be intelligent and well informed. To this end, the free flow of commercial information is indispensable. (p. 765)

Legendary public relations scholar Scott Cutlip (1994) presented a similar societal justification for public relations when he asserted that "the social justification for public relations is to ethically and effectively plead the cause of a client or organization in the free wheeling forum of public debate" (p. xii). Cutlip maintained that in a democratic society the practitioner serves the common good by helping to bring about a process in which "every idea, individual, and institution ... [has] a full and fair hearing in the public forum" (p. xii).

Ethical Problem in Persuasive Communications

It seems clear that proponents believe the persuasive "professions" can serve the public interest and that persons active in those professions can be ethical. Unfortunately, the "can" too often does not translate into a reality of fact. That is, although proponents argue advertising can serve the economic or social system by providing important consumer information, too frequently it operates dysfunctionally by providing misinformation, inflating the cost of goods and services, and inducing individuals to make purchases that are not in either their short- or long-term interest.

The same is true in regard to public relations. Although many practitioners will insist Cutlip (Cutlip, Center, & Broom, 1994) is correct in asserting that practitioners can serve the public interest by helping to make various points of view articulate in the marketplace of ideas, in fact those same practitioners too frequently serve to disrupt that marketplace by serving special interests at the expense of the common good (p. 133). Furthermore, instead of providing useful information, practitioners frequently "clutter ... [the] already-choked channels of communication with the debris of pseudoevents and phony phrases that confuse rather than clarify" (Cutlip et al., 1994, p. 133).

One needs to ask, Why? Why do the persuasive professions at least appear to evoke in persons a proclivity toward acting in a less than ethical manner and in ways that are detrimental to the common good or public interest? Critics argue that such a response is intrinsic to the very nature of much of persuasive communication. That is, efforts to persuade—despite all the efforts at rationalization—can not really be differentiated from manipulation, coercion, propaganda, or all of these.

More supportive of efforts to persuade is the work of Andersen (1978) who defined *ethical* persuasion as "a communication activity that unites people ... [while it] permits maximum individual choice" (p. 3). For Andersen, ethical persuasion centered around an effort "to effect a desired voluntary change in the attitudes and/or actions of" (p. 7) those to whom particular persuasion efforts are directed. For communication ethicists Jaksa and Pritchard (1994), Andersen's emphasis on voluntary change was critical. Jaksa and Pritchard stated

> ... [this emphasis on voluntary change] in the person being persuaded ... distinguishes persuasion from indoctrination and coercion, which do not allow significant choice. But it also suggests that ethically acceptable modes of persuasion do not rely on deceptive manipulative tactics.... [Jaksa & Pritchard] support those forms of persuasion that show respect for individuals as capable of making significant choices ... those capable of rational choice are respected only if manipulative and deceptive tactics are avoided. (p. 76–77)

"The advantage of a lie without telling a literal untruth"

It has been suggested that to allow for voluntary change, the persuader must provide for something at least approaching what Klaidman and Beauchamp (1987) termed *substantial completeness*—"that point at which a reasonable ... [person's] requirements are satisfied" (p. 35). Although ethics may not dictate that the persuader provide a scientifically verifiable summation of a particular issue, one can insist that such efforts "be directed toward genuinely informing ... [others]—not creating false impressions, whether or not what is communicated might be literally, in at least some fashion, true" (Martinson, 1996–1997, p. 44).

It is precisely at this point that problems begin to surface. Advertising and public relations practitioners too often use "torturous linguistic contortions" to achieve what Gaffney suggested was "the advantage of a lie without telling a literal untruth" (Martinson, 1996–1997, p. 43). The case study law books are filled with such examples. Certainly one of the classics in this regard is the Federal Trade Commission order that "ITT Continental Baking Company ... correct a false impression created by a long-term series of advertisements for the company's Profile bread" (Middleton & Chamberlin, 1994, p. 322). Profile advertising had implied

> That consumers could lose weight by eating Profile bread because it contained fewer calories than other breads. Actually, Profile bread contained the same number of calories per ounce as other breads. Therefore, if a person kept a better figure while eating ITT Continental's bread, it was because Profile bread was sliced thinner. (Middleton & Chamberlin, 1994, p. 322)

Is it any wonder that advertisers and public relations practitioners are viewed in such a negative light when one recognizes that examples such as the Profile "fewer calories" campaign are too often more reflective of behavior that is normal for the industry rather than exceptional? Advertisers and public relations practitioners are distrusted because the public—with good reason—has come to recognize that too frequently the goal in persuasive communication centers around exploiting them in a manner that is, in fact, "detrimental to ... [the public's] own preferences, interests, or well being" (Jaksa & Pritchard, 1994, p. 76).

Defining the problem, of course, is less difficult than advancing—from an ethics perspective—an answer. Surely there would not be so much unethical persuasive communication if there were not some benefit in engaging in such wrong actions. Many feel they are "forced" to use less than ethical means because the use of such means are essential to achieving the desired end. Chided for their use of stereotypes, for example, many in advertising are likely to respond "Gee, I'd really like to avoid these stereotypes, but I've got to use them to survive" (DeFleur & Dennis, 1998, p. 337).

The "Relative Last End" of Professional Communications

One will never be able to articulate a practical means to achieving at least something approaching a level of minimally acceptable ethical behavior in persuasive communications until there is greater agreement as to what is that last end toward which persuasive communication is directed.

It is essential to note, in this context, that what is being considered here is a relative last end—but, nevertheless, something beyond increased sales or an improved corporate image. When Cutlip (1994), for example, spoke about assisting clients in an effort to inject their views into the marketplace of ideas, there is an unstated assumption that there is an end that will be achieved in that process. Hopefully, that end goes beyond increased profits for the particular organization the practitioner represents.

For the philosopher, "a thing is intended either for its own sake or for the sake of something else" (Fagothey, 1976, p. 85). There have, of course, been "pitched battles" between teleologists who argue an act should be judged ethical or not based on its consequences, and deontologists who argue an action must be judged ethical or not according to the means utilized to achieve the desired end. Most would agree, however, with Fagothey that "a means always supposes an end" (p. 85). More specifically

> ... [A means] is called a means precisely because it lies on a mean, or middle, position between the agent and the end, and its use brings the agent to the end. The same thing may be both means and end in different respects, for it may be sought both for its own sake and for the sake of something further. This is called an *intermediate* end, and there may be a long series of such intermediate ends, as when we want A in order to get B, B in order to get C, C in order to get D, and so on. (Fagothey, 1976, p. 85)

That is why one speaks of a relative last end as the goal of persuasive communications in the immediate context. In a strict philosophical sense, what is being discussed is an intermediate end—as contrasted with an ultimate or absolute last end. It is, of course, well beyond the scope of this particular effort to consider questions germane to what may be the ultimate or absolute last end of those engaged in persuasive communications—that must be left to philosophers and theologians. What is of primary concern here is examining that relative last end toward which a discussion of applied ethics in the persuasive communication can and should be directed.

The immediate end in some forms of persuasive communication is readily identifiable. Wells, Burnett, and Moriarty (1992) stated that the goal (end) of product advertising is "to inform or stimulate the market about the sponsor's product(s). The intent is clearly to sell a particular product, to the exclusion of competitors' products" (p. 13).

The immediate goal (end) of public relations, on the other hand, is subject to some debate even among practitioners. Cutlip (1994), for example, has consistently identified the practitioner as an advocate—insisting that "the advocate's role is essential in a democracy that must be responsive to the public and dependent on the reconciliation of public and private interests in a mutually rewarding manner" (p. xii). Grunig and Hunt (1984), on the other hand, have advanced what they define as a "two-way symmetric" model of public relations that has as a "goal ... [facilitating] mutual understanding between organizations and their publics" (p. 22).

The Grunig and Hunt (1984) "two-way symmetric" model, in fact, is useful in the context of defining a "relative last end" in all forms of persuasive communication because it is stated in terms that at least begins to move beyond egocentricity—and surely "overcoming, or at least reducing, egocentricity is an essential element" in the cultivating of persons who will engage in what reasonable persons would define as ethical persuasion (Jaksa & Pritchard, 1994, p. 94).

It is for this reason that the relative last end in persuasive communications must not be defined in terms of increased sales or increased profitability or visibility for an organization or client. That is not to suggest that efforts directed toward increased profitability or visibility are illegitimate per se. It is to suggest, however, that the persuader wishing to be ethical must always keep in mind that increased sales or increased visibility are nothing more than a means to some more important social and individual end. If not, persuaders inevitably will begin to embrace something approaching social Darwinism in which the goal too often is to succeed at all costs—or at least to succeed through the use of any means that do not violate the letter of the law.

The last end in persuasive communication (relative to the context of this discussion) must center around respect for that individual to whom the particular persuasive effort is directed. Any persuasive effort must be directed toward providing information that will enable the person to whom it is directed, in Andersen's (1978) earlier cited words, the freedom to make a voluntary choice (p. 7). Although the short-term—or immediate—goal, in the case of advertising for example, may well be increased sales, the ethical persuader will only utilize those messages and methods that demonstrate genuine respect for those to whom the particular advertisement is directed.

Genuine respect dictates that the persuader place the interests of persons to whom a particular persuasive effort is directed before his or her (the persuader's) narrowly defined self-interest. It means, in fact, that the persuader must ethically evaluate his or her efforts from a relative last end perspective, which views a particular persuasive effort as

> Assisting the receiver in attaining that which is already implicitly … in the receiver's interest.… [the persuader] must communicate truthful and substantially complete information … [in a context] that will enable the receiver to make a rational decision to accept or reject that which is being put forth. (Martinson, 1996–1997, pp. 44–45)

That is not to say that all efforts at persuasion must be ethically evaluated from a coldly analytical and scientifically objective perspective. Jaksa and Pritchard (1994), in fact, made an important point when they pointed out that "rational argument is not the only morally acceptable form of persuasion" (p. 77). They were quick to add, however, that "even when evidence or proof is not available, those capable of rational choice are respected only if manipulative and deceptive tactics are avoided" (Jaksa & Pritchard, 1994, p. 77).

This is true because persuaders are engaged in acts of communication and any effort to communicate can be judged as ethical only to the degree with which it provides, as a relative last end, genuinely truthful information. One who communicates false, misleading, or deceptive information in a serious circumstance, from a moral philosophy perspective, does wrong because to do so perverts the very purpose of speech (communication). Certainly society would quickly come to a grinding halt were deception to become the norm. Fagothey (1976) made this point succinctly when he stated

> By nature ... [each man and woman] is a social being, and the gift of speech is perhaps the chief means by which ... [our] social life is carried on. Like all other gifts, speech may be used or abused. Thus truthfulness is good and lying is wrong.... [To wrongfully deceive] is *morally wrong* because it is an abuse of the natural ability of communication, because it is contrary to ... [an individual's] social nature, which requires mutual trust, ... and because it debases the dignity of the human person, whose mind is made for truth. (p. 241–242)

In final analysis, is that not why advertising and public relations practitioners are viewed so negatively by a large percentage of the population? People distrust "professional" persuaders because they believe—with good reason—that too often those persuaders are attempting to manipulate them in ways that are "detrimental to ... [their] own preferences, interests, or well-being" (Jaksa & Pritchard, 1994, p. 76). Advertisers and public relations practitioners are distrusted because their goals (relative last ends) are defined not in terms of the interests or well-being of those to whom their particular persuasive efforts are directed. In fact, too often their (the persuaders') efforts, as noted, are directed toward goals (ends) that run counter to the interests or well being of those to whom those efforts are directed.

Those engaged in efforts to persuade through advertising and public relations will begin to demonstrate genuine respect for others only when they begin to "demonstrate that they can view a situation through the eyes of listeners as well as their own" (Jaksa & Pritchard, 1994, p. 78). If professional persuaders make an effort to view their work through the eyes of "significant others," surely they will be more likely to avoid the temptation to lie without lying, to be deceptive without telling a material lie, to secure the advantage of a lie without making a literal false statement (Gaffney, 1979, p. 268).

Moral Myopia in The Culture Of Professional Persuasive Communications

Ethics (moral philosophy) is a subject that primarily is not concerned with increased profits or increased company visibility. It is, rather, concerned with what one ought to do—or ought not to do (Fagothey, 1976, p.

3). One might suggest that one can "call those actions right which ... [one] ought to do, and those actions wrong which ... [one] ought not to do" (Fagothey, 1976, p. 2). Ethics further asks that one be able to justify his or her actions from the perspective of others—"to attempt to justify ... is to offer reasons in support of ... [an action that] can be found acceptable to anyone capable of rationally considering ... [that action], not just to oneself" (Jaksa & Pritchard, 1994, p. 108).

Noted contemporary ethicist Bok (1989) agreed that one must be able to justify his or her actions from the perspective of others—what she terms *reasonable persons* (p. 91). "To justify," Bok (1989) argued, "is to defend as just, right, or proper, by providing adequate reasons" (p. 91). She insisted that it is not enough to be able to justify one's actions to one's self. Consulting one's informed conscience, of course, is essential to ethical decision making. Bok (1989) noted, however, that conscience can "be very accommodating and malleable" (p. 94). Those who would engage in unethical conduct often "have a ... [comparatively easy] time in justifying their behavior so long as their only audience is their own conscience or their self-appointed imaginary onlooker" (Bok, 1989, p. 94–95).

> *One's informed conscience, of course, is essential to ethical decision making.*

The key, according to Bok (1989), is to move to a level of "public justification" (p. 97). The individual engaged in a particular persuasive communication effort, for example, would be required—hypothetically—to be willing to "try to convince an audience of representative people that" his or her particular communication efforts were justified (Jaksa & Pritchard, 1994, p. 107). Bok (1989) called this "publicity" (p. 97).

A willingness to meet this "test of publicity" would most likely eliminate a considerable portion of what reasonable persons would define as unethical conduct in persuasive communication. A willingness to meet such a test would also indicate that those engaged in persuasive communication did respect those to whom particular communication efforts were directed the standard that is advanced here.

Application of this test of publicity can perhaps be made more clear by citing the debate surrounding the case of an automobile manufacturer who advertised (promoted) its product "by comparing the quietness of its car to that of a glider ... [while] not saying that a glider is noisy in flight" (Pember, 1981, p. 414). A reasonable person would most likely judge that the advertiser was attempting to use literal truth to manipulate potential customers into buying its particular model. (The great majority of persons have never been in a glider and would naturally assume that a powerless aircraft, high above the hustle and bustle of the working world, must be a virtual citadel of restful peace and tranquility.) That same reasonable person, therefore, would likely conclude that the advertiser was not showing respect for those to whom the communication was directed. In short, that advertiser would fail Bok's (1989) test of publicity.

Similar was the case of the public relations practitioner working for a large conglomerate (Montgomery, 1978, p. 14). He was quoted as saying "It's so damn easy to massage the numbers" (Montgomery, p. 14). Why would one want to "massage numbers"? In the specific instance, he said, because "his company was able to show in the front of its annual report ... that per share earnings were as good as management had predicted they would be" (Montgomery, p. 14). In fact, one "had to wade through some fine print and the heavy financial tables way in the back of the report" (Montgomery, p. 14). At that point, one would find "that earnings were down sharply" (Montgomery, p. 14).

In the process, the macroethical question has been ignored.

A problem for persuasive communication centers around the fact that, despite all the rhetoric to the contrary, unethical conduct—conduct that does not show respect for those to whom particular communications are directed—continues to be far too often the norm. It continues to be the norm because those engaged in particular facets of persuasive communication—including practitioners and educators responsible for the instruction of future practitioners—have too often viewed ethics in microterms. Too often the focus has been on whether or not a particular persuasive effort is ethical or unethical. In the process, the macroethical question has been ignored. That is, what is that relative last end toward which such persuasive communication is directed?

So long as those in persuasive communication continue to focus on the individual "sins" of practitioners and not the broader question of why such sins are so prevalent, the level of ethical conduct in advertising and public relations will not be advanced. People do not so generally and broadly distrust those in persuasive communications because occasionally an advertiser or public relations practitioner will engage in less than ethical conduct. They distrust persuasive communicators—generally and broadly—because they fear those in the field do not respect them as individuals and are interested only in achieving immediate and narrowly defined self-interested goals or objectives—goals or objectives that often are not in the interest of those to whom persuasive communication is directed.

It is the broader working place culture of the persuasive professions that is the major problem, and not so much the individual acts—however reprehensible they may be—of particular practitioners. Because of a cultural myopia that is so pervasive in persuasive communication, practitioners and educators "have not been sufficiently attentive to a need to transcend a narrowly defined *personalistic vision*" (Martinson, 1996, p. 20). One might suggest that to this point far too "much of the effort … [to define ethical behavior in persuasive communications has been] spent paying attention to the ethical trees … [when it] would be more profitably expended if it were focused on the ethical forest from which the trees cannot be separated" (Martinson, 1996, p. 4).

It may, for example, help to soothe a troubled conscience when a practitioner active in advertising or public relations chooses to make a public "confession" as to particular unethical transgressions he or she is guilty of vis-à-vis acts of persuasion. Such an individual may, in fact, be entitled to a certain level of absolution providing they display genuine contrition. Unless, however, a greater number of those active in persuasive communication are willing to confront the broader working place culture question as to why such acts are so prevalent, ethical conduct will not significantly improve because individual acts, as noted, do not take place in a professional or cultural vacuum.

Moral End of Persuasive Communication

Those active in some aspect of persuasive communication would do well to read and contemplate Victor Hugo's (1862/1997) classic novel, *Les Miserables.* In that novel, Hugo schooled the reader—perhaps as well as any novelist in history—that justice, particularly social justice, cannot be defined so much in terms of individual acts, but rather in terms of broader principles. A man who emerges in the novel as an intrinsically good man, Jean Valjean, is convicted of stealing bread. Later, when he escapes, he is pursued in a relentless manner by a cold, unsympathetic and legalistic policeman—Javert.

The lesson is clear. Valjean emerges as a good man because he has a better understanding of that end toward which one's individual acts are directed. Although the act of stealing another's property under ordinary circumstances is wrong, property is but a means to an end. Traditional ethics consistently held, in fact, that one—under extreme circumstances—was entitled to steal food.

It is again a matter of putting means and ends into proper perspective, and this is a particularly important point where persuasive communications are concerned. If means continue to be confused with ends in professional persuasive communications, there is a very real danger that advertisers and public relations practitioners will play an increasingly dysfunctional role in the communications process. Means will continue to be confused with ends unless advertisers and public relations practitioners reach some level of agreement as to that relative last end toward which their efforts should be directed.

In this article we argue that the end must be formulated in a way that places an emphasis on respect for those to whom particular persuasive communication efforts are directed. The advertiser may legitimately hope to increase sales of a particular model of automobile, and the public relations practitioner may legitimately wish to improve the image of a particular client whose business practices have come under assault—but in the attempt to achieve this immediate end, advertisers and public relations practitioners act unethically if they utilize methods intended more to manipulate, exploit, or both, listeners and persuadees than to respect them. They act unethically because no professional persuasive communication effort is justified if it demonstrates disrespect for those to whom it is directed.

Search for Guiding Principles in Persuasion

Communications scholars, practitioners, and observers long have sought to articulate guiding ethical principles for their work. "Ethical principles [for professionals] have proven useful in identifying the conflicting responsibilities in a moral dilemma, bringing clarity to moral thinking, and providing a shared language for discussion" (Fitzpatrick & Gauthier, 2000). Lambeth (1986), for example, has identified for the ethical practice of journalism the principles of truth telling, justice, freedom, humaneness, and stewardship. The Code of Ethics of the Society of Professional Journalists (SPJ) discusses the principles of truth, minimizing harm, independence, and accountability (SPJ, 1996). The Member Code of Ethics of the Public Relations Society of America (PRSA) discusses the principles of advocacy, honesty, expertise, independence, loyalty, and fairness (PRSA, 2000); the National Communication Association's (NCA's) Credo for Ethical Communication lists the principles of human worth and dignity, truthfulness, fairness, responsibility, personal integrity, and respect for self and others (NCA, 1999); and the International Association of Business Communicators (IABC) articulates the principles of human rights, rule of law, sensitivity to cultural norms, truthfulness, accuracy, fairness, respect, and mutual understanding (IABC, 2000). A quite different source, the Pontifical Council for Social Communications, proposed three moral principles for the ethical practice of advertising: truthfulness, dignity of the human person, and social responsibility (Pontifical Council for Social Communications, 1997).

Christians (personal communication, October 14, 2000) has called for establishing a set of prima facie duties (principles) specifically for commercial information (which is inherently utilitarian and consequentialist).

To best serve the public interest in an ethical manner, commercial information needs an ethics of duty to replace its consequentialism. In ethical theory, duty ethics is the radical alternative to utilitarianism. ... I see this theory as the best framework for insuring that commercial information operates in the public interest.... Rather than patch up utilitarianism, or try to make it work—if we adopt a new ethical theory we will transform our profession. (Christians, 1999.)

Our goal in this article was to articulate a set of prima facie principles for persuasion that would operationalize ethical theory, facilitate ethical thinking, be useful pedagogically, and engender the ethical practice of persuasion.

TARES Test: Five Principles for Ethical Persuasion

We propose a five-part test of prima facie duties that defines the moral boundaries of persuasive communications and serves as a set of action-guiding principles directed toward a moral consequence in persuasion. We suggest that these five principles, taken together, comprise the legitimate end of persuasive communications. Each principle focuses on a different element or component of the persuasive act from the perspective of the communicator. (The test does not address the ethical obligations of the receiver of the persuasive message.) We first present each of the principles individually, and then discuss them together as a set of prima facie duties.

The TARES Test is an acronym that consists of the five principles: Truthfulness (of the message), Authenticity (of the persuader), Respect (for the persuadee), Equity (of the persuasive appeal) and Social Responsibility (for the common good; see Figure 1).

In our discussion, we include reflection tables that are meant to communicate the essence of each principle and to stimulate thinking about its application. The TARES Test consists only of the five principles; the questions in the reflection and applications tables are only examples of issues to think about in applying TARES Test principles. The questions can be modified as needed to shed light on various and specific persuasive contexts faced by the practitioner.

Truthfulness (of the Message)

The first principle in the TARES Test focuses on the persuasive message and requires that it be not only true, but truthful.

Among the consistent themes in Bok's (1989) writing is that deception causes harm to individuals and to society, that "trust is a social good to be protected" (p. 26), and that deception undermines that trust. Bok (1989) equated deceit with violence, "the two forms of deliberate assault on human beings" (p. 18).

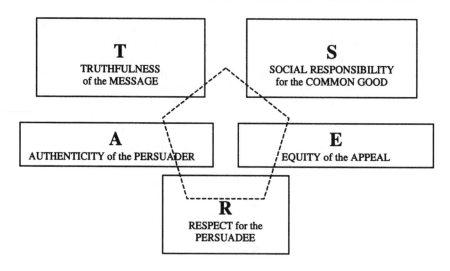

Figure 1   The TARES Test: Five principles for ethical persuasion.

All societies have stressed certain basic injunctions against at least a few forms of wronging other people chief among these "force and fraud," or violence and deceit. From the Ten Commandments to Buddhist, Jain, Confucian, Hindu, and many other texts, violence and deceit are most consistently rejected, as are the kinds of harm they make possible, such as torture and theft. (Bok, 1995, p. 15)

Just as violence takes power and control away from the one assaulted and gives that power and control to the assaulter, so does deception. People rely on information from others to make their choices in life, large or small. Lies distort this information, alter the choices of the deceived, and injure and lead him or her astray. In deception, then, as in violence, there are issues of power, of harm, and of violation of agency. From this perspective, to persuade others through deceptive messages is harmful to persuadees and undermining of their trust, and should be regarded with the same seriousness as an act of violence.

Truthfulness in the TARES Test is a broader standard than literal truth. It is possible to deceive without literally lying. The Principle of Truthfulness requires the persuader's intention not to deceive, the intention to provide others with the truthful information they legitimately need to make good decisions about their lives.

Table 1 provides a list of questions that professional persuasive communicators might ask themselves to guide their moral reflection in application of the Principle of Truthfulness of the Message.

Table 1
Truthfulness (of the Message)

Is this communication factually accurate and true, and also truthful? Does it deceive others either overtly or covertly? Does it lead people to believe what I myself do not believe? (Bok, 1989, p. 13)	Has this appeal downplayed relevant evidence? (Cooper & Kelleher, 2000)
Is this communication consistent with open, sincere, and honest communication? Is it responsive to the persuadees' human need to have truthful information to inform their life decisions?	If this message communicates only part of the truth, what are my justifications for disseminating this selective (incomplete) truth? Are my omissions meant to deceive? (Deaver, 1990, pp. 168–177)
Would I feel that this communication was truthful and nondeceptive if communicated to me in this context?	Am I creating a false image or a false impression with selective information? Will the people receiving this message feel they have been deceived if later they learn the whole truth?
Is this communication substantially complete? Does it satisfy a reasonable person's requirements for information in this situation? (Klaidman & Beauchamp, 1987, p. 35)	Is the information withheld needed by the audience for their own choices and actions? Will not having this information result in any harm? (Fitzpatrick & Gauthier, 2000)
Have comparisons between alternatives been presented in an undistorted and truthful manner? (Cooper & Kelleher, 2000)	Will people have reason to question my honesty and trustworthiness as a result of this communication? What can I do to ensure that this persuasive message is truthful?

Authenticity (of the Persuader)

The Principle of Authenticity in the TARES Test centers on issues related to the persuader. Authenticity is a complicated and variously defined concept, grounded in the philosophical literature of existentialism, that has "develop[ed] in many branches" (Taylor, 1991, p. 66). For purposes of the TARES Test, we carve out a particular connotation for authenticity that combines a cluster of related issues including integrity and personal virtue in action and motivation; genuineness and sincerity in promoting particular products and services to particular persuadees; loyalty to appropriate persons, causes, duties, and institutions; and moral independence and commitment to principle.

In broad terms, as envisioned here, authenticity is about discovering and expressing oneself, self-development, being true to oneself, and "finding the design" of one's own life oneself (Taylor, 1991, pp. 67–68). However, it relates also "to issues of self in situation" (Langan, 1992, p. 3). It is "the opposite of narcissistic" (Langan, 1992, p. 12), and assumes that one finds "genuine fulfillment" only in something that has significance independent of oneself or one's narcissistic desires (Taylor, 1991, p. 82).

Authenticity is "to live genuinely ... to take responsibility for one's actions and to foster true concern for others" (Golomb, 1995, p. 204). It is to act in harmony with one's authentic self "without impeding these processes in others" (Golomb, 1995, p. 205). "Authenticity does not refer to sheer factual life but to the life worth living. [It] cannot be achieved outside a social context ... [it] calls for an ongoing life of significant actions. It is actions that shape our authenticity (Golomb, 1995, p. 201).

Integrity and personal virtue. The Principle of Authenticity in the TARES Test relates to virtue ethics. Instead of focusing on the act, virtue ethics focuses on the actor. "Rather than seeing the heart of ethics in actions or duties, virtue ethics centers in the heart of the agent in his or her character" (Pojman, 1999, p. 158). The goal of life, and thus of one's professional activities, is to live well and achieve excellence (Pojman, 1999, p. 158); "... the unvirtuous (the virtue-indifferent or vicious) life is not worth living" (Pojman, 1999, p. 175). The Principle of Authenticity requires persuaders to evaluate the motivations, intentions, and attitudes that drive their persuasive activities, and to act nobly.

It is important not only to do the right thing, but also to have the requisite dispositions, motivations, and emotions in being good and doing right.... Virtue ethics is not only about action but about emotions, character, and moral habit. (Pojman, 1999, p. 158)

Sincerity and genuineness. The Principle of Authenticity as advanced by the TARES test includes also the requirement that professional persuaders should personally believe in the product, service, or cause they are advancing. They should be able to support and advocate it wholeheartedly and in person, including to people they know and love. They should sincerely believe that the product will benefit persuadees, and that the persuasion campaign is truthful, respectful, fair, equitable, and responsible.

Loyalty and independence. The Principle of Authenticity also requires that persuaders examine carefully their multiple and often conflicting loyalties, and to appropriately balance those loyalties in a given situation and context. One must choose to whom or what one will be loyal. Persuaders often are in the dilemma, for example, of having obligations of loyalty to client or employer that seem to conflict with obligations to truthfulness and the well-being of persuadees and of society. In these cases, practitioners must employ their moral discernment to ascertain when the demands of these loyalties are perverse, and that independence and adherence to personally held moral principles is required.

Table 2 lists questions for professional persuasive communicators to ask themselves in assessing authenticity in the persuasion.

Respect (for the Persuadee)

We have discussed the Principle of Respect for the Persuadee in this article at length. It requires that professional persuaders regard other human beings as worthy of dignity, that they not violate their rights, interests, and well-being for raw self-interest or purely client-serving purposes. It assumes that no professional persuasion effort is justified if it demonstrates disrespect for those to whom it is directed. "Human beings ... should not be treated merely as a means to an end; they are to be respected as ends in themselves. Human beings are 'beyond price'" (Jaksa & Pritchard, 1994, p. 128).

This principle requires further that people should be treated in such a way that they are able to make autonomous and rational choices about how to conduct and arrange their lives according to their own priorities, and that this autonomy should be respected.

> When we communicate to influence the attitudes, beliefs, and actions of others, the ethical touchstone is the degree of free, informed, rational, and critical choice significant choice that is fostered by our speaking. (Nilsen, 1966, p. 38, as cited in Griffin, 2000, p. 203)

Christians (1997) suggested that human dignity (the sacredness of life) is a protonorm ("[a principle] that holds true universally," p. 21), that "our human existence is the touchstone of ethics" (p. 25), and that "reverence for life on earth is the philosophical foundation of the moral order" (C. Christians, personal communication, October 14, 2000).

The Principle of Respect for the Persuadee is at the heart of the TARES Test, and is the underlying foundation and motivation for all of its other principles. Persuaders should disseminate truthful messages through equitable appeals with integrity and authenticity and with an eye to the common good because of their respect for the people to whom they are communicating and for all others who will be affected by the persuasion.

Table 3 provides a checklist for moral reflection relating to the Principle of Respect for the Persuadee.

Equity (of the Persuasive Appeal)

The Equity Principle focuses on the persuasive appeal. In the United States, a large body of law regulates persuasive appeals (laws, for example,

Table 2
Authenticity (of the Persuader)

Does this action compromise my integrity? Does it conform to my highest principles? Is it true to my best self? Does it conform to my religious convictions?

What is the rule or maxim on which I am acting? Is this rule justifiable? Would I want others to follow the same rule in similar circumstances?

Does this action arise out of noble intentions and motivations? (Cunningham, 2000.) Although I may have the right to do this, is it the right thing to do?

Would I ideally want to live in a world in which people routinely engaged in this type of action? If not, what is my justification for engaging in it myself?

Do I personally believe in this product, company, service, event, idea, cause? Can I support and advocate it wholeheartedly and in person, including to people I know and love?

What good reasons and justifications do I have for advocating this product, service, or cause (other than purely self-serving reasons)?

Would I openly, publically and personally be an advocate for this cause? Or am I hiding behind the anonymity of a promotional campaign or the work of others?

By engaging in this action, am I cooperating with evil or encouraging or requiring others to do so? (Martinson, 1999, pp. 120–122.)

Do I feel good about being involved in this action? How will I feel if others find out about my participation? Am I willing to take full, open, public, and personal responsibility for this action? (Waltz, 1999, pp. 127–128.)

Does this action properly and appropriately (without hurting others) balance my loyalties in this situation to self and conscience, employer, society, humanity, clients, supporters, stockholders, profession and professional colleagues, family, friends, and others who have treated me well?

Do I truly think and believe that the persuadees will benefit (or will be doing the right thing) if they are persuaded to act or think in the ways that this persuasive communication suggests they should?

Have I pursued a moral ideal with integrity, despite the behavior of others in society or with whom I work? Am I taking appropriate responsibility for the moral conduct of the organizations with which I work? (Raper, 1999, pp. 123–125.)

Is the motive of my action or communication (or of the secret I am keeping) to hurt, deceive, manipulate, or use others merely for my own or my client's purposes (to the detriment and at the expense of the persuadees)?

What can I do to conduct myself as an authentic person in this situation?

164

Table 3
Respect (for the Persuadee)

Is the persuasive appeal made to the decency in people? Have I respected the receivers of this persuasive message by appealing to their higher inclinations and their basic goodness, by not pandering, exploiting, or appealing to their lower or baser inclinations?	Does this action or communication respect the persuadee as a human being worthy of dignity and respect? Have I taken the rights, interests, and well-being of others into consideration as much as my own?
Is the persuasive appeal made to persuadees as rational, self-determining beings? Does it facilitate persuadees' capacity to reflect and to make responsible choices about their lives?	Is the quality of this information adequate to the information needs of the persuadees? Does this persuasive message facilitate the persuadees' capacity to act well (i.e., to choose, speak, vote, or purchase well)? (Cunningham, 2000)
Does this action conform to my own religious convictions, and to religious perspectives that people should act with a spirit of caretaking and loving kindness toward others (Christians, Fackler, & Rotzoll, 1995, p. 19).	Will the persuadees benefit (will they be doing the right thing for themselves and others) if they are persuaded to act or think in the ways that this communication suggests they should?
What ethical responsibility do I have for the people I am targeting with this persuasion?	Does this action promote raw self-interest at the unfair expense of or to the detriment of persuadees?
What can I do to be more respectful of and more responsible to the people I am persuading, and all others who will be affected by this persuasion?	Does this persuasive appeal contribute to understanding, consideration, reflection, and valid reasoning, and facilitate informed, free-will assent and consent? (Cunningham, 2000)

about deceptive and comparative advertising, celebrity endorsements, etc.), much of which is designed to protect fairness among commercial competitors. The equity principle in the TARES Test considers, instead, fairness to persuadees. It requires that persuaders consider if both the content and the execution of the persuasive appeal are fair and equitable, if persuaders have fairly used the power of persuasion in a given situation or if they have persuaded or manipulated unjustly. Appeals that are deceptive in any way clearly fall outside of the fairness requirement. (Note that although there are conceptual and definitional differences between the terms *equity* and *fairness*, they are used interchangeably for our purposes in this discussion.)

The Equity Principle requires either that there be parity between the persuader and persuadee in terms of information, understanding, insight, capacity, and experience, or that accommodations be made to adjust equitably for the disparities and to level the playing field (the lack of parity must be fairly accounted for and not unfairly exploited). Vulnerable audiences must not be unfairly targeted. Persuasive claims should not be made beyond the persuadees' ability to understand both the context and underlying motivations and claims of the persuader.

Vulnerable audiences must not
be unfairly targeted.

Rawls' (1971) notion of a "veil of ignorance" is a useful conceptual tool for assessing the equity of an appeal. The goal of this approach is to "nullify the effects of specific contingencies which put men at odds and tempt them to exploit social and natural circumstances to their own advantage" (Rawls, 1971, p. 136). The task behind the veil is to find a course of action that will be fair and equitable to all those affected by the decision, and especially to the weaker parties—to ensure "that the interests of some are not sacrificed to the arbitrary advantages held by others" (Cahn & Markie, 1998, p. 621). The veil of ignorance requires professional communicators to step conceptually out of their roles as powerful disseminators of persuasive promotional messages and to evaluate the equity of the appeal from the perspective of the weaker parties (their persuadees).

Persuaders also can contemplate issues of fairness and equity by applying the test of reversibility that is expressed simply in the Golden Rule, a concept "basic to so many religious and moral traditions" (Bok, 1989, p. 93).

> The Golden Rule has been formulated, the world over, either positively, as an injunction to "do unto others as you would have them do unto you" (Matthew 7:12), or negatively, urging that you not do to others what you would not wish them to do to you, as in the sayings of Confucius or Hillel. In either formulation, the Golden Rule represents not so much a moral value or principle in its own right as a perspective necessary to the exercise of even the most rudimentary morality: that of trying to put oneself in the place of those affected by one's actions, so as to counter the natural tendency to moral myopia (Bok, 1995, pp. 14–15).

As these approaches suggest, it would violate the Principle of Equity to use persuasive appeals that would not seem legitimate if the persuader were on the receiving end of the persuasion.

Table 4 provides a checklist by which the persuasive communicator may consider the Principle of Equity of the Persuasive Appeal in professional practice.

Social Responsibility (for the Common Good)

The Principle of Social Responsibility focuses on the need for professional persuaders to be sensitive to and concerned about the wider public interest or common good. It represents an appeal to "responsibility to community over [raw] self-interest, profit, or careerism" (Baker, 1999, p. 75).

The essence of social ethics is to recognize that "humans are accountable to each other, interdependent and not isolated selves" (Christians, et al., 1995, p. 330). Social responsibility ethics recognizes "the human person as a communal being" (Christians, et al., 1995, p. 332). [It] includes "a moral obligation to

Table 4
Equity (of the Persuasive Appeal)

Is the context, nature and execution of this persuasive act fair? Is the power of persuasion used fairly and justly?	Is there parity in this situation between the persuader and persuadee in terms of information, understanding, insight, capacity, and experience? If not, have accommodations been made to adjust equitably for the disparities and to level the playing field?
Would I feel that the persuasion in this situation was fair, just, ethical and appropriate if it were communicated to me or to people I know and love? Am I doing to others what I would not want done to me or to people I care about?	Do persuadees understand what I am claiming my product/service/ company/ position is and can do? Are they able to assess these claims fully and rationally? Do they thoroughly understand the costs and potential harms to themselves and others of what I am advocating?
Is this a persuasion that should not be made, considering the persons and circumstances involved?	Is this persuasive appeal sensitive to the needs, interests, concerns, and sensibilities of the persuadees? (Cooper and Kelleher, 2000.)
Have I unfairly targeted specific (or vulnerable) audiences and made claims outside of their ability to understand the context and underlying claims of the communication? (Patterson & Wilkins, 1998, p. 63.)	Does it allow for both reflection and counterargument? (Wilkins and Christians, 2000.)
Do the receivers of the message know that they are being persuaded rather than informed?	What can I do to make this persuasive appeal more fair and equitable?
Has this persuasion taken unfair advantage of a power differential? (Gauthier, 2000)	

consider the overall needs of society" (Lloyd, 1991, p.199) … personal sacrifice for the benefit of others … and a stewardship toward humanity" (Lloyd, 1991, p.200). Professional communicators are responsible for loyalties to self, profession, organization/employer, and to society, but loyalty to society encompasses all of the others (Parsons, 1993). (Baker, 1999, pp. 75–76)

The Social Responsibility Principle in the TARES Test "assumes that persons in society are interdependent communal beings" and that persuaders "have a responsibility to the societies in which they operate and from which they profit, including obligations of good citizenship in contributing positively to the … health of society" (Baker, 1999, p. 76). Persuaders acting in harmony with this principle would not promote products, causes, or ideas that they know to be harmful to individuals or to society and will consider contributing their time and talents to promoting products, causes, and ideas that clearly will result in a positive contribution to the common good and to the community of mankind.

Bok (1995) wrote that "All human groups, first of all, and all religious, moral, and legal traditions stress some form of positive duties regarding mutual support, loyalty, and reciprocity" (p. 13); Christians (1999) wrote in a related concept that

> All meaningful action is for the sake of community building; the bonding of persons is the epicenter of social formation. Given the primacy of relationships, unless I use my freedom to help others flourish, I deny my own well-being (p. 73).

The Social Responsibility Principle in the TARES Test requires moral conduct by professional persuaders at macrolevels as well as microlevels. The principle would demand, for example, that professional persuaders consider the impact of their communications on society if only a few well-financed and privileged voices are able to dominate the marketplace of ideas and distort the balance of debate on important societal issues (Moyers, 1999).

These are important questions because critics insist that public relations has been used as manipulation by powerful political, economic, and social interests intent on achieving their own narrow goals at the expense of the greater common good. In fact, it is sometimes alleged, public relations as it is practiced is too frequently dysfunctional for society in that it serves primarily to disrupt the "proper" functioning of the marketplace of ideas. (Martinson, 1998, p. 146)

As an example of a macrolevel concern for the common good, Martinson (1998) wrote that distributive and social justice require that public relations practitioners "must take seriously the challenge of defining how they can positively serve the traditionally under-represented in society" (p. 148).

Meeting the demands of the Principle of Social Responsibility ulti-mately comes down to the issue that is at the heart of all the principles in the TARES Test: the question of respect, respect for individuals and for society (Martinson, 1998, p. 149, citing Jaksa & Pritchard, 1994).

Although political and moral philosophers have differed on the pre-cise content of the common good and how to promote it, there is a core meaning that the welfare of all citizens, rather than that of factions or special interests, should be served impartially. Moreover, it is a norma-tive principle, not just the majority results of an opinion poll or voting. The common good cannot be understood statistically, but is a *"fundamen-tal concept of social morality"* (Diggs, 1973, p. 284, italics added; Christians, 1999, p. 68).

Table 5 suggests some questions professional practitioners might ask themselves in considering application of this principle.

TARES Test As A Set of Prima Facie Duties

The TARES Test has been presented here as a set of prima facie duties for professional persuasion (i.e., public relations, advertising, promotional campaigns, and commercial information). Prima facie duties are basic moral obligations (Ross, 1930), the understanding of which may "counter the natural tendency to moral myopia" (Bok, 1995, p. 15). Moral myopia arises from raw self-interest or particularity. As Pojman (2000) said, there is always a tension between particularity and universality (see Figure 2 illus-trating this point). Because public relations and advertising are inherently particular (professionals serving the interests of clients and of self), moral safeguards must be put into place to balance the excesses and harm that can result from rampant particularity.

The five principles in the TARES Test are interrelated moral safe-guards (as the overlapping questions in the reflection and application ta-bles demonstrate); the principles are mutually supporting and validating (e.g., being truthful demonstrates respect for others, respect for others leads the authentic practitioner to social responsibility, the authentic practitioner acts equitably and thus respectfully, the equitable appeal is truthful and socially responsible, etc.).

Ideally, all prima facie duties must be honored at all times in all of one's actions. There may conceivably be times, however, in which adherence to one principle will cause one to violate another. For example, truthfulness may sometimes be disrespectful of individuals or result in inequities (see Martinson, 2000, on this problem for journalists).

When prima facie duties conflict, a moral dilemma emerges. Kidder (1995) used the term *ethical dilemma* "to stand for those right-versus-right situations where two core moral values come into conflict" as distin-

Table 5
Social Responsibility (for the Common Good)

Does this action recognize the interdependency of persons in society, of persons as communal beings? (Christians et. al., 1995, p. 332) Is the action/communication responsible to individuals, society, the public, and the public interest?	Does this action take responsibility to promote and create the kind of world and society in which persuaders themselves would like to live with their families and loved ones? (Baker, 1999)
Will the product or issue I am promoting cause harm to individuals or to society? Does this action conform to the ethical requirement to do no unnecessary harm or to prevent harm?	Have I legitimately and fairly participated in the marketplace of ideas such that competing ideas fairly can be heard and considered by the public? Have I considered the responsibility to fairly represent issues and to allow and foster public consideration of alternative views? (Moyers, 1999)
Has this action's potential negative impact on individuals and the common good been taken into account and responded to appropriately?	Have I taken seriously the challenge of defining how I can positively serve the interests and views of the traditionally underrepresented in society? (Martinson, 1998, p. 148)
Does this persuasive communication promote (or strain) understanding and cooperation among constituent groups of society? Does it enhance or deplete public trust? (Bok, 1989, p. 26)	Have I unfairly stereotyped constituent groups of society in this promotion/communication campaign?
Will this action (or not having this information) cause disproportionate harm to any person, group, or interest? (Fitzpatrick & Gauthier, 2000)	Does this persuasive communication elucidate issues, dispel confusion and ignorance, and encourage public dialogue based on truthful information? (Cunningham, 2000)

guished from "right-versus-wrong issues that produce what can usefully be called *moral temptations*" (Kidder, 1995, pp. 113–114). "A moral dilemma occurs when a choice is required among actions that meet competing commitments or obligations, but there are good reasons for and against each alternative" (Fitzpatrick & Gauthier, this issue, p. 207).

Bonhoeffer (1962), for example, wrote about the problem of competing commitments and obligations with regard to truth telling, holding that truth is sensitive to context (see Martinson, 2000, on Bonhoeffer and journalism). "Every utterance or word lives and has its home in a particular environment. ... Telling the truth ... [has] respect for secrecy, confidence, and concealment" (Bonhoeffer, 1962, pp. 329, 334). This does not mean that

Particularity <--> Universality
(Sole focus on well-being of   (Sole focus on well-being of
self/client/employer.)   persuadees/society.)

Figure 2   Particularity/universality continuum.

truth is relative or that it "can and may be adapted to each particular situation in a way which completely destroys the idea of truth and narrows the
gap between truth and falsehood, so that the two become indistinguishable" (Bonhoeffer, 1962, p. 329). It does mean that in applying principles to
situations one must take the context into consideration.

Martinson (1997–1998) suggested that there is a difference between situational ethics and taking the nuances of the situation into account in one's
moral deliberations. In the latter, one applies "accepted ethical principles
… to particular acts" (Martinson, 1997–1998, p. 42).

> *In applying principles one must
> [consider] context.*

If practitioners are to behave ethically in the "real world," it is essential
they be able to identify the basic principles and values that are universally
relevant to defining what will be acceptable conduct in persuasive
communication. They must then apply those principles and values under
specific circumstances. It is vital that they recognize the difference between
doing that and practicing situational ethics (Martinson, 1997–1998, p. 43).

In situations in which prima facie duties conflict, one must decide
which of the principles has the greatest moral claim on one in a given context. Violation of one of the principles can be justified only by well-moti-
vated adherence to another of the prima facie duties. Fitzpatrick and
Gauthier (this issue) have written on this topic that

> It is important to recognize that these are *prima facie*, and not absolute, princi-
> ples. They are principles that hold generally unless they conflict with one an-
> other. When only one of the principles is implicated in a moral choice, that
> principle should be taken as the controlling guideline for ethical conduct.
> However, moral dilemmas often involve conflicts between the principles. In
> these cases, the decision maker must employ his or her own values, moral in-
> tuition, and character to determine which principle is most important and
> most controlling in the particular context (p.207–208).

Morality, as Pojman observed, is sometimes ambiguous. "When you really have a dilemma, you must use your moral intuition" (Pojman, 2000). Kidder (1995) wrote similarly that "there can be no formula for resolving dilemmas, no mechanical contraption of the intellect that churns out the answer" (p. 176).

> The more we work with these principles, the more they help us understand the world around us and come to terms with it. … In the act of coming to terms with the tough choices, we find answers that not only clarify the issues and satisfy our need for meaning but strike us as satisfactory resolutions. (Kidder, 1995, p. 176)

The authentic persuasive communicator will thoughtfully and successfully traverse these murky waters by keeping in mind the pivotal Principle of Respect for persuadees (and all others affected by the persuasion) on which the TARES Test is grounded, and by recognizing that "the only acts that are morally good are those that proceed from a good motive" (Ross, 1930, p. 4).

Conclusions

It was our goal in this article to identify the legitimate and moral end of professional persuasive communications. We argued that although professional persuasion is a means to an immediate instrumental end (such as increased sales or enhanced corporate image), ethical persuasion must rest on or serve a deeper, morally based final (or relative last) end.

Toward that goal, we have proposed a five-part test that defines the moral boundaries of persuasive communications and serves as a set of action-guiding principles directed toward a moral consequence in persuasion. We suggest that these five principles, taken together, comprise the legitimate end of professional persuasive communications and that these communications are ethical and morally justified if they adhere to the principles of Truthfulness (of the message), Authenticity (of the persuader), Respect (for the persuadee), Equity (of the persuasive appeal), and Social Responsibility (for the common good).

References

Andersen, K. E. (1978). *Persuasion: Theory and practice*. Boston: Allyn & Bacon.

Baker, S. (1999). Five baselines for justification in persuasion. *Journal of Mass Media Ethics, 14*, 69–81.

Bok, S. (1989). *Lying: Moral choice in public and private life*. New York: Vintage.

Bok, S. (1995). *Common values*. Columbia: University of Missouri Press.

Bonhoeffer, D. (1962). *Ethics*. New York: Macmillan.

Cahn, S., & Markie, P. (1998). *Ethics, history, theory, and contemporary issues.* New York: Oxford University Press.

Christians, C. (1997). The common good and universal values. In J. Black (Ed.), *Mixed news: The public/civic/communitarian journalism debate* (pp. 18–35). Mahwah, NJ: Lawrence Erlbaum Associates, Inc.

Christians, C. (1999). The common good as first principle. In T. L. Glasser (Ed.), *The Idea of public journalism* (pp. 67–84). New York: Guilford.

Christians, C., Fackler, M., & Rotzoll, K. (1995). *Media ethics: Cases & moral reasoning* (4th ed). New York: Longman.

Cooper, T., & Kelleher, T. (2000). Remarks in discussion among Fellows. Colloquium 2000: The Ethics of Persuasion. Park City, Utah, October 10–14, 2000.

Cunningham, S. B. (October 10–14, 2000). Remarks in discussion among Fellows. *Colloquium 2000: The Ethics of Persuasion.* Park City, Utah.

Cutlip, S. M. (1994). *The unseen power: Public relations. A history.* Mahwah, NJ: Lawrence Erlbaum Associates, Inc.

Cutlip, S. M., Center, A. H., & Broom, G. M. (1994). *Effective public relations.* Englewood Cliffs, NJ: Prentice Hall.

Deaver, F. (1990). On defining truth. *Journal of Mass Media Ethics, 5,* 168–177.

DeFleur, M. L., & Dennis, E. E. (1998). *Understanding mass communication.* Boston: Houghton Mifflin.

Diggs, B. J. (1973). The common good as reason for political action. *Ethics, 83,* 283–284.

Fagothey, A. (1976). *Right and reason: Ethics in theory and practice.* St. Louis, MO: Mosby.

Fitzpatrick, K., & Gauthier, C. (October 10–14, 2000). Remarks in discussion among Fellows. *Colloquium 2000: The Ethics of Persuasion.* Park City, Utah.

Gaffney, J. (1979). *Newness of life.* New York: Paulist Press.

Golomb, J. (1995). *In search of authenticity: From Kierkegaard to Camus.* London: Routledge & Kegan Paul.

Griffin, E. (2000). *A first look at communication theory* (4th ed.). Boston: McGraw-Hill.

Grunig, J. E., & Hunt, T. (1984). *Managing public relations.* Fort Worth, TX: Holt, Rinehart & Winston.

Gauthier, C. (October 10–14, 2000). Remarks in discussion among Fellows. *Colloquium 2000: The Ethics of Persuasion.* Park City, Utah.

Hugo, V. (1997). *Les Miserables.* New York: Knopf. (Original work published 1862)

International Association of Business Communicators. (2000). *International association of business communicators code of ethics for professional communicators.* Retrieved December 29, 2000, from the World Wide Web: http://www.iabc.com/members/joining/code.htm

Jaksa, J. A., & Pritchard, M. S. (1994). *Communication ethics: Methods of analysis.* Belmont, CA: Wadsworth.

Kidder, R. M. (1995). *How good people make tough choices: Resolving the dilemmas of ethical living.* New York: Morrow.

Klaidman, S., & Beauchamp, T. L. (1987). *The virtuous journalist.* New York: Oxford University Press.

Lambeth, E. B. (1986). *Committed journalism: An ethic for the profession.* Bloomington, IN: Indiana University Press.

Langan, T. (1992). *Tradition and authenticity in the search for ecumenic wisdom.* Columbia, MO: University of Missouri Press.

Lloyd, S. (1991). A criticism of social responsibility theory: An ethical perspective. *Journal of Mass Media Ethics, 6,* 199–209.

Martinson, D. L. (1996, August). *Thomas Schindler and the social dimension of ethics: Serious questions for the public relations 'culture'.* Paper presented to the Public Relations Division of the Association for Education in Journalism and Mass Communication, Anaheim, CA.

Martinson, D. L. (1996–1997). Truthfulness in communication is both a reasonable and achievable goal for public relations practitioners. *Public Relations Quaterly, 41*(4), 42–45.

Martinson, D. L. (1997–1998, Winter). Public relations practitioners must not confuse consideration of the situation with "situational ethics." *Public Relations Quarterly, 42*(4),39–43.

Martinson, D. L. (1998). A question of distributive and social justice: Public relations practitioners and the marketplace of ideas. *Journal of Mass Media Ethics, 13,*141–151.

Martinson, D. L. (1999). The public interest must take precedence. *Journal of Mass Media Ethics, 14,* 120–122.

Martinson, D. L. (2000). Dietrich Bonhoeffer and communicating "the truth": Words of wisdom for journalists. *Journal of Mass Media Ethics, 15,* 5–16.

Middleton, K. R., & Chamberlin, B. F. (1994). *The law of public communication.* New York: Longman.

Montgomery, J. (1978, August 1). In public relations, ethical conflicts pose continuing problems. *Wall Street Journal,* pp. 1, 14.

Moyers, B. (1999). Free speech for sale. In Public Affairs Television (Producer), *Free speach for sale.* (Available from Films for the Humanities & Sciences, Princeton, NJ, 1–800–257–5126).

National Communication Association. (2000). NCA credo for ethical communication. *Media Ethics: The Magazine Service Mass Communications Ethics,* Spring 2000, *11*(2), 39.

Nilsen, T. R. (1966). *Ethics of speech communication.* Indianapolis, IN: Bobbs-Merrill.

Parsons, P. (1993). Framework for analysis of conflicting loyalties. *Public Relations Review, 19*(1), 49–57.

Patterson, P., & Wilkins, L. (1998). *Media ethics: Issues & cases* (3rd ed.). Boston: McGraw-Hill.

Pember, D. R. (1981). *Mass media law.* Dubuque, IA: Brown.

Pojman, L. (1999). *Ethics: Discovering right and wrong.* Belmont, CA: Wadsworth.

Pojman, L. (October 10–14, 2000). Remarks in discussion among Fellows. *Colloquium 2000: The Ethics of Persuasion.* Park City, Utah.

Pontifical Council for Social Communications. (1997). *Ethics in advertising.* Boston: Pauline Books & Media.

Public Relations Society of America. (2000). *Public Relations Society of America member code of ethics.* Retrieved December 29, 2000, from the World Wide Web: http://prsa.org/profstd.html

Raper, M. (1999). Expose myths and focus on the miracle. *Journal of Mass Media Ethics, 14,* 123–125.

Rawls, J. (1971). *A theory of justice.* Cambridge, MA: Harvard University Press.

Ross, W. D. (1930). *The right and the good.* Cambridge: Hackett.

Society of Professional Journalists. (1996). SPJ Code of Ethics. Retrieved December 29, 2000, from the World Wide Web: http://spj.org/ethics/code.htm

Taylor, C. (1991). *The ethics of authenticity.* Cambridge, MA: Harvard University Press.

Virginia State Board of Pharmacy v. Virginia Citizens Consumer Council, Inc., 425 U.S. 748 (1976).

Waltz, S. L. (1999). A list of acid tests. *Journal of Mass Media Ethics, 14,* 127–128.

Wells, W., Burnett, J., & Moriarty, S. (1992). *Advertising: Principles and practice.* Englewood Cliffs, NJ: Prentice Hall.

Wilkins, L., & Christians, C. (October 10–14, 2000). Remarks in discussion among Fellows. *Colloquium 2000: The Ethics of Persuasion.* Park City, Utah.

Journal of Mass Media Ethics, *16*(2&3), 176–192
Copyright © 2001, Lawrence Erlbaum Associates, Inc..

Better Mousetrap?
Of Emerson, Ethics, and
Postmillennium Persuasion

Thomas Cooper
Emerson College

Tom Kelleher
University of Hawaii at Manoa[1]

❑ *Ralph Waldo Emerson reputedly said, "If you build a better mouse trap, the world will beat a path to your door." In this article, Emerson's actual quote is seen to infer a simple rule: quality supply attracts quantity demand. Such a rule could imply that enitre businesses related to persuasion, such as public relations, advertising, and marketing seem at best unnecessary and at worst unethical. However, Emerson's logic may not apply in modern market places driven by multiple competing images. This article proposes eithical thresholds for persuasion and examines the relationship of these thresholds to public relations theory. Two case studies are analyzed in which better-mousetrap logic is applied to test the viability of these thresholds.*

If a man can write a better book, preach a better sermon, or make a better mousetrap than his neighbor, though he builds his home in the woods, the world will make a beaten path to his door.

> Ralph Waldo Emerson
> (Yule and Keane, 1889/1891, p. 88)

This quotation, first attributed to Ralph Waldo Emerson in print in 1889, has a curious history. It is based on notes taken during an Emerson lecture in San Francisco or Oakland in 1871 (Stevenson, 1935). Sarah S. B. Yule or Mary S. Keene recorded notes at the lecture and then transcribed the brief excerpt in their coauthored quotation anthology *Borrowings* (1889/1891).

Although it is now impossible to know how accurate the Yule and Keene (1889/1891) transcription from memory was, Emerson did write a passage within his essays that conveyed the same spirit as the now famous "better mousetrap" proverb. In *Common Sense,* published in 1855, Emerson wrote

> If a man has good corn, or wood, or boards, or pigs to sell, or can make better chairs or knives, crucibles, or church organs, than anybody else, you will find a broad, hard-beaten road to his house, though it be in the woods. (Emerson, 1909, p. 528)

Inherent within both of these quotations, one hearsay but popular, the other actual but obscure, is this implication: There is a direct relation between product quality and customer demand. From a strictly Emersonian perspective, professional persuasion is unnecessary to promote quality products, services, or ideas. Quality speaks for itself through customer satisfaction, which affects word-of-mouth publicity. The sense behind Emerson's two dicta is that quality products come to dominate the market by forces similar to the laws of natural selection. Ostensibly the fittest products—that is, those of greatest craftsmanship and stamina—will flourish in the marketplace without the need for persuasive promotion.

Thus, in a strict Emersonian-cum-Spencerian/Darwinian universe, persuasion is probably inherently unethical. Persuasion appears to be a form of conning or manipulation only necessary to interest customers in second-rate products. On reflection such persuasive practices seem in direct conflict with ethical ideals such as "tell the truth"; "improve the lot of others"; "recognize merit"; "maximize good, minimize harm"; "do the greatest good for the greatest number"; and "do unto others as you would have them do unto you."

If we strictly apply Emersonian logic inferring that superior products and services will automatically succeed, it follows that persuasive communication is inherently deceptive. Clients and customers are persuaded to buy mediocre and inferior products not for the reasons they are told ("this is the best," "it is good for you"), but rather, in many cases, to magnify corporate profits (Marx, 1900), growth (Galbraith, 1967), or image (Boorstin, 1972).

To be fair to Emerson, he does not say, "If you build an inferior wagon, chimney, or fruitcake, it would be unethical to sell it." Nor does he say, "If you build a better mousetrap, you need not initially persuade people to sample it." Nor does he write, "People should never buy lower quality products occasionally to save money, trouble, or time." Such statements seem to be corollaries to his better-known expressions, but they raise questions about whether his implied marketplace is ruled by absolute laws or permits exceptions.

Perhaps Emerson would have been realistic in allowing such exceptions. One cannot be certain in his absence. However, if it is implied that his general rule—quality supply invites quantity demand—is typically accurate, then entire businesses related to persuasion, such as public relations, advertising, and marketing, seem at best unnecessary and at worst unethical. A discussion of how Emerson's logic may be interpreted and applied in modern marketplaces introduces possible ethical thresholds for persuasion. A look at two cases in which his better-mousetrap logic may apply tests the utility of those thresholds.

Postmillennium Ethics

Emerson's idealized, transcendental logic may well have been more appropriate within a 19th-century preelectric America. In the global realities of the 21st century, several questions are not easily answered by the implications of Emerson's vision. Consider these contemporary queries.

What is better?

In an age of mixed yet culturally diverse values, competing product designs, long-term versus short-term needs, price wars, and a mixture of human needs and personalities, is "better" an absolute that may be easily identified in every case? Does not the current question of "What is a better mousetrap?" evoke others such as "Does better mean 'environmentally friendly'? Nontoxic? More 'humane' to mice? Longer lasting? Cheaper? Less visible? More attractive? More customer friendly? Better track record with *Consumer Reports*? Instantly lethal?" In India cows are sacred, so is a better hamburger an oxymoron, or does it mean a vegetarian burger, or, given that many beef eaters do live in India, does it mean tastier, healthier, prepared quicker, more nutritious, cheaper, less fattening, more energizing, or all of these?

Does natural selection occur in the mass mediated marketplace?

Do the laws of natural selection apply in a world where artificial rules supercede natural ones, in which mass media dominate word-of-mouth, in which "image" (Boorstin, 1972) may overpower substance? For example, if an unknown Alaskan candidate is running for U.S. President without money, image makers, media appearances, or travel, how will voters "make a beaten path to his door"? No matter how much integrity, experience, statesmanship, and expertise this candidate possesses—perhaps even with a PhD in foreign policy and 20 years in the state senate—how may he, as an unknown, compete favorably with wealthy, media-savvy, household-word candidates? Persuasion seems essential not only to counteract other forms of persuasion (such as the ad campaigns of known candidates) but also to achieve visibility in the first place. If dozens of mousetraps already have high-quality public relations (PR) campaigns worldwide (as opposed to high-quality products), how may a start-up company, seeking to obtain legal, copyright, and union protection, give customers a fresh choice without significant investment in media exposure?

Does natural selection work in a world of language inflation? Bok (1978) and Schneider (2000) noted the pressures on professors to write letters of recommendation that inflate the accomplishments and potential of candidates for graduate school. If a professor knows that other letters of recommendation will inflate the value of other candidates, then writing an honest letter about a candidate will create an unfair playing field. To level the playing field, the professor is tempted to lie or inflate the worth of the candidate. Similarly, if several products each claim to be "the best" on national television, how will a product that is truly the best stand out? Products do not compete so much with other products as with the images of other products (Boorstin, 1972). Can a product described without any persuasive or inflated rhetoric survive?

"Perception" becomes central to the 21st-century approach to persuasion. If a mousetrap is perceived as better, why should consumers be tempted to purchase another within the same price range and degree of availability? Moreover, if a mousetrap is perceived as better, it may be purchased without any evidence of superiority. Such perception relates to Boorstin's (1972) world of pseudoreality in which convincing images substitute for truth.

Although it may be difficult, after decades of experimentation, to make yet another better soap or orange juice, it is not so difficult to make a better perception, such as that the soap will improve your sex life or the juice will keep you young forever. Persuaders wish to sell the perceived fulfillment to customers' wants and desires. Because there is a competitive one-upmanship among persuaders to appeal to deeper and deeper human desires, the escalation of pseudoreality images about products also fuels the increasing language inflation.

Responsibilities

Such a norm of rhetorical escalation does not relieve the modern publicist, PR firm, advertiser, or sales force from ethical responsibilities. Each must reckon morally with the use and implications of the notion of better. Baker (1999) listed five baselines for the moral justification of persuasion. If a PR firm or other persuader wishes to be, in Baker's terms, at the higher end of the moral menu, the firm must be at least socially responsible and at best exemplify what is called the "kingdom of ends." Baker elucidated that the second highest system, "social responsibility," means one has a higher responsibility to community (cf. customers, clients, humanity) than to self. The highest or most virtuous system for Baker, kingdom of ends, like Kant's Categorical Imperative, calls for living one's life as if it were the role model for the world. People and actions are treated as ends in themselves, not justifications for unethical means to someone else's ends.

If professional persuaders wish to be publicly accountable through a kingdom of ends, or even practice social responsibility as described by Baker (1999), they must carefully evaluate their claims of a better mousetrap in this way:

1. Clear definition: Ethically, persuaders ought not to make claims of better without definition and clarification to the consumer. Is a better cigarette an oxymoron? If not, is it a cheaper, tastier, bigger, fresher, or healthier one? Is bigger better? Is it faster? Is more pain killer within a drug automatically better or might it produce side effects or blind a consumer to the hidden messages of pain? Persuaders must clearly articulate the meaning of *better*. Although the Federal Trade Commission and Food and Drug Administration (FDA) may legally allow "puffery," unsubstantiated claims of better, what is legal in one country is not necessarily ethical in that country or elsewhere.

2. Scientific evidence: Although better is often subjective as in a better tasting coffee, better often implies that there is objective data, such as when a car is said to be better because it is safer. Persuaders ought not to imply better in an objective sense unless there is independent, replicable, valid scientific evidence. Whenever possible, professional persuaders should provide the source and nature of the evidence. Failure to reveal the source and current status of full evidence may lead to deception by omission as can failure to disclose the absence of scientific evidence. Such failure may also lead to lawsuits, loss of credibility, and harm to both consumers and clients.

3. Context for comparison: *Better* and kindred terms *faster, cleaner, cheaper, softer, easier,* and so forth imply a comparative state between a product and its competition. Ethically, persuaders ought to declare the answer to the question, "Better than what?" It should be clear whether the product is arguably better than all comparable brands or only better than last year's predecessor model. Is it better than similar products within its price range or best of all? Is it better than it once was (i.e., "improved"), better than it always was, or is it being compared to one or more competing brands? Or, is using the product simply better than using no such product at all?

4. Audience sensitivity: Professional persuaders have an obligation to consider the nature of their audiences. A better condom may be an oxymoron to audiences who do not condone birth control. The multicultural and mixed-gender nature of most mass media audiences makes many claims of better questionable or inappropriate. For example, in Fiji women left the room when TV ads for tampons were shown. They were embarrassed to see the ads shown when men were present but also shocked to have such intimate, private matters made public among other women. No product or ad can be better if people refuse to purchase or view it. Ethically and ethnically, persuaders must ask, "To whom might the product be objectionable? Offensive? Worse? Better?" and "Why?"

Summarily, professional persuaders, to be ethical, ought to be accountable to consumers and clients alike. Persuaders may and ought to determine thresholds regarding the notion of better by clear definition, scientific evidence, context for comparison, and audience sensitivity. Thresholds are not only based on ideals but may be established according to such criteria as safety records, laboratory testing, comparative consumer satisfaction (e.g., *Consumer Reports*), and relative value within a culture.

21st-Century Policy

Emerson's claims may well have been true in the 19th century and are probably still accurate in a publicity vacuum in cases in which a product is demonstrably better to the satisfaction of all. However, within the 20th century described by Boorstin (1972) and Bok (1978), and now within the even more surreal hyper-bowl (cf. hyperbole) competition among 21st-century persuaders, there is no longer a justification for the implication that "All publicity claims are unethical." Instead the question has become, "Which claims are unethical?"

Barney and Black (1994) articulated well the postmodern realistic necessity for contemporary persuaders. Within a sea of products and persuaders, there must now be an ethics of advocacy. Without advocates, current products and services may not even become available, let alone visible and competitive.

Advocates, however, are also bound by ethical guidelines. Barney and Black (1994) correctly argued that persuasion advocates must, for example, abide by Bok's (1978) three tests for deception. These three tests of when to use deception are

> ... first whether there are alternative forms of action which will resolve the difficulty without the use of a lie; second, what might be the moral reasons brought forth to excuse the lie; and what reasons may be raised as counter-arguments. Third as a test of these two steps, we must ask what a public of reasonable persons might say about such lies. (Bok, 1978, pp. 111–112)

When professional persuaders ask these three questions, they rarely find justification to deceive the public about the meaning of *better, best,* and similar superlative and comparative language. Professional persuaders must take pains to make sure that they are not practicing deception by defining what they mean by *better.* "Better according to what evidence?" "Better than what?" "Better in what way?" "Better according to whom?" "Better within which cultural context?" It is also important that such practitioners make sure their claims of better are internally consistent within all their own organization's communications.

Of PR Theory

Succeeding ethically in the marketplace requires communicators to work effectively within an adversarial marketplace as discussed by Barney and Black (1994) while realizing the moral responsibilities to society evident in Baker's (1999) discussion of ethical baselines for persuasion. The task of persuading people to buy products, services, and ideas by claiming superiority may fall within the domains of advertising, marketing, and PR. Although these functions are often integrated to increase sales and corporate profits, the idea of treating people and actions as ends rather than means fits best with the theoretical ideals of PR.

Marketers, advertisers, and PR people should all be held responsible for defining competitive claims, citing valid evidence, and clarifying the context for such comparisons. However, our final method for determining thresholds for ethical persuasion—seeking to understand audience sensitivities—falls squarely in the domain of PR. This is not to say that marketers and advertisers are not concerned with audience feedback, demographics, and psychographics. To be sure, focus groups and test marketing strategies are among the firmly established tactics within marketing and advertising. Nor does this mean that public relations people do not practice two-way communication with strong one-sided motivations. Such two-way communication activities, however, are solely designed as means to profitable ends for the organization that sponsors them. These activities, driven by self-interest, occupy the lower, if not lowest moral ground among Baker's (1999) baselines for ethical persuasion.

Grunig (1993) examined the ethics of two-way communication by developing models of PR that feature two types of two-way communication that an organization may have with its publics: two-way asymmetrical communication and two-way symmetrical communication. In Grunig's (1993) two-way *asymmetrical model* of PR, PR people primarily use feedback and research to persuade publics. That is, they use communications tactics and they use the people with whom they communicate primarily as means to the organization's ends (usually bottom-line profits). In contrast, the two-way *symmetrical model* depicts how publics and organizations may communicate more often in a balanced manner; publics have the same opportunity to influence organizations as organizations have to influence publics.

Grunig's (1993) model of two-way symmetrical communication may be more often prescriptive than descriptive in the field of PR, but it is clearly unique to PR among those industries promoting mousetraps. Symmetrical communication meshes with the third part of Bok's (1978) three-part test for deception: the test of "publicity." Bok's (1978) test of publicity requires professional communicators to shift perspectives and consider "what a public of reasonable persons might say" about ethical decisions. Although this shift in perspectives may be practiced in the form of a careful thought experiment, it requires that professional communicators rise above their roles as advocates and tellers of selective truth and consider how their own opinions may be biased. Communicators who see publics only as means to profitable ends will be hard pressed to predict what publics of reasonable persons might say about their decisions. However, those who primarily communicate with publics in a symmetrical manner will have a more accurate and less biased perspective from which to identify ethical claims.

Likewise, our test of audience sensitivities in determining the validity of a better-mousetrap claim means that professional persuaders should consider what their publics consider to be better before promoting their goods as such. This shift in perspectives requires two-way symmetrical communication with publics. Although such balanced communication at the moment of strategic decision making may be impractical—as when an unexpected question is asked at a live press conference—immediate decisions may be informed by past communication with the people potentially affected by the claim.

The PR practitioner who practices symmetrical communication will be in an optimal position to inform an organization's management team about those products, services, or ideas that are better from the perspective of the organization's publics. He or she will also be uniquely suited to decide those claims that are unethical in promoting his company's mousetraps in the competitive marketplace.

Of Persuasive Practice

Grunig's (1993) public relations models provide a good starting point for discussing how professional communicators can balance on the ethical tightwire between responsible collaboration with publics and successful advocacy in the marketplace (e.g., Grunig, 2000). Yet continuing the discussion of practical thresholds for making ethical claims in the competitive marketplace requires real cases. We examine two cases.

McNeil Consumer Healthcare's Benecol®

"Benecol Prelaunch: Laying the Foundation for Phenomenon" is presented by McNeil Consumer Healthcare in Jerry Hendrix's (2000) *Public Relations Cases*. McNeil Consumer Healthcare, a unit of Johnson & Johnson®, hired PR firm Hill & Knowlton to "help create a phenomenon" by introducing Benecol into the market for "cholesterol lowering functional foods" (p. 283).

Clear Definition

McNeil Consumer Healthcare defined *Benecol* as a "new line of cholesterol lowering functional foods" (as cited in Hendrix, 2000, p. 283). Trade media such as *Food Processing* magazine categorize this type of product as a "nutraceutical," a health food–drug hybrid (Zind, 2000). The unique point of comparison made between Benecol and other margarine-like spreads is an ingredient called *plant stanol ester.* Press materials described it as "an ingredient that helps promote healthy cholesterol levels.… Plant stanol ester is derived from natural plant sources. Stanol ester is also present in small amounts in foods such as corn, wheat, rye, oats, and olive oil" (as cited in Hendrix, 2000, p. 292).

The product was described by Diane Toops (2000), news and trends editor of *Food Processing* magazine, as one of the food and packaged goods industry's "genuinely new and different products". Benecol, then, was positioned as better than competing products based on its cholesterol-lowering ingredients.

Benecol was positioned as better than competing products.

Scientific Evidence

Plant stanol ester had already been tested in more than 24 scientific studies including reports published in *New England Journal of Medicine* and *Circulation.* McNeil and Hill & Knowlton analyzed these studies to conclude that the dietary ingredient was "clinically proven to reduce total cholesterol levels on average by 10%" and that "Benecol reduces LDL, or 'bad' cholesterol, on average by 14%" (as cited in Hendrix, 2000, pp. 283–284). The product had also been used in Finland for several years before becoming available in U.S. markets. Although evidence of Benecol's long-term health effects is still inconclusive, results from recent studies clearly demonstrate its short-term, cholesterol-lowering effects (Law, 2000).[2]

To get cholesterol-lowering results like the ones achieved in the scientific studies, however, consumers with high cholesterol must eat two to three servings of the product a day—a fact Benecol promoters didn't hide.

> Two to three servings a day with meals providing 3.4 grams of Plant Stanol Esters daily, as part of a diet low in saturated fat and cholesterol may reduce the risk of heart disease. Benecol Spread contains 1.7g Stanol Esters per serving. (Benecol, 2000)

Besides displaying this message prominently, the Benecol Web site for U.S. consumers includes a direct link to the FDA's "Talk Paper" on related issues. The paper, dated September 5, 2000, announced more leeway for Benecol and competing products in making promotional claims to include claims about "reducing the risk of coronary heart disease" (FDA, 2000).

Context for Comparison

McNeil's published case study referred only to a "formidable competitor" that announced a similar product in the same year. A November 8, 1999 American Heart Association news release reveals more about the competing product called *Take Control®*. "There are two FDA-approved cholesterol-lowering spreads.... Take Control contains vegetable oil sterol esters from soybeans.... Benecol contains plant stanol esters, which come from wood pulp from pine trees" (American Heart Association, 1999). Neither the American Heart Association nor the McNeil PR team made much of this difference. Rather, the McNeil PR team planned to compete with Take Control on the basis of name recognition rather than distinctive chemical properties. Their first objective was to "establish the Benecol brand and McNeil food/nutrition credentials with key science and consumer media and our primary audiences" (Hendrix, 2001, p. 284). Their second objective was to "preempt competitive threats by being the first to capture the public's 'mind share'" (Hendrix, 2000, p. 284).

Apparently the context for comparison with traditional margarine-type spreads was the efficacy of Benecol in lowering cholesterol, and the competition between Benecol and Take Control was based more on name recognition than any substantial difference between the two products themselves. Any claim that Benecol was better than Take Control was only implied by Benecol's highly publicized entry into the marketplace. For example, a May 17, 1998 news release issued by McNeil touted Benecol's FDA approval and referred to its "success in Finland since 1995 and its phenomenal launch in the United Kingdom earlier this year" (as cited in Hendrix, 2001, p. 288).

However, both Benecol and Take Control contain fat. Three servings of Benecol contain 27 g of fat. Some doctors caution against eating this much, whereas others emphasize that consuming Benecol or Take Control is better than eating regular margarine products ("Functional Foods," 2000; Mirkin, 2000). Another caveat for both products is that they are expensive. They cost about four to six times more per ounce than light margarine ("Functional Foods," 2000).

Audience Sensitivities

Authors of the case study mention several publics that were considered critical by Benecol promoters: consumers; nutritional scholars and advocates; media; regulatory agencies; "key McNeil players from the Regulatory, Professional Marketing, Medical, and Communications departments"; and grocery retailers. In communicating with each of these publics—McNeil's internal stakeholders as well as those outside of the organization—campaign planners were positioned well to practice two-way symmetrical communication. Obviously, regulatory agencies such as the FDA had the potential to influence the McNeil organization. One issue of "considerable bluster" was the content of health claims McNeil made in promoting Benecol (Neff, 1999). The FDA Talk Paper mentioned previously and Benecol's link to the FDA Web page suggest that the two organizations reached a resolution on the health-claims issues that was acceptable to both.

Yet how symmetrical was McNeil's communication with the other groups in determining if or how Benecol was a better mousetrap? Internal publics were consulted to produce a book of resources to help identify areas of potential crisis, or "what-if scenarios." And "Benecol briefings" were organized to encourage dialog between "a cadre of credible, recognized advocates, and thought leaders" (Hendrix, 2001, p. 285) and national and international media. Given the clear definition of Benecol and the scientific evidence presented, these tactics of communication meet our ethical requirements for audience sensitivity. That is, employees, Benecol advocates, news media who cover this industry, retailers, and the scientific community were all presumably willing and able to understand the issues involved and ready to participate in a fair discussion of the product.

A greater ethical challenge for McNeil, however, was to communicate openly with consumers to determine whether Benecol was better to them. McNeil conducted focus-group research to define their target audience as "Health/Diet Actives, a group comprised of about 40% of primary grocery shoppers, skewing strongly female with an average age of 52" (Hendrix, 2001, p. 284). The well-defined demographic profile continued: "Women within this category were diet-conscious yet had difficulty achieving health goals due to feelings of deprivation" (Hendrix, 2001, p. 284). From this profile, McNeil developed a strategy. "Hence all press materials to consumer media reflected the ease of incorporating Benecol into any daily lifestyle and the health benefit—with no deprivation—of doing so" (Hendrix, 2001, p. 284). McNeil also used data collected from survey research to "craft consumer messages" (as cited in Hendrix, 2000, p. 284). Given that consumers were not consulted for any other reason than to sell the product, this type of two-way communication is asymmetrical. But should consumers have been consulted?

Discussion

It can be argued that McNeil's advocacy for Benecol in the marketplace, which followed product development with input from professional, scientific, and regulatory publics, is part of a broader strategy of symmetrical communication. Even Grunig (2000) held that there is ethical room for what he called "mixed-motive" models of public relations in which collaboration and advocacy are both valued. According to Grunig (2000), symmetry "involves two-way advocacy—of both organizational and public interests" (p. 43). Bok (1978) also supported the idea that advocacy, and even deception, is justifiable if all parties involved are aware of and agree to the rules of conduct. Courts of law and games of poker are examples. Is the consumer marketplace different? Did McNeil and its agency Hill & Knowlton break any of the commonly understood rules of product promotion by implying that Benecol was better than Take Control? Or better than regular margarine?

The success of the Benecol PR effort lies in the fact that it flashed on the radar of the American consumer bright and early. How long will it survive the marketplace? Consumers of Benecol will have their say now. And knowing that the product has FDA approval and that no major protestors have made their voice heard in the marketplace, Benecol's target audience will likely make up their minds based on individual taste and cost benefit as much as promotion.

Nestlé's® Infant Formula

Whereas the Benecol case was documented as an example of effective public relations, Nestlé Corporation's marketing of infant formula products in Third World countries is documented as "a case of failed corporate responsibility" (Heath, 1997, p. 124).

Clear Definition

Infant formula is a substitute for a mother's breast milk, allowing mothers to feed their babies using a mixture of powdered formula and water. Apparently, Nestlé does not deceive mothers about the contents of the breast milk substitute itself. However, Nestlé's promotional strategies implying that formula is better than natural breast milk have been a source of controversy. The main points of contention between Nestlé and its critics are how the product is marketed and to whom.

Scientific Evidence

The question of whether baby formula is better than natural breast milk has been an issue for decades. However, evidence in favor of natural breast milk is most pronounced in underdeveloped countries. In documenting the origin of boycotts against Nestlé, James E. Post (1985) described the problems that physicians and established medical organizations such as the World Health Organization have observed.

Sanitation and refrigeration are not generally available to the population in many such countries. Water supplies are unpurified, thereby increasing the probability that a formula mixed with local water will produce diarrhea and disease in the bottle-fed child. Poverty encourages the over-dilution of powdered formula, thereby reducing the amount of nutrition the child receives from each bottle. Once a mother's ability to breastfeed "lets down," the baby must be fed in an alternative way. If the mother is too poor to afford formula, which is an expensive product, there is the temptation and need to place other products in the baby bottle. These products may range from powdered whole milk (which is unsatisfactory for a baby's digestive system) to white powders such as corn starch. (p. 115–116)

According to Post (1985), the controversy over the use of baby formula has brought the attention of advocate groups, health professionals, and government agencies throughout the world and resulted in a "medical consensus about the desirability of breastfeeding as the best way to provide infant nutrition" (p. 115). On its Web site, even Nestlé (2000) acknowledges that "Breast milk is best for babies", and Nestlé encourages consumers to "consult your doctor or clinic for advice" before using formula (p. 115). However, Third-World consumers are not likely to purchase Nestlé products based on information delivered via the World Wide Web. In addition, Nestlé's promotional strategies have often contradicted their formal statements.

Context for Comparison

Nestlé promoted its products in impoverished areas with advertising that showed healthy, smiling, robust children. They used healthcare systems to distribute samples and posters. "Milk nurses," who were paid by commission by Nestlé, walked the halls of maternity wards in uniform advising mothers to use formula. Nestlé baby formula was featured in radio jingles, posters, and baby books. The healthy, smiling babies in the ads provided a sharp contrast to the undernourished babies of Third-World populations. "The advertising created an idealized image of what infants should look like and a clear concept of how the ideal could be achieved by even the most destitute of families" (Post, 1985, p. 116). The implied comparison, then, was that Nestlé's formula was better than natural breastfeeding as well as other brands of formula.

Audience Sensitivities

No evidence was found to suggest that Nestlé considered consumers in Third-World countries as anything more than means to profitable ends. This unbalanced relation became an issue Nestlé had to face, however, when activists organized a boycott against Nestlé products in 1977. The boycott remained in effect for many years and "many key publics" entered the fray, including "industry members, media, federal authorities, foreign governments, medical experts, and the World Health Organization" (Heath, 1997, p. 124). By 1981, Nestlé had hired and fired two PR agencies to try to change the company's image with no significant change in the company's practices.

Nestlé eventually cooperated with others in the industry and the World Health Organization to develop a code of marketing practices. Nestlé hired an outside organization to audit its efforts to improve marketing practices, and by 1984 the major boycotts were lifted.

Yet Nestlé's management strategy was far from a two-way symmetrical model of communication and understanding. Nestlé's extended initial resistance to change and eventual compromises with organized activists do not suggest any genuine concern for the mothers Nestlé and other industry leaders target in their Third World promotional campaigns. Heath (1997) documented the continuing opposition Nestlé faced in the early 1990s. Taylor (1998) studied and compared marketing practices in Bangladesh, Poland, South Africa, and Thailand and found that violations to the industry codes resulting from the baby formula controversy are still prevalent in underdeveloped countries. For example, the surveys revealed that formula companies still commonly give free samples of breast milk substitutes, infant formula, bottles, or teats to new mothers and use health facilities as distribution channels for promotional information.

*Finally, consumer sensitivities
and interests were ignored.*

Discussion

Nestlé's persuasive promotion of baby formula in underdeveloped countries appears unethical on all counts. Nestlé failed to encourage mothers to make informed decisions by clearly defining how and when baby formula is better than natural breast milk. Nestlé downplayed relevant evidence that revealed the product's potential for harm. The image Nestlé created to promote its product in comparison to natural alternatives was presented in a distorted and deceitful context. Finally, among our four tests, consumer sensitivities and interests were ignored. That is, the mothers targeted for formula sales were clearly treated as means to profitable ends. Indeed, the PR and marketing practices employed by Nestlé are far from the ideals of Grunig's (1993) two-way symmetrical model of communication. The result is a case study in how not to practice public relations, evident in this case's inclusion in Stauber and Rampton's (1995) *Toxic Sludge is Good for You: Lies, Damn Lies and the Public Relations Industry.*

Better Is in the Eye of the Beholder?

Although better depends on the case, thresholds can be determined by considering the consumers and publics affected by a product, idea, or service in the marketplace. An optimistic perspective on the Benecol case study is that postmillennium persuasion does not have to be totally removed from Emerson's refreshing logic. If persuaders consider their publics when carefully evaluating their claims of better by considering the thresholds of clear definition, scientific evidence, context of comparison, and audience sensitivities, our capitalistic marketplace may remain somewhat grounded. The four thresholds offer practical opposition to the totalitarian *Image* of which Boorstin (1972) warned. In an adversarial marketplace, the final decisions on which products are indeed better will be based on consumer trial. Based on the ethics of Bok (1978), Baker (1999), and Grunig (2000), persuaders will be wise to communicate openly with those most affected by their claims.

As illustrated in the Nestlé case, however, the better mousetrap can be defeated in the marketplace when reliable, comparative information is withheld or distorted. This brings us back to our second question regarding Emersonian logic in the new millennium.

Does natural selection occur in the mass mediated marketplace? The Benecol case suggests that if persuaders operate ethically, the laws of natural selection will eventually manifest. Clever promoters will find a way to get their mousetraps noticed in the marketplace. They may even sustain interest for prolonged periods of time using strategic marketing, advertising, and PR. However, if persuaders remain ethical in their claims as discussed previously, informed consumers will eventually choose the mousetrap that is truly fittest for their own needs.

The Nestlé study, on the other hand, demonstrated how unethical persuasion interrupts the process of natural selection in the marketplace. Nestlé's images of robust, healthy babies posted in maternity wards of Third-World countries promoted formula to impoverished women using strategic images Boorstin (1972) would likely describe as extravagant even for wealthy American consumers. And the strategies worked. Rather than losing profits as a result of the controversy, the infant formula industry continued to thrive in developing nations (Post, 1985). Nestlé touts itself as the world's largest food company, with products marketed in nearly every country. This level of success, despite persuasive practices that do not meet the aforementioned thresholds for ethical behavior in the marketplace, contrasts with the optimistic thesis that solid business means solid ethics.

Does this mean that natural selection doesn't work in the mass mediated marketplace? Neither one of these case studies can provide a conclusive answer, but the implications are still encouraging. As in the theory of evolution of species, lasting changes are a product of numerous generations, not single cases. Persuaders on both ends of Baker's (1999) continuum may profit in today's marketplace. Yet those who observe these ethical thresholds are more likely to enjoy morally sound, long-term relationships with their audiences. Allowing for exceptions, they will also be more likely to predict those mousetraps that will be deemed fittest.

Notes

1. Dedicated to Larry Rasky.
2. Law (2000) reviewed the scientific literature related to plant sterol and stanol margarines. The British Medical Journal Web site that hosts Law's article also includes responses to Law's review.

References

American Heart Association. (1999, November 8). *New sterol can reduce bad cholesterol.* Retrieved June 16, 2000 from the World Wide Web: http://www.americanheart.org/Whats_News/AHA_News_Releases/11-08–99_2-comment.html

Baker, S. (1999). Five baselines for justification in persuasion. *Journal of Mass Media Ethics, 14,* 69–81.

Barney, R. D., & Black, J. (1994). Ethics and professional persuasive communications. *Public Relations Review, 20*(3), 233–248.

Benecol. (2000, September 5). *FDA today announces plant stanol esters in Benecol(lower cholesterol and may reduce risk of heart disease.* Retrieved October 24, 2000 from the World Wide Web: http://www.benecol.com/press.html

Bok, S. (1978). *Lying: Moral choice in public and private life.* New York: Pantheon.

Boorstin, D. J. (1972). *The image: A guide to pseudo-events in America.* New York: Atheneum.

Emerson, R. W. (1909). *Journals of Ralph Waldo Emerson: With annotations.* Boston: Houghton Mifflin.

Evans, B. (1968). *A dictionary of quotations.* New York: Delacorte.

Food and Drug Administration. (2000, September 5). *FDA authorizes new coronary heart disease health claim for plant sterol and plant stanol esters.* Retrieved October 24, 2000 from the World Wide Web: http://www.fda.gov/bbs/topics/ANSWERS/ANS01033.html

Functional foods' address health problems. (2000, August 14). *Houston Chronicle.* Retrieved August 31, 2001 from the World Wide Web: http://ipn.intelihealth.com/IPN/ihtIPN/WSIPN000/22883/7197/294779.html.

Galbraith, J. K. (1967). *The new industrial state.* Boston: Houghton Mifflin.

Grunig, J. (1993). Implications of public relations for other domains of communications. *Journal of Communication, 43,* 164–173.

Grunig, J. (2000). Collectivism, collaboration, and societal corporatism as core professional values in public relations. *Journal of Public Relations Research, 12,* 23–48.

Heath, R. L. (1997). *Strategic issues management: Organizations and public policy changes.* Thousand Oaks, CA: Sage.

Hendrix, J. A. (2000). *Public relations cases* (5th ed.). Belmont, CA: Wadsworth.

Law, M. (2000). Plant sterol and stanol margarines and health. *British Medical Journal, 320,* 861–864. Retrieved October 25, 2000 from the World Wide Web: http://www.bmj.com/

Marx, K. (1900). *Das capital.* New York: Modern Library.

Mirkin, G. (2000, February 25). *Benecol and take control.* Retrieved October 18, 2000 from the World Wide Web: http://www.drmirkin.com/heart/8137.htm

Neff, J. (1999, July 1). Benecol, take control cases crumble FDA regulatory walls. *Food Processing.* Retrieved August 31, 2001 from the World Wide Web: http://www.foodprocessing.com/Web_First/FP.nsf/ArticleID/DTOS-4LNNHQ/

Nestlé. (2000). *In your life.* Retrieved July 23, 2000 from the World Wide Web: http://www.nestle.com/in_your_life/

Post, J. E. (1985). Assessing the Nestle boycott: Corporate accountability and human rights. *California Management Review, 8*(2), 113–131.

Schneider, A. (2000, June 30). Why you can't trust letters of recommendation. *The Chronicle of Higher Education,* A14–A16. Retrieved August 31, 2001 from the World Wide Web: http://chronicle.com/free/v46/i43/43a01401.html

Stauber, J., & Rampton, S. (1995). *Toxic sludge is good for you: Lies, damn lies and the public relations industry.* Monroe, ME: Common Courage.

Stevenson, B. (1935). *Famous single poems and the controversies which have raged around them.* New York: Dodd, Mead.

Taylor, A. (1998). Violations of the international code of marketing of breast milk substitutes: Prevalence in four countries. *British Medical Journal, 316,* 1117–1122.

Toops, D. (2000, March 1). Build a better mousetrap. *Food Processing.* Retrieved June 16, 2000 from the World Wide Web: http://www.foodprocessing.com/Web_First/FP.nsf/ArticleID/MEAT-4L8NSX/

Yule, S. S. B., & Keane, M. S. (1891). *Borrowings.* San Francisco, CA: Murdock. (Original work published 1889)

Zind, T. (2000, April 1). Youth through consumption: Can food products really turn back the clock? *Food Processing.* Retrieved August 31, 2001 from the World Wide Web: http://www.foodprocessing.com/Web_First/FP.nsf/ArticleID/RDAT-4JZH73/

Journal of Mass Media Ethics, *16*(2&3), 193–212

Toward a Professional Responsibility Theory of Public Relations Ethics

Kathy Fitzpatrick
University of Florida

Candace Gauthier
University of North Carolina

❑ *This article contributes to the development of a professional responsibility theory of public relations ethics. Toward that end, we examine the roles of a public relations practitioner as a professional, an institutional advocate, and the public conscience of institutions served. In the article, we review previously suggested theories of public relations ethics and propose a new theory based on the public relations professional's dual obligations to serve client organizations and the public interest.*

The leading association in the public relations industry defines the purpose of public relations as follows: "Public Relations helps our complex, pluralistic society to reach decisions and function more effectively by contributing to mutual understanding among groups and institutions. It serves to bring private and public policies into harmony" (Public Relations Society of America Foundations, 1991, p. 4). The same association describes the work of the public relations professional: "The public relations practitioner acts as a counselor to management and as a mediator, helping translate private aims into reasonable, publicly acceptable policy and action (Public Relations Society of America Foundations, 1991, p. 4).

These rather vague statements are among hundreds that have been offered to explain the term and function of those working in public relations. Many who have studied or practiced public relations have pondered—but seldom agreed—on just what public relations is or exactly what those who do public relations should be or do. The result is that the field includes a lot of people doing a lot of things for a diverse group of institutions and interests.

Most professionals who provide public relations services offer counsel regarding the public implications of an institution's decisions and actions. They advise the institution on communication strategies and tactics that can be used to gain and maintain the support of important constituents, called *publics* or *stakeholders*. Techniques commonly used to help organizations establish positive relationships with the news media, employees, shareholders, communities, government officials, and other publics involve strategic, often persuasive, communication. In fact, to the embarrassment of many associated with the public relations field, the history of contemporary practices dates back to a time when manipulative publicity stunts frequently were used to influence people's attitudes toward an institution, its products, its services, its ideas, or all of these.

Some public relations scholars and practitioners believe that contemporary public relations has moved beyond persuasion and rhetoric as fundamental concepts, and that professional public relations work is driven by principles of negotiation and mediation as reflected in the preceding industry statement. The purpose of public relations, they say, is not to simply influence publics for the good of the institution. Rather, it is—or at least it should be—to help organizations and their publics accommodate each others' interests with a goal of mutual benefit (see, e.g., Grunig, 1992).

Others argue that persuasion remains at the heart of public relations work. "Despite a few voices to the contrary, public relations practitioners generally and readily accept persuasion and advocacy as their major function" (Kruckeberg & Starck, 1988, p. 4). As such, the paramount interest served is that of the institution.

> *Efforts include both self-*
> *interested ... and benevolent*
> *initiatives.*

In fact, both views are correct. Modern day public relations efforts include both self-interested persuasive tactics as well as genuinely benevolent initiatives. Still more involve mixed-motive communication programs and campaigns designed to benefit both institutions and their publics (see Murphy, 1991). In brief, the practice of public relations involves a multitude of communication strategies and tactics designed to influence the attitudes and behaviors of targeted audiences, generally for the good of the "sponsoring" organization and sometimes for the good of both the organization and others.

Throughout public relations' brief history, the partisan efforts of some practitioners have drawn criticism and raised questions concerning the ethical conduct of those who call themselves "public relations professionals." In some cases, criticism may be justified because of unprincipled practices. Just like guns, strategic communication can be used for legal and ethical purposes as well as for illegal and unethical purposes. Often, however, the criticism results from either a misunderstanding of or lack of appreciation for the function of public relations. The field has done a poor job in defining what public relations professionals do and in justifying their value and worth to society. The result is that public relations professionals continue to be plagued by charges of unethical conduct.

This state of the industry is the result of several factors. First, as noted earlier, the parameters for public relations work have not been—perhaps cannot be—clearly defined. Confusion regarding the role that public relations professionals should perform creates still more confusion regarding the ethical standards that should define public relations practices.

Second, public relations has not fully extricated itself from its journalistic roots. Many still believe that because public relations evolved from journalism—and is still taught primarily in schools and colleges of journalism and communication—public relations practitioners should share their journalistic counterpart's passion for objectivity. Of course, when measured by that yardstick, public relations professionals will never size up. Although advocates can be fair, they are seldom objective.

Third, there are no established minimal standards for the practice of public relations. States do not require practitioners to qualify for a license before hanging out a shingle. In the absence of such regulation, it is left to the industry itself to define standards of performance. Although industry associations have done a laudable job in developing codes of conduct for their members, the codes stop short of providing a theoretical basis for ethical decision making.

Finally, the values and ethics of the institutions represented by public relations professionals often are confused with the values and ethics of the individuals who provide counsel on such matters. When an institution is the subject of public criticism for perceived irresponsible behavior, the public relations representative shares the blame—regardless of his or her involvement in or knowledge of alleged bad acts. This "guilt by association" has become increasingly detrimental to the public relations industry as more and more organizations fail to meet public expectations.

Unfortunately, these problems are not easily resolved. Many have spent years trying to establish public relations as a legitimate and credible profession. A big step in achieving that goal will be the development of a universally accepted theory of public relation ethics. In that regard, much work remains to be done.

Although a number of theories of public relations ethics have been advanced, few have been fully developed. In fact, a review of public relations textbooks led one scholar to conclude that "there is no accepted conceptual framework from which to study public relations ethics" (Bivins, 1989, p.

39). In a doctoral dissertation on public relations ethics, Pearson (1989x) concluded that "...many practitioners and scholars of public relations are capable of philosophical thought, but few seem to develop basic philosophical theory to under gird their discussion of public relations" (as cited in Grunig & Grunig, 1996, p. 20).

So begins this study, which is a first step toward the development of a "professional responsibility theory" of public relations ethics. First, we briefly review existing theories of public relations ethics, pointing out weaknesses that limit each model's usefulness as a universal standard. We then consider the role of a public relations practitioner as a "professional," asking what special obligations attach to professional status and how such status does or should influence public relations practices.

Next, we explore the concepts of institutional advocate and "social conscience." Just what is a *social conscience*? Although the term frequently is used in reference to public relations practitioners, it has not been fully defined, nor seemingly widely accepted. Certainly the words suggest that public relations professionals have obligations that extend beyond a client organization's bottom line. Yet just what those obligations are and how they are realized is unclear.

We conclude the article with suggested principles that might serve as ethical guideposts for the responsible practice of public relations.

Theoretical Bases for Public Relations Ethics

Attorney Adversary

According to the attorney-adversary model, public relations performs the socially necessary role of professional advocacy within the adversary process essential to free enterprise and competition. It is argued that in the free market system, the public relations advocate functions the same way as does a lawyer who zealously represents his or her client in a court of law (Barney & Black, 1994, p. 233).

Several questions raised by this model demonstrate its inadequacy as a standard for ethical public relations practice. In a court of law fairness is presumed. There is no such presumption in the media-driven court of public opinion. This court operates without specific rules of evidence and procedure that, in law, are designed to prevent undue prejudice against either side.

Judicial process rests on the assumption that, if both parties are adequately represented, the truth will emerge and justice will be served. Thus, when an attorney is appointed in criminal cases in which the defendant cannot afford one, the outcome is morally and legally questionable when a defendant is represented by incompetent counsel. In the court of public opinion, there is no guarantee that all interested parties will be represented or heard.

Defenders of this model have suggested that the public has a responsibility to gather and evaluate information that is relevant to their lives and choices (Barney & Black, 1994, p. 241). Yet, when opposing voices are silent or important information is withheld, how will the public obtain information that challenges an institution's version of the truth? With access to only one version of the truth, how can the public take responsible action?

Finally, in a court of law the information that juries and judges receive and evaluate—the persuasion that they experience—and the truth that they discover through the adversary process will rarely have consequences for their own lives. On the other hand, the persuasive communication by public relations professionals potentially has far-reaching consequences for people's choices and actions.

Enlightened Self-Interest

According to the enlightened self-interest standard for persuasive communication, "… businesses do well (financially) by doing good (ethically), and it is, therefore, in their bottom-line interest to engage in good deeds and ethical behavior" (Baker, 1999, p. 73). This standard would allow corporate decisions and actions to be represented as in the public interest, even if their ultimate motivation is the financial benefit of the company.

In defense of enlightened self-interest, one commentator suggested that this form of justification is similar to utilitarian reasoning in which all of the options are weighed and the costs and benefits to all concerned parties are considered (Whalen, 1998, p. 6). However, there is an important methodological difference between the two. Enlightened self-interest clearly makes institutional benefits the priority and the ultimate motivation for decisions that benefit other groups or interests in society. After all, it is through these social benefits that an organization's benefits are attained. According to classical utilitarianism, however, an action's benefits and costs to all concerned parties are to be considered and weighed impartially (Mill, 1861/1979, pp. 16–17). Impartiality requires that the interests of those making the decision about an action are not to be valued any higher than the interests of others who will be affected by that action.

Critics of this model for public relations practice have pointed out several ethical problems. Representing corporate actions as based on "corporate social responsibility" implies that actions are done out of a sense of duty rather than from selfish motives (L'Etang, 1994, p. 117). From a Kantian perspective, such programs treat their beneficiaries as mere means to the end of corporate image and profits (L'Etang, 1994, p. 121). Moreover, representing the corporation's aims in terms of a duty or desire to benefit the community, rather than in terms of marketing strategy, may involve the public relations practitioner in blatant deception of the public (L'Etang, 1994, p. 121).

As David Martinson (1994) argued, ethical standards include considerations such as the welfare of others, the avoidance of injustice, respect for self and others, and the common good (pp. 104–105, 107). Based on these criteria, enlightened self-interest is not truly an ethical standard, as its focus is clearly on the self-interest of the company. Thus, this model will not be sufficient to guide the difficult ethical decisions that public relations professionals have to make (Martinson, 1994, p. 103).

Community/Communitarian/Social Responsibility

In comparison with enlightened self-interest, true social responsibility is taking actions and instituting policies that are morally right for that reason alone, without an ulterior self-interested motive. It is based on values such as honesty, respect, fairness, the avoidance of harm, and justice in the distribution of the benefits and burdens of living together in a democratic society. Social responsibility means first that one recognizes, accepts, and acts on a general responsibility to one's society. More specifically and more realistically it requires responsibility to those persons and interests who will be impacted by one's actions.

Baker (1999) proposed the "social responsibility model" as one possible baseline for professional persuasive communication. Such a model, she said

> Assumes that persons in society are interdependent communal beings; that corporate citizens have a responsibility to the societies in which they operate and from which they profit, including obligations of good citizenship in contributing positively to the social, political, environmental, and economic health of society; and the focus of one's actions and moral reasoning should be on responsibilities to others and to community rather than on one's individual rights. (Baker, 1999, p. 76)

It would be difficult to find a public relations professional who disagreed with the concepts espoused in ethical theories based on the need for enhanced social responsibility, good citizenship, and improved community relations. All of these concepts focus on the need for public relations to contribute to the betterment of both communities in which their clients and employers operate. Indeed, service to society is an important aspect of each model.

Kruckeberg and Starck (1980) went so far as to suggest that an ethical approach to public relations might be found through an emphasis on the restoration of community. Because many of the problems that public relations professionals concern themselves with in modern mass society stem directly from the loss of community, they argued, "[a]n appropriate approach to practicing community (and public relations) must be derived through an active attempt to restore and maintain the sense of community that has been lost in contemporary society" (Kruckeberg & Starck, 1988, p. 111).

Such thinking is reflective of the "communitarian" approach later suggested by Leeper (1996). Concluding that "the primary 'code of conduct' by which our behaviors are judged will focus on our social responsibilities to strengthen community and promote traditional American values including fairness, democracy, and truth" (p. 168), she somewhat hesitantly proposed that these "responsibilities and values, then, can be examined as a basis for a public relations ethical system" (p. 168).

Although laudable, theories of ethics based on the concept of social responsibility are particularly limiting in the effort to develop standards of practice in public relations because the primary focus is on the obligations of institutions rather than on the ethical obligations of public relations professionals. In addition, the lack of a clear definition of social responsibility confuses rather than clarifies what appropriate—ethical—counsel would require on the part of the public relations professional. Is participation in philanthropic endeavors enough to meet an institution's obligation to operate in the public interest? If not, what else is required? And is it public relations' role to decide such issues?

Another significant concern is that these approaches do little to resolve the inherent ambiguity in such phrases as "serve the public interest" or "serve society." As we discuss next, all professionals are deemed to serve the public interest. A significant question in the development of a theory of public relations ethics is how public relations professionals fulfill their social role. More specificity is needed to provide the public relations professional the intellectual tools needed for ethical reasoning.

Sullivan's (1965) Partisan Values Versus Mutual Values

The theory of public relations ethics set forth in 1965 by Albert Sullivan and later reviewed by Pearson (1989) rests on what Sullivan defined as the technical, partisan, and mutual values in public relations. According to Sullivan, "mutual values" that reflect respect for human rights should be viewed as "higher" than "partisan values" that can lead to too much commitment and too much obedience (Pearson, 1989, pp. 57). Because technical values are morally neutral, Pearson argued, the focus of public relations ethics lies at the point where partisan and mutual values intersect. Under this theory, partisan values rest on concepts of commitment, trust, loyalty, and obedience. Sullivan (1965) suggested that although a public relations practitioner's commitment to his or her client or employer is important, many take their partisanship to extremes, relying too heavily on the views of the organization while ignoring or minimizing the viewpoints of others (see Pearson, 1989).

Mutual values—or the "higher values," as Sullivan called them—are necessary to balance partisan values, because they "take into account the viewpoints, interests, and rights of others" (Pearson, 1989a, p. 57). Sullivan proposed a "principle of mutuality," which states "If one has a right, another...has an obligation to respect that right, to fulfill that right" (Pearson, 1989, p. 57). According to this theory, "because a person is rational, that person has a right to the preconditions for rationality," which involves access to accurate and complete information in matters that affect him or her (Pearson, 1989, p. 58). And because a person is free, "that person has a right to participate in decisions which affect him or her" (Pearson, 1989, p. 53). Pearson (1989) observed that "[p]erhaps Sullivan's most important contribution to ethical theory in public relations in his argument for institutional obligation to publics" (p. 57).

Certainly, as Pearson (1989) pointed out, Sullivan identified the thorniest ethical challenge for public relations professionals both then and now. Balancing the special interests of institutions represented with those affected by those institutions is the issue that seems to defy resolution. Also, Sullivan's rejection of zealous advocacy places him among many of today's commentators who call for increased attention to social responsibility on the part of both public relations professionals and the institutions they serve.

A significant question raised—but not answered—by Sullivan's theory is when it is appropriate, if ever, for public relations advocates to place the interests of others above the interests of institutions they represent. Pearson (1989a) noted that although Sullivan criticized public relations for excessive partisanship, he also said that it "would be the height of cynicism to advocate that practitioners should have no commitment to an employer" (p. 56).

Two-Way Symmetrical Model

Another theory of public relations ethics that rests on principles of mutuality is that proposed by Grunig and Grunig (1996), who offered an ethical theory based on symmetric public relations. Under this approach, practitioners "play key roles in adjusting or adapting behaviors of [institutional] dominant coalitions, thus bringing publics and dominant coalitions closer together" (Grunig & Grunig, 1996, p. 6). This "win-win" approach provides an ethical basis for public relations, they argued, because it "provides a coherent framework for socially responsible practices" (Grunig & Grunig, 1996, p. 6).

Of course, it could be argued that in order for true symmetry to result, both sides must consider and weigh the effects of institutional decisions and actions and have the power to affect a particular outcome. In fact,

Grunig and Grunig (1992) acknowledged that a symmetrical approach to public relations does not guarantee all parties equal benefit.

Symmetrical public relations provides a forum for dialogue, discussion, and discourse on issues for which people with different values generally come to different conclusions. As long as the dialogue is structured according to ethical rules, the outcome should be ethical—although not usually one that fits the value system of any competing party perfectly. (Grunig & Grunig, 1992, p. 308)

The fact that the institution most often sets the "rules," however, raises concerns regarding the ethics of a process in which the power to establish the operating principles lies in the hands of one party.

In addition, this model might be criticized for going too far in requiring practitioners to meet the needs of constituents. As institutional advocates, public relations professionals represent a particular point of view that may or may not be harmful to those influenced by it. Is the responsibility to ensure that mutual benefit is gained or is it, rather, to ensure that no harm results from an anticipated decision or action?

In other words, just how far should public relations professionals should go in counseling their clients and employers to address the needs of constituents? As Grunig and Grunig (1992) themselves observed, "Practitioners of the two-way symmetrical model are not completely altruistic; they also want to defend the interests of their employers—they have mixed motives" (p. 320).

In summary, these previously proposed theories of public relations ethics make significant contributions to our understanding of the ethical challenges encountered in the practice of public relations. Yet, for various reasons, each falls short of providing a universally acceptable philosophy on which standards of ethical public relations practice might be based.

Toward a Professional Responsibility Theory of Public Relations Ethics

"Central to the importance of ethics in American public relations is the reality that, most of the time, practitioners have the voluntary choice of whether to be ethical or not" (Wright, 1989, p. 3). This statement by public relations scholar Don Wright captures the need for the development of a philosophical foundation for ethical decision making in public relations. Practitioners need some basis on which to judge the rightness of the decisions they make everyday. They need ethical principles derived from the fundamental values that define their work as public relations professionals. They need guidance in reconciling the potentially conflicting roles of the professional advocate and the social conscience.

An important first step in developing such standards is recognition of the public relations practitioner's position as a professional. Notwithstanding the debate about whether the field's members have achieved professional status, we presume such standing. Thus, the special ethical obligations of a professional must be addressed. As Goldman (1992) observed, "[Professionals must be committed to] some overriding value that defines both expertise and service, whether it be health, salvation, the protection of legal rights, or the provision of public information, knowledge, and education" (p. 1019).

In reviewing the professions literature, four criteria emerge as the defining characteristics of a professional: membership in an occupational organization, special expertise, a service orientation, and autonomy. In writing about the professions in 1960, W. J. Goode stated what is still true today

> If one extracts from the most commonly cited definitions all the items which characterize a profession ... a commendable unanimity is disclosed, ... core characteristics are a prolonged specialized training in a body of abstract knowledge, and a collectivity or service orientation. (p. 671)

Another states

> [A] professional service requires, among other things, advanced intellectual training, mastery of technical subject matter, the exercise of skilled and responsible judgment. These attributes are beyond appraisal by the client ... the client must take the professional man [sic] on faith—faith in his competence and faith in his motives. (Carey, 1957, p. 7)

Put another way, "Professionals are charged by their clients with making important decisions on their behalf, and they are compensated for assuming this decision making responsibility and bringing their knowledge to bear on the decisions" (Wolfson, Trebilcock, & Tuohy, 1980, p. 191). "A qualified professional is supposed to be an authority on his subject as a body of knowledge and an expert on the application to the solution of particular problems presented by clients" (Moore, 1970, p. 106).

> Professionalism involves the application of a general system of knowledge to the circumstances of a particular case. In treating a client's problem, this knowledge is necessary (1) to identify the precise nature of the problem (diagnosis), (2) to determine the best way of dealing with it (prescription), and (3) to provide specialized services so as to solve the problems (therapy). (Wolfson et al., 1980, p. 190–191)

The professional services provided by public relations professionals include expert counsel on matters involving institutional relationships with constituents and the management of communication between the two.

Special knowledge regarding the formation of public opinion, social science research, media channels, and communication strategies and tactics is assumed.

In rendering these special services, "the professional proceeds by his own judgment and authority; he thus enjoys autonomy restrained by responsibility" (Moore, 1970, p. 6). Public relations professionals—as professionals—have obligations that extend beyond the profitability (however defined) of the organization represented. Responsibility to the public—or in the case of public relations, to multiple publics—must be balanced with responsibility to a client or employer.

Indeed, public service always has been the hallmark of the professions, which serve society by providing essential services. Carey (1957) concluded that professionals enjoy the prestige of professional status because "they are presumed to accept a special obligation to place service ahead of personal gain" (p. 7). In a recent study, Reynolds (2000) observed that "society grants professional standing to those groups which contribute to the well-being of the broader society" (p. 115).

To summarize, professionals perform an essential public service that is realized through the provision of specialized services to clients or employers who retain them because of their special expertise and trust them to represent their interests. Because of this special relationship, the professional owes the client his or her loyalty. In fact, some would go so far as to define such associations as "fiduciary" relationships to which legal liabilities attach (see *Black's Law Dictionary*, 1979, defining a "fiduciary" relationship as one in which there exists a "reposing of faith, confidence, and trust, and the placing of reliance by one upon the judgment and advice of another," p. 6).

Thus, as professionals, it would seem that public relations practitioners owe a higher duty to client organizations and employers than to these institutions' constituents. This would support the role of public relations professionals as advocates of—and voices for—institutional interests. By definition, an *advocate* is one who pleads another's cause or who speaks or writes in support of something" (*Webster's New World Dictionary*, 1979, p. 20).

Now, how does this jibe with the oft assumed function of the public relations practitioner as the institutional *social conscience*? The term suggests that one who serves in such a capacity counsels an institution regarding the social implications of decisions and actions and—as a "conscience"— advises the institution to take actions that are in the best interest of society and to avoid those that are not. The concept seems simple in language and, on its face, seems to be in line with the professional's obligation to serve the public interest. However, the vagueness of such responsibility may be the reason public relations professionals struggle with this concept.

How does an institution best serve society? This is the question that public relations professionals must resolve if they truly are to serve as the social consciences of the organizations they represent. It's a big question and, indeed, one that business leaders throughout the world have not been able to answer. Following a 10-year study in the corporate arena on issues related to corporate social responsibility, Clarkson (1995) concluded that there is "[no] general agreement about the meaning of these terms from an operational or a managerial viewpoint" (p. 92).

Scholars in public relations have reached the same conclusion. The question, as posed by public relations scholar Tom Bivins (1993), is "How can a practitioner advocating a discrete point of view serve the interest of the greater public" (p. 120)?

Bivins (1993) suggested four possible paradigms:

> First, if every individual practicing public relations acts in the best interest of his or her client, then the public interest will be served.
>
> Second, if, in addition to serving individual interests, an individual practicing public relations serves public interest causes, the public interest will be served.
>
> Third, if a professional or professionals assure that every individual in need of or desiring its/their services receives its/their services, then the public interest will be served.
>
> Fourth, if public relations as a profession improves the quality of debate over issues important to the public, then the public interest will be served. (p. 120)

Noting that none of three approaches provides the definitive answer, Bivens (1993) concluded that

> In its dual role as mediator and advocate, public relations has the opportunity both to engage in and to encourage public debate. By doing so, it also has the opportunity, and the obligation, to lessen the obfuscation often surrounding the mere provision of information. It must develop clear guidelines and formal mechanisms by which issues important to society are clarified and presented to the public for open, democratic debate. (p. 121)

Bivins's (1993) focus on the value of ethical communication to open public debate captures the essence of public relations' social role. By providing voices for special interests, public relations contributes to the harmonization of diverse points of view, thereby promoting "mutual understanding and peaceful coexistence among individuals and institutions" (Seib & Fitzpatrick, 1995, p. 1).

To get beyond the general concepts of social responsibility or public service, however, we must focus on public relations practitioners as professionals rather than as communicators. Although, as noted earlier, we reject the idea that the attorney-adversary model is fully appropriate as a moral foundation for public relations, the professional service model employed in the legal profession may be an appropriate guide for determining the ethical—and morally justifiable—role of the public relations professional.

Lawyer jokes aside, people in and outside the legal profession recognize the value of the legal profession in the functioning of a democratic society. Attorneys represent clients to ensure that they are treated fairly in the criminal and civil justice systems, to ensure that their legal interests are protected. Lawyers serve as zealous advocates of their clients, with no special obligation to the opposing party. In other words, they serve the public's interest by serving their clients' interests. A former federal judge put it this way:

> To the client [the lawyer] owes loyalty, undivided and undiluted, zeal and devotion and some additional obligations. … His object is to achieve for his client the best which is available within the law by means compatible with the canons of ethics. (As cited in Gillers & Dorsen, 1989, p. 22)

The judge went on to say that the lawyer also owes duties to the profession and to the community. "From the community, the lawyer derives his special status, special franchise, his unique accessory role" (Gillers & Dorsen, 1989, p. 22).

In applying this analogy to public relations, it can be argued that public relations professionals best serve society by serving the special interests of their clients and employers. Like other professionals, however, they must balance such service with their obligations to operate in the public interest. In public relations this means that the special interests of the institution served must be balanced with the interests of those directly affected by the institution.

Such balancing begins with the recognition that the public relations professional's greatest loyalty is to his or her client. At the same time, he or she ensures that the institution hears and considers the interests of its stakeholders. We contend that serving the public interest simply requires public relations professionals to consider the interests of all affected parties and make a committed effort to balance them to the extent possible while avoiding or minimizing harm and respecting all of the persons involved.

As such, a significant aspect of professional responsibility means responsibility to publics. In this way, we borrow from the meaning of *public interest* in the public policy arena:

> [P]ublic interest is part of our political language—a term we use to express concern for all interests affected by a decision and for a set of fundamental social principles. Invoking the public interest requires all parties to a discussion to make their arguments in terms of these interests and these principles, and it

requires that the consequences of all proposals be shown and discussed in a public forum. (Wolfson et al., 1980, p. 84)

Thus, the views of those affected by an institution's decisions and actions should be heard before decisions are made or action is taken.

In further developing this idea, we propose that the term *social conscience* be eliminated from the public relations literature. Such terminology simply contributes to the confusion about the proper role of public relations. In addition to the fact the term appears to be indefinable, many contemporary practitioners reject the title as an accurate reflection of their work (see, e.g., Katzman, 1993). Additionally, there is some evidence that public relations is not viewed by institutional leaders as the appropriate function to serve in the capacity of a social conscience. Many organizations that have taken steps to institutionalize ethics have turned to legal or other advisors outside public relations for advice in this area (see, e.g., Fitzpatrick, 1996). At the same time, only a third of corporate Chief Executive Officers participating in a recent survey said they sought the counsel of public relations advisors on matters related to social responsibility (Fitzpatrick, 2000).

Next, we propose that the term *social conscience* be replaced with the term *public conscience.* Although the terms *social* or *society* are acceptable in reference to the groups of people affected by institutional decisions and actions, they carry a sense of the "greater society" rather than of those specifically and directly affected by or, alternately, who affect an institution in a given situation.

In the context of public relations, the term *public* is widely defined as "a specific part of the people; those people considered together because of some common interest or purpose" (*Webster's New World Dictionary,* 1979, p. 1148). Thus, the use of the term *public conscience* better captures the more focused obligation of public relations professionals to best serve society by balancing their clients' and employers' interests with the interests of those directly associated with their clients' decisions and actions.

A social conscience provides moral limits or checks on decision-making power within an institution that has effects (good and ill) on society, both individual members and the society as a whole. A public conscience weighs the effects of decisions and actions on specific parties, thereby serving society by serving these special interests.

A theory of public relations ethics based on responsibility to specific publics not only helps to resolve the ambiguity of such phrases as "serve the public interest" and "social responsibility." It also reflects what recent studies in the field have concluded—that "relationships ought to be at the core of public relations scholarship and practice" (Ledingham &

Bruning, 2000, p. xiii). By focusing on relationships between an organization and its constituents—rather than on an organization's relationship with or obligation to serve an intangible society—scholars and public relations professionals can begin to define an organization's ethical responsibilities to its publics. Then practitioners can go further in defining standards of performance that are appropriate to the ethical practice of public relations.

Principles of Responsible Advocacy in Public Relations

For the public relations practitioner, as for most professionals, moral dilemmas arise when loyalties and responsibilities conflict and a course of action must be chosen. A moral dilemma occurs when a choice is required among actions that meet competing commitments or obligations, but there are good reasons for and against each alternative.

For other professionals, such as health care providers, ethical principles have proven useful in identifying the conflicting responsibilities in a moral dilemma, bringing clarity to moral thinking and providing a shared language for discussion.

Three principles that could provide the foundation for a theory of professional responsibility in public relations are

1. The comparison of harms and benefits: Harms should be avoided or, at least, minimized, and benefits promoted at the least possible cost in terms of harms.
2. Respect for Persons: Persons should be treated with respect and dignity.
3. Distributive Justice: The benefits and burdens of any action or policy should be distributed as fairly as possible.[1]

Principles hold generally unless they conflict.

It is important to recognize that these are prima facie, and not absolute, principles.[2] They are principles that hold generally unless they conflict with one another. When only one of the principles is implicated in a moral choice, that principle should be taken as the controlling guideline for ethical conduct. However, moral dilemmas often involve conflicts between the principles. In these cases, the decision maker must employ his or her own values, moral intuition, and character to determine which principle is most important and most controlling in the particular context.

As Aristotle (1975) pointed out, determining the morally right action is difficult based on reasoning alone, as with the application of ethical theories and principles. We must learn to discern the morally relevant particulars in each situation and ultimately, "the decision rests with perception" (Aristotle, 1975, *Book II*, Section 9, p. 47).

Moreover, the use of ethical principles in approaching moral choice and action does not ignore the importance of virtues or the character of the decision maker. Aristotle (1975) argued that a good character is the product of habit. One becomes virtuous by practicing virtuous actions over a lifetime (*Book II*, Section 1, pp. 28–29; Section 4, pp. 34–35). Ethical principles can guide us in the recognition of the morally right or virtuous act and, acting accordingly, over time we can develop both the moral discernment and the habits of morally right action that comprise a good character.

Application of the first principle requires the identification and comparison of harms and benefits expected to result from a proposed course of action or policy.[3] All of the affected parties and interests must be considered and weighed impartially (Mill, 1861/1979, pp. 16–17). The probability and seriousness of the possible harms must be determined, as must the probability and extent of the expected benefits. According to this principle, causing harm is worse than not providing a benefit. In a true moral dilemma some harm or risk of harm is often anticipated, so that when harm cannot be avoided, it should at least be minimized to the extent possible. Because this principle requires a comparison of harms and benefits, its application will rely on the perception of particulars and the values of the decision maker.

Respect for persons requires that persons be treated with respect and dignity, so that their decision-making abilities, choices, and actions are supported rather than interfered with, to the extent consistent with equal respect for others.[4] This principle prohibits deception, manipulation, and coercion, as these forms of influence interfere with the decision-making process.

The principle of justice is based on the value of fairness. It requires that benefits and burdens, in terms of risk of harm and actual harm, be distributed among the affected parties as fairly as possible. This principle is particularly useful as a supplement to the first two principles.

These three principles often work in combination, supporting and supplementing each other to provide more concrete guidance in moral decision making. For example, fairness requires that benefits for one group or interest should not be secured at the cost of disproportionate harms to another group without adequate justification, and everyone affected should be treated with respect and dignity. Similarly, when harm is unavoidable, it should be minimized to the extent possible, and those harmed deserve an explanation out of respect for their value as persons. They may also deserve compensation based on the principle of justice.

Once actions are taken and their effects are known, the professional responsibility theory further requires that those whose decisions resulted in these actions and effects must fully accept and admit responsibility for them. Here, the communication specialist role for public relations becomes particularly important. When organizational actions or policies turn out badly and when harm is done, the public relations professional will shoulder the task of explaining and perhaps attempting to justify those actions or policies to those who have been adversely affected, as well as to the wider public.

Whether the public relations communicator is announcing actions or policies at their inception or explaining and justifying them when something goes wrong, respect for persons and the avoidance of further harm will be particularly relevant. Although respect for persons requires honesty, this does not mean that selective communication and persuasion are automatically ruled out. They do, however, require some limits and careful consideration of their purposes and how they are meant to influence target audiences.

Selective communication is morally suspect when it is intended to mislead or when it is used to conceal information that others need to make their own life decisions. Yet, not everything that is known, believed, or communicated within an organization needs to be made public.

Questions that may assist in a moral evaluation of selective communication in a particular case include the following: For what purpose is selectivity in communication being employed here? What was not selected for release and why not? Is the selective release of information meant to mislead or deceive the target audience? Is the information held back needed by the audience for their own choices and actions? Will not having this information risk or cause harm to any person, group, or interest?

Persuasion need not be deceptive or harmfully manipulative to be effective. It is possible to use persuasive communication to appeal to the rational faculties of a target audience, to affect attitudes and beliefs through honest conviction, and to point out good reasons for specific choices and actions. Rational persuasion respects persons when it contributes truthful, relevant information in the form of facts and reasons to the decision-making process. This is quite different than deception or manipulation that operate by interfering with that process.

Questions that may assist in a moral evaluation of a specific use of persuasion include the following: For what purpose is persuasion being employed here? Toward what choices and with what consequences for individual lives is persuasion being used? Does the persuasion in this case contribute to or interfere with the decision-making process for its target audience?

Conclusions

A professional responsibility theory of public relations has advantages over other theories in part because it attempts to reconcile the dual roles of the public relations professional as institutional advocate and public conscience for that institution. The inclusion of responsibilities to the various publics affected by institutional actions and policies, in addition to the institution itself, broadens the more narrow focus on institutional interests found in both the attorney-adversary and enlightened self-interest models. Conversely, the emphasis on public rather than social responsibility narrows the overwhelming and unrealistic focus of a communitarian model on the community or society as a whole.

The ethical principles that form the philosophical foundation for the professional responsibility theory also may provide more concrete guidance than do other approaches in resolving ethical dilemmas caused by conflicting obligations to a variety of competing interests. These principles also suggest a series of questions that may assist the public relations practitioner in serving both as institutional advocate and public conscience in a morally responsible way.

The next step in developing a professional responsibility theory of public relations will be to apply these principles and questions to real moral dilemmas and ethical issues that arise in public relations practice. As many who work in other disciplines have realized, the interaction between principles and cases in practical application is indispensable for both the development of practical judgment and the grounding and refinement of ethical theory (Jonsen, 1991).

Notes

1. Tom Beauchamp and James Childress (1994) are responsible for developing the four basic principles of health care ethics: Respect for Autonomy, Beneficence, Non-Maleficence, and Justice. The three principles discussed here are modifications of their model developed specifically for public relations ethics. See also Lisa H. Newton (1989, p. 21). This study guide was prepared for the *Ethics in America* television series, produced by Columbia University Seminars on Media and Society. The ethical principles, "Do Good, or at Least Do No Harm, Observe the Requirements of Justice, and Respect Persons" were meant to guide professional conduct in politics, medicine, business, journalism, the military, and the law. For business ethics specifically, see Richard T. De George (1995, pp. 60–109) and Thomas Donaldson and Patricia H. Werhane (1996, pp. 1–12). In both texts, ethical analysis is based on (a) utilitarian or consequential theory in which benefits and harms are compared, (b) deontological or Kantian theory in which respect for persons is paramount, and (c) considerations of justice.

2. This conception of the principles as prima facie is borrowed from the prima facie duties of W. D. Ross (1930).
3. This principle is a combination of Non-Maleficence and Beneficence in Beauchamp and Childress (1994). It originates in Mill (1861/1979).
4. This principle is similar to Respect for Autonomy in Beauchamp and Childress (1994). The change to "persons" and the emphasis on respect and dignity refer back to its original source in Immanuel Kant (1785/1959, pp. 46–47).

References

Aristotle. (1975). *Nicomachean ethics* (Sir David Ross, Trans.). London: Oxford University Press.

Baker, S. (1999). Five baselines for justification in persuasion. *Journal of Mass Media Ethics, 14*, 69–81.

Barney, R., & Black, J. (1994). Ethics and professional persuasive communications. *Public Relations Review, 20*(3), 233–248.

Beauchamp, T., & Childress, J. (1994). *Principles of biomedical ethics.* New York: Oxford University Press.

Black's Law Dictionary (5th ed.). (1979). St. Paul, MN: West.

Bivins, T. H. (1989). Are public relations texts covering ethics adequately? *Journal of Mass Media Ethics, 4*, 39–52.

Bivins, T. H. (1993). Public relations, professionalism, and the public interest. *Journal of Business Ethics, 12*, 120–121.

Carey, J. L. (1957, March). Professional ethics are a helpful tool. *Public Relations Journal.*

Clarkson, M. B. E. (1995). A stakeholder framework for analyzing and evaluating corporate social performance. *Academy of Management Review, 20*, 92–117.

De George, R. (1995). *Business ethics* (4th ed.). Englewood Cliffs, NJ: Prentice Hall.

Donaldson, T., & Werhane, P. (1996). *Ethical issues in business* (5th ed.). Upper Saddle River, NJ: Prentice Hall.

Fitzpatrick, K. R. (1996). The role of public relations in the institutionalization of ethics. *Public Relations Review, 22*(3), 249–258.

Fitzpatrick, K. R. (2000). CEO views on corporate social responsibility. *Corporate Reputation Review, 3*, 290–300.

Gillers, S., & Dorsen, N. (1989). *Regulation of lawyers: Problems of law and ethics* (2nd ed.). Boston: Little, Brown.

Goldman, A. H. (1992). Professional ethics. In C. Becker & C. B. Becker (Eds.), *Encyclopedia of Ethics* (Vol. 2), pp. 1018–1020. New York: Garland.

Grunig, J. E. (Ed.). (1992). *Excellence in public relations and communication management.* Hillsdale, NJ: Lawrence Erlbaum Associates, Inc.

Grunig, J. E., & Grunig, L. A. (1992). Models of public relations and communications. In J. Grunig (Ed.), *Excellence in public relations and communication management.* Hillsdale, NJ: Lawrence Erlbaum Associates, Inc.

Grunig, J. E., & Grunig, L. A. (1996, May). *Implications of symmetry for a theory of ethics and social responsibility in public relations.* Paper presented to the Public Relations Interest Group, International Communication Association, Chicago, IL.

Jonsen, A. (1991). Of balloons and bicycles or the relationship between ethical theory and practical judgment. *The Hastings Center Report, 21*(5), 14–16.

Kant, I. (1959). *Foundations of the metaphysics of morals* (L. W. Beck, Trans.). New York: Bobbs-Merrill. (Original work published 1785)

Katzman, J. B. (1993). What's the role of public relations? Profession searches for its identity. *Public Relations Journal, 49*(4), 11–17.

Kruckeberg, D., & Starck, K. (1988). *Public relations and community: a reconstructed theory.* New York: Praeger.

Ledingham, J., & Bruning, S. D. J. (2000). Introduction: Background and current trends in the study of relationship management. In J. Ledingham & S. D. F. Bruning (Eds.), *Public relations as relationship management: A relationship approach to the study and practice of public relations* (p. xiii). Mahwah, NJ: Lawrence Erlbaum Associates, Inc.

Leeper, K. A. (1996). Public relations ethics and communitarianism: A preliminary investigation. *Public Relations Review, 22*(2), 163–179.

L'Etang, J. (1994). Public relations and corporate responsibility: Some issues arising. *Journal of Business Ethics, 13,* 111–123.

Martinson, D. (1994). Enlightened self-interest fails as an ethical baseline in public relations. *Journal of Mass Media Ethics, 9,* 100–108.

Mill, J. S. (1979). *Utilitarianism.* Indianapolis, IN: Hackett. (Original work published 1861)

Moore, W. (1970). *The professions: Roles and rules.* New York: Russell Sage Foundation.

Murphy, P. (1991). The limits of symmetry: A game to symmetric and asymmetric public relations. *Public Relations Research Annual, 3,* 115–132.

Newton, L. (1989). *Ethics in America study guide.* Englewood Cliffs, NJ: Prentice Hall.

Pearson, R. (1989). Reviewing Albert J. Sullivan's theory of public relations ethics. *Public Relations Review, 15*(2), 52–62.

Public Relations Society of America (1991). Public relations: An overview. *PRSA Foundation Monograph Series, 1*(3).

Reynolds, M. A. (2000). Professionalism, ethical codes and the internal auditor: A moral argument. *Journal of Business Ethics, 24,* 115–124.

Ross, W. D. (1930). *The right and the good.* London: Oxford University Press.

Seib, P., & Fitzpatrick, K. (1995). *Public relations ethics.* Fort Worth, TX: Harcourt Brace.

Sullivan, A. J. (1965). Values in public relations. In O. Lerbinger & A. Sullivan (Eds.), *Information, influence, and communication: A reader in public relations.* (pp. 412–439) New York: Basic Books.

Webster's New World Dictionary, Second College Ed. (1979). New York: William Collins.

Whalen, P. (1998, August). *Enlightened self-interest: An ethical baseline for teaching corporate public relations.* Paper presented to the Public Relations Division, Association for Education in Journalism and Mass Communication.

Wolfson, A. D., Trebilcock, M. J., & Tuohy, C. J. (1980). Regulation of the professions: A theoretical framework. In S. Rotenberg (Ed.), *Occupational licensure and regulation* (pp. 180–214). Washington, DC: American Enterprise for Public Policy Research.

Wright, D. K. (1989). Ethics research in public relations. *Public Relations Review, 15*(2), 3–5.

Journal of Mass Media Ethics, 16(2&3), 213–233

Communication in the Unfettered Marketplace: Ethical Interrelationships of Business, Government, and Stakeholders

Robert I. Wakefield
Brigham Young University, Hawaii

Coleman F. Barney
Solution Bank International

❑ *As technology redefines relationships, new assumptions are emerging about the ethics of persuasion. In an increasingly global economy, technology is forcing greater transparency onto businesses and governments as the moral context of their communications is inseparable from the competitive nature of the business world. This article suggests that moral boundaries will be set naturally, that consumers have a moral obligation to excercise "due diligence" in their acceptance of messages, and that no one is in charge of the global economy's conventions and morality. The system ultimately depends on participants to keep their own self-interested boat in the race.*

Globalization of Economics and Information

As a so-called global economy spreads, breaking down nationalistic barriers for production, distribution, and consumption, thousands of formal and informal cultural and political rules are under assault. If "controlled economy" is an oxymoron, then by definition the emerging global economy matrix will likely challenge most of the long-standing parochial rules that have preserved local stability for centuries.

In the wake of globalization, then, highly developed economic systems with affluent consumers are being jammed up against subsistence cultures with cheap and plentiful supplies of labor and huge potential mass markets.

Relatively wealthy consumers who shudder at the thought of earning less than $20 per hour are snapping up running shoes, clothing, DVD players, and television sets produced in factories whose maximum wage ranges in the pennies, rather than dollars, per hour.

From this unprecedented mix rise three questions:

1. What universal moral mandates can usefully serve both the sophisticated (even predatory) and relatively open and competitive economic systems of the United States, Britain, France, and Germany and traditionally conservative systems of such disparate nations as China, India, Mexico, Japan, and scores of others?
2. What will protect consumers and existing systems as the new economic realities gallop through the world?
3. In an economic revolution that threatens protective national barriers, who will be in charge of the emerging global economy? For how long, for example, will China (or any other country) be able to regulate internet content with all the product offerings and ideas that flow through its spreading channels? Tangentially, who can (or should) regulate the internet?

In this article, we describe the prospects of a generally unfettered global economy and offer a detailed argument for a morality of a strongly competitive business climate as one serving the best interests of all shareholders in the mix, including consumers and even vulnerable producers unable to compete in the marketplace. It is an uncomfortable proposition for those who would protect the weak and advocates of the legislated level playing field, for it argues the importance in these new conditions of an open competition that ultimately allows the collective consumer to be in charge.

Is a New Ethical Model Needed for Global Society?

By answering these questions, it may be possible to account for global, free market ethics. We believe it is imperative to understand the ethical interrelationships of businesses and their stakeholders in the context of globalization. It also is important to examine ethics in light of new media, including the Internet, which render information so accessible. With this accessibility, traditional gatekeepers are replaced by the ability of individuals to both receive and spread information (and to directly pressure corporations rather than relying on media or governments). This creates an entirely different communication system that, combined with a truly free market unleashed globally, may need modified ethical constructs.

Unchained Marketplace

The free enterprise ideal is that there is no need to restrict business behaviors. The marketplace governs itself by rewarding strong companies and forcing weaker ones out of business. Companies are obligated to work vigorously against competitors to wrest away customers, revenues, and market share, even though it may result in competitors folding and people losing their jobs. By contrast, people destroy their own jobs if they fail against their competitors. In return for championing this survival-of-the-fittest mentality, the successful company will reward employees and investors for capturing an industry.

As the theory goes, this vigorous competitive environment should also reward consumers. A successful company creates new and improved products and expanded production capacity. This in turn fosters investment and job creation. Competition accelerates these benefits by increasing product choices and pushing the limits of technology. This has occurred in various industries, but has been particularly apparent in recent surges in the capacities of personal computers, the varieties and reach of mobile telephones, and other technological advances.

---

*A vigorous economic
environment rewards consumers.*

Entire societies can benefit from the competitive marketplace. One observer said that the existence of multinational firms is "a necessary good" in many societies:

> Domestic savings are simply not enough to sustain high economic growth. So we need direct foreign investment. [Multinationals] bring international standards and technologies and help us become attuned to the patterns of different markets, and they also bring foreign partnerships, which themselves bring technology transfers and new markets of their own. (Friedman, 1999, p. 135)

Free Enterprise Can Be Self-Regulating

Recent examples indicate how free market competition regulates itself without government interference. In fact, formal intervention can do more damage than good. Competition has been especially aggressive in the technology sector. Andy Grove, former executive officer of Intel, the world's largest manufacturer of computer chips, recently observed that paranoia drives the fiercest competitors to win. Even when a corporation is winning, its employees need to hear the footsteps of their competitors. This keeps the firm sharp and aggressive.

When C. F. Barney (one of the authors of this article) worked at Microsoft®, employee banter was always about winning. Even when this high-tech giant was a dominant force in the software marketplace, in-house conversation was not about having won but about needing to do more to gain even greater dominance against competitors like WordPerfect® and Lotus®.

Microsoft chief executive Bill Gates felt it was imperative to eliminate Netscape®, which was trying to advertise its Navigator browser as the next, and supposedly superior, computer operating system. Yet the marketplace perceived the Microsoft Explorer browser as the "better mouse-trap," and Netscape could not respond. Therefore, Netscape failed in this free market battle due to weak product offerings and a lack of ability to execute on ambitious product design plans.

Microsoft's dominance produced several benefits. With a focus on the operating systems that host applications on desktop computers and network servers, the company's dominance resulted in a standard that led to thousands of new software programs being created that sparked the purchase of millions of computers worldwide, which caused costs to drop. So both software and hardware developers benefited. Also, Microsoft employees could continually upgrade their product, keep prices down, and, because most computers were sold with Microsoft Windows®, receive substantial revenues.

Unfortunately, the mousetrap that captured market share and allegedly drove Netscape out of the business also caught the government's attention when competitors of Microsoft banded together and lobbied an end to Microsoft's grip. Netscape and its allies pressed the Justice Department to prosecute Microsoft. After months of wrangling, the company was convicted of monopolistic behavior and ordered to divide into two separate firms.

Yet, as Microsoft was enduring federal scrutiny over browser dominance, the sheer competitive force of the Internet was shifting attention in the computer industry away from desktop and server operating systems. The value of computers moved to software and moved to business-to-business applications that unleashed a new way for computers to communicate and automate commerce and transactions over the Web. Oracle® and Sun® had already jumped into Internet applications, and "up-and-comers" like Ariba® also raced to lead the software industry. Regardless of what Microsoft may have done as a monopolist, its stock plummeted to a 52-week low and, for the first time, market analysts questioned its relevance. This shift hinted that the government did not need to interfere with Microsoft. Although many people reveled in Microsoft's defeat, others questioned the long-term impact of federal intervention.

While Microsoft was losing market share by government edict, Novell®, Inc., another darling of the NASDAQ 100, saw its dominance in another technology category erode through normal market forces. As recently as 1997, Novell was the largest networking operating system in the world; now it is only Number 4. It has gone through several major layoffs, including in September 2000. Within days after the most recent round of cuts, a job fair was conducted to help ex-Novell employees find new positions.

Ironically, many of the new positions were in dynamic new businesses started and operated by other former Novell employees.

Free Enterprise Attracts Motivated Individuals

Through free enterprise, successful companies create jobs, intense competition, and wealth. Managers of capitalist firms labor for more than a paycheck; they have a strong desire to maximize their potential. Such people expect to succeed and to be measured on their success. When they accomplish the goals set by themselves, owners, and investors, they reap substantial rewards. If unsuccessful, they expect to be replaced with more competitive management. Abraham Maslow (1970) described five levels in his Hierarchy of Needs. Maslow described how everyone is driven to achieve the initial level of supporting Basic Needs. Also, most people will reach the second level of Safety and Security. However, the number of people in the world who ever progress into the upper levels of the hierarchy are limited. The top level of the hierarchy, Self-Actualization, is populated by the smallest proportion of people but arguably is the level attained by most successful capitalists and business leaders. Because these individuals are mostly motivated by the desire to maximize their own potential, they are the least likely to tolerate regulations and controls designed to temper or moderate their progress. A serious trade-off occurs whenever regulation is introduced. Although regulations may be designed to "protect" the masses of the population, they restrict the ability of self-actualizing leaders to be successful, and this success is ultimately what we rely on to provide jobs and wealth to those masses. Goal-oriented, confident people with the skills to embrace their own visions flourish in dynamic firms that reward self-actualization; they don't respond well to regulatory boundaries meant to equalize or normalize the way businesses compete. Figure 1 illustrates this.

Corruption Is Inevitable in Any Market System

Despite the positives of free enterprise, government officials and other business observers have offered many reasons to regulate commerce. Stability seems to be the main incentive. Regulations (including restrictive moral restraints) supposedly preserve jobs and maintain stable incomes for families and communities. They are intended to keep unsafe or unsatisfactory products out of the marketplace. Such restraints can help sustain the environment and can protect the economies of given countries from foreign influences.

Regulations, however, can promote false security. Japan's regulated economy could not deter unprecedented layoffs during recessions, and

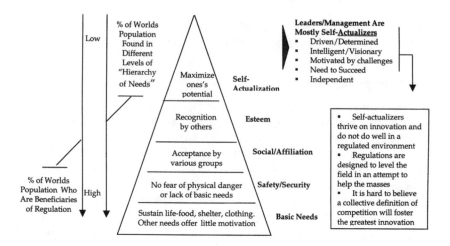

Figure 1   Self-actualization in business management.

laws failed to eliminate dangerous tires that resulted in Bridgestone's tire calamity. The collapse of the Soviet economies in the late 1980s starkly illustrated the failures of purposive economic regulation (Friedman, 1999) or the planned economy. These highly regulated economies stifled production and innovation. "Winners" typically were companies in collusion with the regulators to install market protection, price supports, and capacity planning. However, under these constraints gains were short lived. Meanwhile, consumers were stuck with less innovative products, limited offerings, higher prices, and, eventually, drastically weakened and noncompetitive states (Vogl & Sinclair, 1996).

Certainly, free enterprise is not immune from corruption. As mentioned, motivated individuals are naturally attracted to competition. So when regulatory bodies have attempted to artificially balance power, these individuals have been known to figure out ways to skirt the regulations to preserve their ideas and obtain their "share" of wealth. Among multinationals, these regulatory side steps include moving from country to country in a continual search for cheaper labor and less stringent manufacturing constraints. In such a world, it is unreasonable to assume that any economic system will remain free of corruption.

Coping With the Inevitable Corruption of the Unregulated?

We certainly do not condone any organization skirting the laws or their own moral obligations. Society should be concerned about how decent people can lose their means of family support. We should be concerned about economic disparities between countries and about the hundreds of thousands of people who go to sleep hungry every night despite arguments that developing nations are catching up (Vogl & Sinclair, 1996). We should be disturbed when corporations pursue profits without any seeming compassion.

Yet a free global system favors altruism, not profitability, and when money is the goal, corporations will communicate in a way that fosters maximum opportunity to make and retain profits. This means they will want to hide certain information if for no other reason than to keep competitors from knowing about it. They will try to "put their best foot forward," to convince their stakeholders that they are profitable, that their products are "the best" on the market, and that they are a good investment. It also means that many companies will withhold the complete truth or even lie outright to stay above the competition.

Therefore, what restraints are available to protect society against businesses that will not adhere to the rules? Furthermore, who is responsible for protecting consumers and other members of society if the unfettered, free market has no rules?

We believe that the answers transcend corporate walls. Companies function within a societal context that has the capacity to monitor and influence corporate behaviors. Ethical codes relevant to global business should reflect this context, as explained hereafter.

Ecosystem of Market Segments

A corporation is part of an ecosystem of five key market segments that determine how the entity creates new products, settles on prices for its offerings, and markets its wares. The segments are similar to what others call *stakeholders* (Freeman, 1984). To be successful in the long term, a firm must recognize and interact with these segments, which are

1. The Company: The entity responsible for identifying market needs and generating and delivering products or services that are seen as innovative and worthy of consumption. This segment is controlled by its management, which controls the destiny of the entity. Employees often have different priorities.

2. The Customer: The primary consumer of the product or service created by the company. A customer may be an individual or another firm. Buying motives vary depending on the product or service, but every customer follows a formula of benefit plus price equals value. If the value is sufficient, a purchase will occur.

3. The Investors: The group that has an equity stake in The Company, either through investing of capital directly in a private firm or the purchase of stock on the public market. The investments carry an expectation of greater profits in return.

4. The Employees: The people who rely on the company for their livelihood. Employees have a personally vested interest in the company's success. The interests of managers, as officers of the entity, may be different from the rank-and-file staff, but the entire employee group is still treated as a key segment.

5. The Community (or Communities): The broader group of businesses, individuals, media, interest groups, or government entities who have a stake in the company—not necessarily as primary consumers or as investors, but because they have some interest in whether the company succeeds (or fails) and how it fits into society.

Obligations of the Market Segments

With the five segments identified, it seems necessary to explain why they correlate to the ethical foundations underlying business decisions. This might be done best by examining the interactions of two of these segments: the company and customers.

In the United States, where competition has endured for decades, companies and consumers seem to understand their moral obligations. Companies offering products or services are morally obligated to not defraud buyers. Consumers have the obligation to assert self-preservation by conducting due diligence before buying. When a contract between buyer and seller is not fulfilled, the wronged party has legal recourse.

The obligation of the seller to be forthright and of the buyer to be informed rests on the ability of both parties to understand what motivates the other actor in the transaction. It also places importance on what is communicated and on the capability of consumers to decipher that communication. For example, if the company (or seller) understands that consumers (or buyers) have access to both positive and negative information about its products and services, the seller will tend to avoid being untruthful for fear of being caught. If consumers understand that fraud occurs, they will be more wary of each seller and more prone to conduct due diligence. Therefore, information again becomes an important factor in today's economic transactions. Relationships also exist between the company and the three other market segments—the investor, the employee, and the community. Each of these segments has expectations of business responsibilities. We refer to these responsibilities as *business virtues,* as described following.

Fundamental Business Virtues

Business virtues can be defined as attributes that bring value to each market segment in the company's environment. The five virtues in the competitive environment are

1. Profitability: To successfully compete, a company must have a plan for profitability and processes that direct how it will generate and meet market demand for its products or services.
2. Vision: This is long-term strategy to maintain viability as conditions change. Vision helps firms exceed industry growth norms. Firms without vision are not rewarded with higher capitalization or recognition from customers and investors.
3. Safety: This dictates the need to create products or services that meet or exceed margins of safety to protect the consumer against harm, which in turn would lead to dissatisfaction or even liability.
4. Stability: This refers to a business model that is economically and institutionally sound, eliminating unsettling gyrations in capacity, demand, and performance.
5. Credibility: This is a reputation of integrity related to a firm's activities that not only facilitates the selling process but reduces outside scrutiny.

These virtues reflect what the market segments expect of the company. Each segment will prioritize the virtues differently and respond accordingly to the business. The priorities even can be contradictory from segment to segment. A successful company will understand these differing priorities from segment to segment and will organize its strategies to accommodate the differences. All of these priorities and interactions are shown in Table 1.

Profitability is the core of business; thus, the virtues are pragmatic as well as theoretical. Yet a visionary business will acknowledge that each segment's prioritization of virtues carries enduring implications. If the firm responds to each virtue, it increases its chances for success. For example, long-term vision can bring stability, thus protecting the welfare of employees and consumers. Such vision also should engender sensitivity toward safe products. Each of these virtues, in turn, builds and preserves a good reputation, which again enhances the other virtues. This creates a continual "cycle of virtue" for an entity that desires long-term success.

Ignoring or Artificially Manipulating Virtues

Often, business leaders view profitability as no more than providing solid products and reaping the returns. This could be viewed as an "inside-

Table 1
Market Segments and Their Business Virtues

| Company | Equity Stakeholders | | Interested Parties | |
	Investors	*Employees*	*Customers*	*Community*
1. Profitability	1. Profitability	1. Stability	1. Credibility	1. Safety
2. Vision	2. Vision	2. Safety	2. Safety	2. Stability
3. Safety	3. Credibility	3. Profitability	3. Stability	3. Credibility
4. Credibility	4. Safety	4. Vision	4. Vision	4. Profitability
5. Stability	5. Stability	5. Credibility	5. Profitability	5. Vision

Note. Examples:
• Investors rank priorities like the company. The rewards of pleasing investors have the most influence in how a company behaves because of its relationship to investors.
• The staff of a company often is powerless to impact its direction and to make it stable.
• A company must be profitable to stay in business but this is not a priority interst to any other segment beyond investors.
• Companies will tailor messages to reflect sensitivity toward the particular segment being communicated with.
• Interested parties tend to look at companies in a more personified way. They want a sense of personality to judge the company as a partner.
• The company will invest in branding that formulates opinions of target segments.

This table shows how each market segment prioritizes virtues. Companies plan their behaviors toward each segment based on its priority of virtues. They create messages and programs to influence each segment's view of the company. Therefore, when a firm introduces a product (priority 1: profitability), a customer (priority 1: credibility) must assess the truthfulness of the firm's message through independent verification of its ability to deliver a quality product.

out" approach to decisions in which the other market segments are ignored in the rush for profits. There is ample evidence, however, that ignoring the priority virtues of the other segments can quickly create harsh consequences.

In 1999, Coca-Cola® suffered a dramatic blow to its reputation and its profits when consumers alleged that products from a Belgium plant were laced with dioxin. Within 24 hr, the allegations spread around Europe. Eight nations banned Coke products and the firm scrambled to repair the damage. Yet it was too little, too late: The company suffered widespread negative publicity, and the company's sales and stock prices plummeted (Holsendolph, 1999).

Coca-Cola executives should not have been caught by surprise. Had they monitored the priority virtues of European market segments along with their incessant pursuit of profits, they would have had plenty of warning. The crisis occurred during an ongoing dioxin scare over agricultural goods. Coke also misjudged the resentment it had accumulated in Europe over previous unfair competitive practices (Roughton & Unger, 1999).

Government intervention serves only to artificially alter the rankings of the virtues. Government subsidies helped make Utah-based Geneva Steel Corporation a stable source of employment, thus satisfying the employee and community segments' needs. However, for several years, although employees made sacrifices to remain employed, Geneva has still failed to compete with the lower wages and production costs of their foreign counterparts. Operating at the margins, Geneva's product quality has suffered along with its credibility. As a result, the firm cannot remain viable in the competitive world, even with the subsidies.

Ethics of Communication in the New World

Beside the question of competition between companies, it is important to consider how companies communicate with their various market segments, and how the market segments judge that communication. It also is important to understand how, in today's society, the market segments can influence business communication.

Company's Obligation to Communicate

In a competitive marketplace, corporations must communicate with their stakeholders. To do this effectively, the company crafts messages to have maximum impact in informing, building understanding, and driving sales. Messages often are targeted to the prioritized virtues of each market segment. Although ethical frameworks would suggest that communication be open and forthright, it is common for manipulation to occur. Manipulation is not limited to deliberate misrepresentation. It includes what companies do not say, as well as what they say.

Many corporations still operate under the Cold War rules regarding information, as outlined by Friedman (1999)—information is power, so its distribution must be controlled. Positive information is distributed widely and perhaps embellished to make the seventh minor upgrade look new or vastly improved. Negative information, by contrast, is hidden in some remote corner so that only the most trusted insiders know about it. To be fair to the corporate world, such practice is pervasive even among individuals. Few people, for example, would boast on a resume of the D+ they received in their freshman physics class.

Today's instantaneous and global spread of information has rendered these old rules of communication utterly ineffective. No longer are the media confined to a few major networks; now they are targeted to the smallest groups of individuals linked around the narrowest of common causes. The same is true of print media. Information is not limited to newspapers and a few magazines in major metropolitan centers. Never has the array of publications and electronic media been so vast as it is today in almost every country.

However, the real change is the unprecedented reach of the Internet that alters the very nature of communication. A short time ago, one-way communication between a business and its market segments was the norm and two-way communication was considered progressive. Corporations could easily control the timing, content, and vehicles for its messages. Now, information flows are "multiway." It is no longer just firms communicating to their constituents but, like it or not, their constituents communicating with them and with each other.

As a result of these changes, it is much more difficult to stonewall information. Firms may keep secrets for a few weeks or even months—but long-term prospects for hiding sensitive information are disappearing. Many multinationals have learned that, unlike in past days, it is difficult to hide problems in one plant from media in other locations; negative information unearthed in one country can quickly spill over borders and even into the global media.

---

*Internet alters the very nature of
[corporate] communications.*

It might be easy for readers to claim moral high ground over corporations who do not communicate the whole truth in this new environment. They may argue that the firms deserved what eventually came their way, and such an assessment may be accurate. Yet the argument also oversimplifies much more complicated and constant interrelationships between companies and their other key market segments.

Obligations of Other Market Segments to Assess Communication

Once a company has communicated, people in each market segment have a responsibility to properly assess the information and make their own decisions about the firm and its offerings. To do this effectively, they must understand that companies will craft information positively as explained previously and become discerning consumers of information. Most people are skeptical of paid advertisements, but how many exercise that same judgment on articles or network news reports? If they act on that information (with a vote or purchase, for instance), then who is at fault for believing what turned out to be inaccurate or untruthful? Such discernment—even a "cooperative" effort between sender and consumer—must persist through every opportunity to evaluate information.

The different priority businesses give to the virtues mentioned earlier often guide their communication. Individuals who know this can filter corporate information and supplement it from other sources for a more complete and balanced view of a situation. At the same time, they must recognize that these sources will reflect their own priority biases. For example, a local station may air the community's concerns over safety in a local plant rather than delving into the plant's revenues. Therefore, if people can sort through these different and often conflicting priorities in assessing communication, they should be able to make better decisions.

Levels of Truth—Barometers for Assessing Communication

Knowing that communication from different sources can be confusing, some scholars have devised guidelines to help judge its veracity. Deaver (1990) described four levels of truth ranging from *pure truth* (unembellished facts) to *deceit* or outright lies. Between are *selective truth* and *invented truth*. In Table 2, we modify Deaver's categories to fit this discussion and suggest moral implications for each level.

Note that only deceit is classified as immoral, whereas the other levels of truth can be good or bad, depending on the situation. For example, even intimate communication between friends ranges mostly in the selective or invented categories. Most people don't want to absorb pure truth, considering a listing of facts and figures to be mundane and uninviting. Therefore, companies spend considerable money to research those selective or invented truths that will entice the market segments to pay attention to their messages.

So herein lie the moral interconnections between businesses and their market segments. The company is obligated to communicate in a morally responsible way, but in the competitive world, where profitability is the prime priority for companies, there is no guarantee that this will occur. Therefore an additional responsibility lies with information recipients to accurately judge what they absorb. Understanding the levels of truth can help in sorting out the vagaries of communication to accurately assess a company and make good choices related to it.

With the myriad information channels and multiway communication described previously, it seems more appropriate than ever to assign ethical responsibility to the market segments as well as to businesses. Information needed to make purchases or to build relationships or to pressure a company no longer need come from the company alone. A variety of checks and balances are built into today's information system, and most individuals can use any or all of these in making decisions. If recipients believe the information is truthful and it convinces them that a product is sound, for example, they likely will buy the product. If they conclude that the information is false, or withheld, whether they buy the product or not—or that the company is manipulating them—they may choose to go elsewhere, complain to the company, pressure the firm to change its behavior, or tell other potential buyers.

A recent Amazon.com case offers one example of how multiway communication between segments and levels of truth have stifled attempts to manipulate information. In an effort to boost profits (Virtue 1 for companies), Amazon.com executives decided to conduct a "dynamic pricing" test. Such a test determines whether a company can charge different prices for the same products, depending on where customers live, their income levels, and other demographics that can now be monitored through the worldwide web (Martinez, 2000).

Amazon.com's test was brief and might have been successful. However, through their own communication channel, DVDTalk.com, customers who had purchased DVDs from Amazon.com compared notes and found that regular customers were charged more (Streitfeld, 2000). This sparked a flurry of protests, and the company spent the next 2 weeks issuing apologies and refunds to former loyal but now angry consumers (Martinez, 2000).

It is difficult to know whether this one incident significantly damaged Amazon.com, but today the company is suffering huge losses in profits and stock prices and has received poor ratings from stock analysts. Thus, the company's Number 1 priority, profitability, has been dramatically affected by the Number 1 priority of its consumers, credibility.

Market segments also reacted when Volvo® was prosecuted in Texas for false advertising in the early 1990s. At a real-life monster truck rally, oversized trucks drove over and crushed a line of cars. Afterwards, a Volvo fan noticed that an old Volvo wagon was visibly less smashed than the other cars. This prompted the company to recreate the event for a TV commercial to demonstrate the safety of Volvo vehicles. However, at the recreation, the advertising agency decided the Volvo didn't look as uncrushed as it should after the first pass of the truck. So the crew reinforced the roof of a second Volvo, then cut the roof supports of the other cars in the subsequent lineup. Satisfied that this would reflect the required contrast between smashed, unsafe cars, and sturdy, safe Volvo's, the filming proceeded. Just then, someone from the Texas attorney general's office walked in, confiscated the props, and closed the operation.

Therefore, where did Volvo officials go wrong? When they decided to do a reenactment? When they propped up the Volvo's roof structure, or cut the support bars on the other cars? The whole scenario was an invented

Table 2
Levels of Truth and Their Moral Implications

	Pure Truth	Selective Truth	Invented Truth	Deceit
Type of truth	• A statement of facts with no embellishment • A good example would be fact sheets of a product size, weight, capacity, etc.	• Selling messages that use hyperbole surrounding some facts • It becomes more important to look for what is not said than what is said	• Stories and examples are gathered and combined into a powerful message • Example: Use the name of a client and the specifics of another custome, combining these facts into a powerful selling message	• An outright lie • Statements or acts designed to improve the situation of the seller at expense of the buyer.
Moral issues	• No moral issues, but this kind of communication leaves it up to the listener to draw conclusions and benefits for products or services	• You don't know if the seller is hiding a problem by withholding information or just trying to reduce complexity by giving only "relevent" information	• Is it moral to "makeup" stories in an attempt to make a powerful point? • Is it the invented truth being used to reinforce truth or embellish a weak story? • Morality is always questionable	• No question this tactic is morally wrong and improper

truth, according to Table 2. It was based on truthful eyewitness accounts but staged to maximize drama for a powerful message. Volvo targeted customers with a message about safety (customer Virtue 2) to maximize sales (company Virtue 1: profitability). However, as the film crew reinforced the car frame they regressed from invented truth to deceit, which caused people to call the authorities. Volvo sacrificed its credibility (Virtue 1 for customers and Virtue 4 for companies) when it crossed the line ethically, morally, and legally.

If Volvo had not been caught and the commercial had aired, consumers would have been responsible for distinguishing between pure truth, invented truth, and deceit. Individuals in each market segment would have had to decide what actions they should take in the situation based on their respective prioritization of virtues. Rather then just trusting the advertisement and buying a Volvo, they could have reviewed *Consumer Reports.* They could have searched the Internet for alternative information and reports. They could ask a friend or acquaintance who owned or had previously owned a Volvo. Armed from various sources, their subsequent purchase of a Volvo would then be an informed choice.

Executives of today should understand that decisions are made in this manner and that those decisions ultimately have an impact on profitability. With such understanding, they may be less likely to risk their profits on invented truths or deceit that destroys credibility. Thus, ideally, the free market rights itself, whether through competition or communication.

Informed Assent and Significant Neglect—Testing the Truth Levels

In the examples just given, both Amazon.com and Volvo were caught in acts of deceit because someone cared about the communication in the first place. In today's world of information overload, businesses try to target communication to customers who need to make positive decisions about their products or services (decisions that will enhance the profits of the company). They also must communicate with those who can harm a company or impede its progress, such as regulators, media, and activist groups. Sometimes, as with Amazon.com and Volvo, positives become negatives when information they attempt to hide gets out anyway. This raises the question of when is enough information given, and when does hidden information become damaging? This may depend on the relative importance of the information.

We believe there is a correlation between how much the market segments scrutinize communication and the possible impact of decisions that arise from that information. When the stakes are small, people seem more willing to accept invented truths or even deceits. For example,

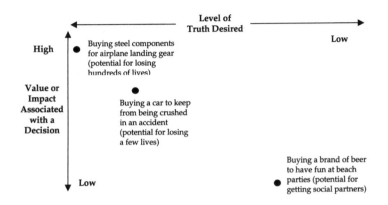

Figure 2   The sliding scale of scrutiny in truth telling.

most people in the United States believe that the *National Enquirer* stretches credibility, but they do not care because the information is of little consequence. Most people also accept that corporate advertisements embellish the truth and thus fall into the selective or invented truth categories. However, when significant dollars or lives are at stake, discerning consumers of information demand much more truthfulness and accuracy. This is illustrated in Figure 2.

Perhaps the level of truth chart could better help information consumers assess truth if two more concepts were included in the decision-making process. These concepts are informed assent and significant omitted truth. Informed assent would operate on the positive end of the truth-telling scale, whereas significant omitted truth is in the negative end. If people have sufficient information (positive or not) by which to make appropriate decisions, then those decisions are based on informed assent. If, however, a company hides information that is critical to making decisions and no other source is able to reveal the information, then information recipients are making decisions in the face of significant omitted truths. The omitted truths become significant because they curtail informed assent and the results are harmful. The Bridgestone tire crisis was an excellent example of significant omitted truths. The company omitted crucial information about unsafe tires for long periods of time, apparently intending to be spared financial loss and undue embarrassment. No other source was able to learn enough about the impending danger or the company's omissions in time to force resolution of the problem. By the time the truth was revealed, hundreds of deaths already had been attributed to the faulty tires. The irony is that with the truth out, Bridgestone suffered worse damage than it tried to avoid, in terms of credibility, profitability, and perhaps even survival.

Considering that most business communication is less than pure truth and that each market segment shares responsibility for assessing communication in line with its own priority virtues, informed assent and significant omitted truth provide distinct separation of where ultimate responsibility for truth rests. If individuals fail to assess the typical selective or inventive truths, and this leads to poor decisions, they must suffer the consequences of their choices. However, if a company has omitted significant truths and put individuals or society in harm's way, then that company should be subjected to full legal and reputational liability.

What About the Disenfranchised?

Before ending this discussion, it must be acknowledged that even with today's omnipresent and instantaneous communication, billions of people in the world still lack access. Should these people just be ignored in this equation of global business ethics? We believe the answer is "no"; in fact, the widening disparity between wealthy nations and the disenfranchised increases the need for a global business communication ethic.

When Nestlé® received global sanctions for placing infant formula into developing nations, it was marketing and communication mistakes, not the product itself, that caused severe damage. When mothers in these nations bought the formula and mixed it with unsafe water, they had insufficient information for exercising informed assent. This was not necessarily a result of significant neglected truths from Nestlé, but from inadequate information and education channels in these underdeveloped nations.

Ironically, the lack of access for the disenfranchised exemplifies the value of an ethic based on the obligation of each market segment to discern truth. Nestlé attempted to market its infant formula in developing countries to satisfy its number one business virtue, profit. In doing so, company officials failed to consider the number one priority of community—in this case, a global community—product safety. Had they possessed the vision to consider this long-term priority, they would have realized the danger of a product that requires whatever water is available. With this vision, they could have avoided future damage to their own credibility and ultimately to their profits. Nike® and Wal-Mart® suffered similar damage due to market segment scrutiny of alleged human rights abuses in developing nations.

In a society where more and more groups have access to more and more information, disenfranchised citizens who previously had little ability to speak for themselves are beginning to access interest groups who can speak for them. Without global watchdogs who constantly communicate with each other and who cooperate to impose change, there would have been no means for mothers to pressure Nestlé, or for young female workers in Indonesia and Malaysia to put pressure on Nike or on their own authoritarian governments.

It is this global activism, even where disenfranchisement has been prevalent, that is forcing corporations to rethink policies regarding what to communicate and what to hide. This global activism is what renders businesses fearful of stonewalling significant neglected truths or of otherwise being unethical in their communication to the outside world, and global activism is what indicates that when the market segments bear responsibility for making decisions about communication, a consumer-based ethic can be successful.

Summary and Conclusions

In this treatise, we have outlined the moral interrelationships between businesses and their market segments, or stakeholders as some call them. The communication arena has changed considerably as the world has progressed from the Cold War to the age of globalization. During the Cold War, those in power were able to control information. Today, the variety and global reach of information has rendered it widely accessible. This forces greater transparency onto businesses and governments, whether they wish for it or not.

We believe that the moral context of business communication cannot be separated from the competitive nature of the business world. With globalization comes evidence that governments are losing the power to intervene, and free enterprise is winning out over controlled economics. This creates a greater competitive urgency among companies that are driven not only to survive, but to thrive within the rigors of unfettered capitalism.

Businesses by nature seek profitability, and communication about products and services will always be designed to that end. To a lesser degree, they also value the virtues of vision, credibility, safety, and stability. Four other market segments that have interests in the company—investors, employees, customers, and the community—share these virtues, but each with different priorities. Relationships between these groups are contingent on communication, and the more knowledge individuals or companies have about the priorities of the other segments, the more they will be able to understand information coming from those segments.

The moral imperative in communication between businesses and their market segments is that each of them carries certain obligations. Companies are obligated to inform their market segments, and individuals within those market segments are equally responsible for deciphering the information in terms of its truthfulness. Because companies naturally steer toward positive information, their truth levels can range from pure truth, to selective or invented truth, to deceit. It is then incumbent on the recipients of that information to evaluate its truthfulness and to make decisions related to the company and its products based on those evaluations.

With the many channels of information through which individuals can receive and share information today, there is little excuse for them to misjudge the information. If they can make decisions based on informed assent, they usually should suffer the consequences of their own poor choices. However, if they conduct due diligence in the information gathering process and still are deceived by companies who have significantly omitted truths related to these choices, and the choices lead to disastrous individual or societal consequences, there are proper avenues of recourse through the legal system. In these instances, the company that purposely omitted significant truths should be held fully accountable.

At the beginning of this article, we proposed three main questions. The first was, are there ethical boundaries in unfettered competition? The answer to that is "yes," but those boundaries can be determined by the natural course and consequences of competition in today's less-regulated environments. Is it morally responsible for one company to drive the other out of business? Some examples listed herein indicate that when this happens, the fault may rest not so much in the aggressor as in the vanquished.

The answer to the second question we discussed in greater detail. Although firms are obligated to communicate with their market segments, the responsibility to make good choices based on that information might ultimately rest with the recipient, and today there are plenty of sources by which to receive and evaluate information. If an individual understands that businesses communicate with varying levels of truth, then he or she is in a better position to evaluate those levels and act accordingly. The decision may range from purchasing a company's products or using its services, patronizing a competitor, filing a lawsuit, or joining other individuals to force the firm to change. In a society of free communications, any of these choices are available and appropriate.

The third question asked, who is in charge of the global economy and its conventions? The answer would appear to be that no on is in charge, but that stakeholder groups affect each other by keeping their own boats in the race.

No doubt proposing that ethical choices ultimately rest with the recipient of business communication, rather than placing responsibility on businesses to ethically communicate, can generate controversy. The purpose of this article was not to absolve businesses of any blame for intentionally manipulating their market segments. Indeed, we believe that ethical codes for business conduct and communication should be strengthened. However, the typical ethical code in circulation today imposes moral values on businesses while ignoring the responsibilities that rest with those who associate with the companies or receive their communication. For free enterprise to be ultimately free, information consumers must accept that responsibility.

References

Deaver, F. (1990). On defining truth. *Journal of Mass Media Ethics, 5,* 168–178.

Donaldson, T. (1989). *The ethics of international business.* New York: Oxford University Press.

Freeman, R. E. (1984). *Strategic management: A stakeholder approach.* Boston: Pittman.

Friedman, T. L. (1999). *The Lexus and the olive tree.* New York: Anchor.

Holsendolph, E. (1999, June 18). Owning up can cut the damage. *The Atlanta Journal-Constitution,* p. H–2. Retrieved September 18, 2001 from the World Wide Web: http://www.ajc.com

Martinez, M. J. (2000, September 29). Amazon answers to 'test pricing' claims. *The Provo (Utah) Daily Herald (AP Business Writer),* p. B7.

Maslow, A. (1970). *Motivation and personality* (2nd ed.). New York: Harper & Row.

Naughton, K., & Hosenball, M. (2000, September 18). Ford vs. Firestone. *Newsweek,* pp. 26–28.

Roughton, B., Jr., & Unger, H. (1999, June 22). Multi-front effort seeks to restore confidence. *The Atlanta Journal-Constitution,* p. D–1. Retrieved Retrieved September 18, 2001 from the World Wide Web: http://www.ajc.com

Streitfeld, D. (2000, Sept. 28). Web asks, how much can you pay? *International Herald Tribune,* p. X. Retrieved Retrieved September 18, 2001 from the World Wide Web: http://www.iht.com

Vogl, F., & Sinclair, J. (1996). *Boom: Visions and insights for creating wealth in the 21st century.* Chicago: Irwin.

Wilson, L. J. (1996). Strategic cooperative communities: A synthesis of strategic, issue management and relationship building approaches in public relations. In H. M. Culbertson & N. Chen (Eds.), *International public relations: A comparative analysis* (pp. 67–80). Mahwah, NJ: Lawrence Erlbaum Associates, Inc.

Woller, G. M. (1997). Business ethics, society, and Adam Smith: Some observations on the liberal business ethos. *Journal of Socio-Economics, 25,* 311–332.

Journal of Mass Media Ethics, *16*(2&3), 234–243

Cases and Commentaries

The *Journal of Mass Media Ethics* publishes case studies in which scholars and media professionals outline how they would address a particular ethical problem. Some cases are hypothetical, but most are from actual experience in newsrooms, corporations, and other agencies. We invite readers to call our attention to current cases and issues. (There is a special need for good cases in advertising and public relations.) We also invite suggestions of names of people, both professionals and academicians, who might write commentaries.

The following case comes from a report by ComputerWire of London.

Louis W. Hodges, Editor
Knight Professor of Ethics in Journalism
Washington and Lee University
Lexington, VA 24450
(540) 463–8786

Was Microsoft's Ad Unacceptably Deceptive?[1]

Microsoft® Corporation is embroiled in a dispute with the Federal Trade Commission (FTC) over claims that the company last year ran an over-aggressive advertising campaign against Palm Inc. to promote its rival Windows-based Pocket PC.

The FTC has found that Microsoft's "Can your Palm do that?" advertisement last year was deceptive because it failed to disclose that certain features offered by Pocket PC were available only if buyers spent more for wireless capability. Palm's devices had wireless capability built in. Consumers were told of the wireless matter only in almost unreadable print at the bottom of the advertisement.

A Microsoft spokesperson said the case is a matter of "font size and graphics." Microsoft and the FTC are now in discussions over how to settle the case. One possible deal could see the company forced to run disclaimers at the bottom of advertisements for the Pocket PC that use larger type than before.

Note

1. ComputerWire of London has given permission for use of this case as it is written here. It was excerpted from ComputerWire's Web site and slightly edited. I

express gratitude to Mr. John Desler of the Public Relations Department of Microsoft for his help in sending me a copy of the advertisement in question. Also, Mr. Desler informed me that the case has been settled to the satisfaction of both the FTC and Microsoft.

Commentary 1
Small Print May Satisfy Demands of Law, but Not of Ethics

One theorist recently said, "Critiquing … is somewhat like playing 'king-of-the-hill'" (Griffin, 2000, p. 417). Someone puts up a flag, then the critics and scholars try to pull it down. So, to some extent, I feel this is a bully's role to steal Microsoft's flag by assessing its advertising claim as described in this case. On the other hand, there is some pleasure in critiquing the ethics of a company that has thrived as king of its own hill.

Before we are too quick to criticize, however, it must be remembered that the United States is the home of the brave and the land of free enterprise. This country reveres unfettered capitalism, where each company must survive in a rough-and-tumble competitive arena. Those with the best instincts prosper, whereas the lesser herd struggle along and risk eventual consignment to the competitive landfill.

In this respect, there is nothing inherently wrong with aggressive advertising of a new product; it simply advances a pawn along the play board of capitalism. Yet the Microsoft case rests with the FTC, so there are legal implications. Fortunately, this review can leave those concerns to the attorneys while examining underlying ethical considerations.

The real ethical issues arise in the allegations that Microsoft was overaggressive or deceptive in its advertisement. There are distinct differences in these categories: Overaggressiveness relates to Microsoft's ethical stance against its competitor, Palm Inc.; deceptiveness concerns the company's moral obligations to consumers. Also, although it is possible to refute the claim of overaggressiveness, it seems easier to agree with the FTC that deception occurred. Let us address these claims individually.

In assessing whether Microsoft's practices were overaggressive, one must ask two questions. The first is what renders a company or its communications overaggressive? Also, if this can be determined, did Microsoft then violate acceptable bounds?

The answer to the first question seems simple, according to what is implied in this case. Apparently, Microsoft was challenged not because it created advertisements to compete with another product (a widespread daily occurrence), but because the ads specifically named and challenged the competitor: "Can your Palm do that?" By so doing, Microsoft implied that the Palm device was inferior to its new Pocket PC.

Is it really overaggressive to assert superiority over another clearly identified brand? If so, maybe we should challenge the very ethical framework of our individualistic society, where from our earliest ages we are conditioned to stand out from peers and to strive for individual excellence (and perhaps that framework is flawed, but that is another discussion).

I see nothing unethical in a company claiming its mousetrap is best through comparison to a competitor's mousetrap if the claims are accurate and truthful. In fact, ethical foundations set up by Adam Smith obligated businesses to be profitable by providing better products and convincing consumers to buy them. Competitors embarrassed by such a comparison should improve their products and do some of their own convincing.

In this case, however, there is reason to doubt that Microsoft's claims were truthful. This leads to the other ethical issue broached previously, that of deception. In the details supplied, one phrase is critical: Microsoft's pitch was deemed deceptive "because it failed to disclose" certain facts. The disclosure that was needed concerned a crucial distinction between competitive products wireless capability that was built into the Palm device but available in the Pocket PC only at an added cost. Microsoft argued that this was explained in the ad's fine print, and therefore the company did not deceive. Like the FTC, I disagree.

I have said that deception is related to an entity's obligation to consumers. For enterprise to remain free of corruption, there must be a bond of trust between entities and consumers (Donaldson, 1989). Corporations are bound to supply safe and sound goods and to truthfully tout their benefits.

Yet, Black (2000) observed that people expect corporate messages, including advertisements, to be "non-objective … if not outright biased" (p. 23). Consumers therefore are responsible for learning about product offerings and making informed choices about which are best for them. Executing these mutual obligations, businesses and consumers can both benefit; but when an organization purposefully deceives, consumers can be significantly harmed.

To determine whether deception was involved in this case, it is important to probe Microsoft's intent. Was it purposeful? Obviously, the company wanted to convince readers that Palm's product, a popular forerunner in the handheld market, was somehow deficient. Thus the headline, "Can your Palm do that?" The intimation was that Microsoft had now created a better mousetrap. Maybe, but to obtain that better mousetrap consumers would have to pay much more. Only in print that is difficult for most people to decipher were those conditions mentioned.

When an entity places barely decipherable text in an advertisement, its goal is not to communicate with consumers but to avoid legal entanglements. Indeed, the small print is included with the hope that consumers will not bother with it. The smaller the print, the less chance that the begrudgingly outlined condition will turn consumers away from the product. So, the very text in question is what could make the difference between consumers choosing that product or the competitor's offering. Therefore, to satisfy the demands of law, the entity has violated the mutual moral bond between the organization and consumer.

I believe that Microsoft did intend to place doubt on Palm's product and lure consumers toward the new Pocket PC. In doing so, Microsoft set forth an unbalanced comparison and communicated unfairly with consumers to satisfy legal possibilities. To me, this is deceptive and therefore unethical. However, perhaps the more important consideration here is not what verdict should be rendered on Microsoft, but why small print disclaimers are allowed in the first place.

References

Black, J. (2000, October). *The ethics of propaganda and the propaganda of ethics.* Paper presented at the Mass Media Ethics Colloquium 2000: The Ethics of Persuasion, Park City, UT.

Donaldson, T. (1989). *The ethics of international business.* New York: Oxford University Press.

Griffin, E. (2000). *A first look at communication theory* (4th ed.). Boston: McGraw Hill.

By Robert I. Wakefield
Brigham Young University, Hawaii

Commentary 2
Microsoft Acted Unethically

At first glance, you may have several reactions to this case. I did. At different points I thought, "They did print the truth, after all." Then, "What's the big deal, you see this in advertisements all the time." Next, "What's the harm? Who's really hurt, anyway?," and finally, "Don't the consumers have a responsibility here, too? Shouldn't they keep informed?"

Each of these is a natural response to the Pocket PC ad and its tiny type outlining the extras consumers must purchase to keep up with the rival Palm. However, as I argue, our natural reactions don't excuse what Microsoft did. This advertisement violated some basic ethical standards.

First, the company did print the truth. There's no lie here, no false statement. Legally (and ethically), of course, it can't lie. Commercial advertising is an area of speech where we are not allowed to make provably false statements, but there's more to it. Crucial here, as far as ethics is concerned, is Microsoft's intent. According to Sissela Bok (1989), "The moral question of whether you are lying or not is not settled by establishing the truth or falsity of what you say. In order to settle this question, we must know whether you intend your statement to mislead" (p. 6). Of course, we can't really know the thoughts of those who created the ads, but Microsoft's response to the FTC is telling: Rather than apologizing for misleading customers, the company was defensive. Clearly Microsoft knew the Palm was already ready for wireless communication, whereas their Pocket PC was not. The ad's caption— "Can your Palm do that?"—certainly appears misleading.

Because nothing appears in an ad by accident, it seems that Microsoft did indeed intend to mislead. In this, it acted unethically.

Second, we do see this in ads all the time. Diet plans use small print to note "these results not typical." Cars appear in ads "with added options." It doesn't matter. The intent here was to have consumers believe that the Pocket PC includes certain capabilities—unlike the Palm—when it does not, at least not without extra cost. A related argument is that consumers will recognize that this is a comparison of two similar, but not identical, products and will know intuitively that there are differences. True, likely they will. Yet the ad is based on a false comparison, in which Pocket PC is promoted as better when it isn't. If the ad had simply highlighted the Pocket PC's features, it would have been fine. As it is, though, the ad contributed to cynicism among consumers, who have been deceived so often by ads of this type that they are no longer surprised.

This leads to the next argument favoring the ad, "What's the harm? Who's hurt, anyway?" Consumers and citizens, that's who. True, it's not likely that any individual would buy a Pocket PC solely on the information in this ad, but seeing ads like this repeatedly leads to a distrust of the individual company, of advertising, and of media in general. One of my students, during a discussion of this case, said, "When I see ads with the tiny disclaimers at the bottom, I get so disgusted I turn the page." She's not alone. Bombarded with questionable claims, consumers first tune out ads, become skeptical, then cynical. They learn to distrust advertisements, then to distrust other media as well, and a citizenry that does not, cannot, trust media also cannot make good decisions about products or policy. In adding to consumer mistrust of the media, Microsoft failed in its stewardship of our media system.

Finally, shouldn't consumers have some responsibility here, too? Shouldn't they take it on themselves to become informed before they purchase a Pocket PC or Palm? Absolutely. Most probably will. Some may go to published product reviews, and many will get information from other literature or a salesperson. However, if they've used this ad for basic first information, they begin their search one step behind—misinformed already. In addition, Bok (1989, pp. 19–20) noted that deception harms our ability to make choices by giving power to the deceiver, obscuring alternative choices, and changing the degree of certainty or uncertainty about a particular choice. When consumers believe that the Pocket PC is better than the Palm because of this ad, they cannot make informed choices. So although consumers do indeed bear some responsibility for the choices they make, they also deserve accurate information on which to base their decisions. Again, through its deception, Microsoft did not give accurate or full information.

This advertisement was true in the literal sense. We do see ads like this frequently. Many people would quickly recognize the disclaimer and understand the true differences between the products, and consumers do have responsibility to inform themselves. Yet Bok (1989) wrote that a message is intentionally deceptive if it is "meant to make [its audience] believe what [the sender does] not believe" (p. 13). Microsoft was, in all likelihood, intentionally deceptive. It doesn't matter that the ad was factually true, or that others do the same thing, or that consumers have responsibility, too.

In this ad, Microsoft acted unethically.

Reference

Bok, S. (1989). *Lying: Moral choice in public and private life.* New York: Vintage.

By Elizabeth Blanks Hindman
Department of Communication
North Dakota State University

Commentary 3
More Blunder Than Deception

Advertising the full features on an electronic device (or a modular lawn mower for a home improvement example) and disclaiming that add-on options are required at extra cost is a common advertising practice. As the features of these kinds of products and technologies increase in complexity, the advertiser is frequently challenged with how to communicate the full potential value of the product in a limited ad space. How to do this without confusing the consumer is an even greater challenge.

Most advertisers agonize over how to balance the amount of information in an ad with how to get the main idea across. At Home Depot, we use a concept called a "creative brief" to prioritize product features and benefits into the simplest, most compelling advertising message. The final line of our creative strategy document asks the question, "What is the single most persuasive idea we can convey?" as a device to keep the advertising message simple, focused, and on target. Shuffling through the thousands of great things we could say about a product to get to just one big idea is tough—really tough. It is where advertising folks really earn their money.

We know that a big headline will catch people's attention. We also know that a paragraph of copy will never be read. That is why Home Depot—

and most other retailers—use disclaimer copy. Keep the big idea big and let the details be available for those who need the additional information.

We try to think of the disclaimer in terms of priority. If the information is useful, but not critical to making a purchase, put it in the small type at the bottom of an ad. If it is required for making a purchase, we try to bring it into the body of an ad. It is not an issue of deceptive information, or an attempt to hide data points of which we are ashamed. Instead, it is trying to get the customer to the information they need in the most accessible way.

Where it shows up at Home Depot most often is in financing information. We frequently run an ad showing deferred interest on selected product categories (6 months same as cash, for example). The disclaimer paragraph is seven lines of descriptive text, which is important but way too much to include in the body of the ad itself. Because we know that most customers find these financing offers attractive—even a service to helping them complete their home improvement projects without financial hardship—we feel that the small type disclaimers are the best course of action. Some customers have been confused by the offers, and many treat all fine print with suspicion.

There is a BMW dealer in Atlanta who advertises their "fine print" with the headline "Our not so fine print," very cleverly using consumer fears to their advantage. It is interesting to note that their financing offers are better than many of their peers, and their ads make it clear they are not ashamed of the terms.

In Microsoft's ad, it appears that the "big idea" behind the campaign was that the portable assistant device was now convertible into a wireless Web tool. Yet the price they advertised did not offer that feature. It would be interesting to read their version of a creative brief; my guess is that it said something like, "Let people know that ubiquitous wireless Web technology is now available." Choosing to disclaim the fully loaded price seems like more of an advertising blunder than a deceptive ad strategy because value was less of an issue than the new technology.

Well, if it were easy to make great, simple, hard hitting advertising, it wouldn't be any fun, would it?

**By John Ross
Vice President Advertising, Home Depot**

Commentary 4
I Can Get You a Laptop PC Free*

*But first, you'll have to give me your children.

We've all seen it. The offer you can't believe. If you follow the asterisk down to the bottom of the page, however, you'll find that you shouldn't believe it. There, in indecipherably small print, are the conditions that eliminate much of the offer's initial appeal. My own favorites are the amazing monthly leasing price on a car, with the asterisk that tells you that you first must put down several thousand dollars, or the unbelievably cheap computer on condition that you sign up for Internet service for life.

Now it seems that Hewlett-Packard (HP) and Microsoft have been nailed by the FTC for similar advertising practices. Both companies ran ads in the *Wall Street Journal* and *New York Times* inviting readers to compare the features of HP's Jornada PDA with those of its Palm competitor. Among the Jornada's selling points, according to the ads, was its ability to access the Internet and e-mail "anytime." Only in the small six- to eight-point print at the bottom of the page did you learn that to do this the Jornada required a separate modem costing between $130 and $350. This significantly changed the comparison with the Palm unit, which included the modem in its price.

In my mind, practices like this represent American business ethics at its worst. True, there is not much direct harm. This is not the dumping of toxic waste in public waterways. Yet these practices are harmful in a deeper and more pervasive sense because they foster consumer mistrust of all advertising claims. They also send the message that businesses think the consumer is there to be gulled. Ultimately, such disrespect for the consumer rebounds on the business system and creates widespread consumer cynicism.

I realize that arguments can be offered for ads like this. "Not everything can be said in the main text," "We can't allow secondary details to distract the reader from the main information," "The relevant information is there on the page," or merely "buyer beware."

Yet surely one doesn't have to be a computer scientist to know that information directly relevant to supporting or qualifying the ad's central claims should not be disguised, hidden, or placed in type too small for many people to read. Jodie Bernstein, director of the FTC's bureau of consumer protection makes the point. "The legal standard for disclosures is clear and conspicuous.... Consumers shouldn't have to use a magnifying glass to read them."

We probably have an FTC imposed legal standard in this area because so many advertisers have failed in the past to respect what is a fairly self-evident moral standard. This is a further consequence of practices like the one that HP and Microsoft engaged in. Ultimately this misconduct invites intrusive and sometimes poorly conceived government regulation. Overregulation is properly criticized by the business community, but shoddy practices like this invite it.

The biggest losers, of course, are HP and Microsoft. Neither company needs the bad publicity. HP cherishes its reputation for business integrity, whereas Microsoft has enough problems. From the standpoint of business and advertising ethics, the really interesting question remains to be answered. How did these ads ever make it into print?

By Ronald M. Green
Director Institute for Study of Applied and Professional Ethics
Dartmouth College

Commentary 5
Whatever Happened to the Careful Consumer?

Is there a room in the world in which advertisers may assume some advanced skills on the part of their audiences to sort, filter, and evaluate messages aimed at them, or must advertising play to the lowest common denominator, without the word games of nuance, embellishment, or promotion that make fierce commercial competition between similar products interesting? Incidentally, and arguably, such public word games (even as do parlor word games) elevate the level of discourse (and thinking) in a society and sees to the general progress and development of the culture.

If there is such a room, climatic conditions appear to be most favorable in the moderate caveat emptor commercial culture of the United States. In few countries do the triple characteristics of high educational level, strong sense of individual responsibility, and fairly free-wheeling commercial enterprise converge as they do in this country. Such a combination, if it works well, produces a dynamic economy in which individuals accept responsibility for their daily actions and do not unnecessarily push onto others the responsibility for their own well-being. This is particularly so in media and communications, arenas in which information generally does not cause physical harm but offers continuing textbook instruction to consumers on adapting to the lifetime game of surviving and thriving in a consumer culture.

In this environment of information games, morally justifiable as socially beneficial, it should be expected that Microsoft would adhere to a few basic moral principles in its advertising. Yet it should also be recognized that product advertising should have wide leeway to enhance the competitive stance of the product and to help consumers sharpen their information consumption and evaluation skills.

At the top of the list of principles is that the ad as a whole should not lie. Second, of course, the ad should not be "terminally misleading." That is, it should not contain information that would cause a consumer to purchase the product under the assumption that it contained features that were missing (buying the Pocket PC, for example, expecting built-in wireless capability). The Microsoft ad seemed to meet those requirements, though notification of wireless capability was in very small print, making it necessary for consumers to extend themselves beyond headline and body copy in gathering information about the product.

At best, the careful buyer would be aware that comparisons between the two products did not take into account the absent wireless capability (because the option feature information was in the ad) in the Pocket PC. That buyer would have a realistic expectation about the product, at least within the boundaries defined by the ad. The ad did not promise in large print that the small computers contained flush toilets, so there was no need for small print on that subject because the question was never raised and few consumers would expect to have such a toilet attached.

At worst, an incautious buyer would learn a valuable, and relatively inexpensive, lesson about the realities of commercial competition and would presumably seek more information (which was available in this ad) before making another major purchase. Any consumer is well served who learns that ads are self-serving and not necessarily in the best interest of the consumer, leaving buyers with equally self-serving obligations to find out for themselves the details of a product. That is not an inconsiderable lesson that naive buyers improve their own survival probabilities by learning.

Certainly, one might hope that Microsoft, or any other advertiser, would have a sense of fair play and would make product information easily accessible, particularly when it modified a visible point in the larger ad. However, if the information is contained in the ad and can be read by a person with normal vision without the use of a magnifying glass, it would appear that Microsoft has met minimal expectations. Certainly, if the product were capable of doing a terrible physical harm, one in which the harm far outweighs the economics lesson to be learned, a bold warning on the label is required ("Warning: Keep out of the reach of children," or "Watch out for this combination of tires and SUV" come to mind).

There are some areas in which consumers may legitimately be expected to control their own destinies and not have an artificially constructed level playing field in a highly competitive culture. If consumers have minimal tools required to care for themselves, the advertiser has fulfilled a moral obligation. Consumers can use the ad as only one source, recognize its motivation, make better purchasing decisions, and grow in the process. When they read an ad they will recognize they are playing in an arena the advertiser has defined. Microsoft, though pushing an envelope, appears to have both informed and persuaded (a formal function) and potentially educated (informal, but socially beneficial).

By Ralph D. Barney
Editor, Journal of Mass Media Ethics

Journal of Mass Media Ethics, *16*(2&3), 244–252
Copyright © 2001, Lawrence Erlbaum Associates, Inc..

Book Reviews

The book reviews included in this issue all focus on how the role of the media is misunderstood and how, in turn, the media are misunderstood by various groups and individuals. A review of two books on media and religion, by D. Keith Shurtleff, discusses problems in how Western media report about religion and religion-based stories. In Michael M. Monahan's piece, he rightly appreciates an author who worries that the public is getting shortchanged by commercial interests that control the media. Here is the public that doesn't understand the larger forces that control what we see and don't see. Finally, a review of a book that details the year-in-the-life of a well-known television journalist reveals that a lack of understanding about how to change the media is not limited to the general public.

As always, if you are interested in reviewing a book, contact the guest book review editor, Paul Martin Lester at lester@fullerton.edu

God Is Not Dead, Nor Doth He Sleep:
A Review by D. Keith Shurtleff

Silk, M. (2000). *Religion on the international news agenda*. Hartford, CT: Trinity College. 140 pp., (Pbk).
Kamalipour, Y., & Thierstein, J. *Religion, law, and freedom, A global perspective*. Westport, CT: Praeger. 242 pp., $69.95 (Hbk).

"God is dead" so Nietzsche's mad man proclaimed, placing responsibility for that death on mankind. Many, in what has been termed by some, the "Post Christian West," seem to have taken the mad man at his word. Included among those of the Western industrialized nations, whose secular bent often cause them to overlook religion and its importance in the affairs of humankind, are reporters, publishers, and media producers. At least that is the well-documented contention of the writers of the collections of essays brought forward in these two volumes. The arguments suggest that when news organizations apply the deemphasizing of religion found in Western culture to other cultures of the global community, they miss out on vital understanding.

Taken together, the writers of these essays paint a picture of an increasingly pluralistic world: a world where major or dominating religions and the states they support are being challenged by numerous religious movements seeking to proselytize converts to their faith; a world wherein widely accepted democratic principles such as freedom of worship and conscience are being challenged and stretched as enforcement of those principles bring different religious groups into conflict and threaten orthodoxy. For those raised in a nation where historical suspicion of state religions resulted in the formation of a secular government, these concepts can be difficult to understand.

Thankfully, Eileen Barker illustrates those difficulties in her captivating essay, "The Opium War of the New Millennium: Religion in Eastern Europe and the Former Soviet Union" (Silk, p. 39). In that essay, she outlines the rise of religious plurality in the vacuum left by the collapse of the Former Soviet Union (FSU). It should be noted that Ms. Baker makes an important distinction between "religious plurality" or (the mere presence of various religions), and the North American view of "pluralism" (the peaceful coexistence of multiple religious groups). Ms. Baker chastises the Western press for being so influenced by Western secularization of institutions that they forget that individual religious fervor has not necessarily followed the institutional decline, particularly in other cultures. The inability of the press to fully understand the deep religious fervor of a people and the potentially great conflicts that can arise between orthodoxy and individual faith, can lead the press to "adopt a holier than thou attitude" toward many of the government enacted restrictions on new religions that are being proposed as FSU nation-states try to preserve their indigenous institutionalized religions (Silk, p. 56). The threatened result in what she terms "the opium wars of the new millennium" (p. 56) is that religious conflicts may be exacerbated.

Individual religious fervor has not necessarily followed the institutional decline.

Such a cry for the Western press to acknowledge the importance of, and become more educated on, religious matters and then to incorporate that knowledge in their reporting, seems to be the underlying theme that holds these essays together. For example from *Religion, Law, and Freedom, A Global Perspective*, Hamid Mowlana uses what he sees as a histrionic failure of Western press to understand Islam and the resultant skewed reporting and sometimes unfair portrayals of Muslims as a plea for the development of a Muslim press corps that would contain the understanding required to more fairly and honestly report on incidents arising in Islamic nations (Kamalipour, pp. 124–126). The same sentiment is echoed in N. J.

Demerath III's criticism (Silk, pp. 3–16) that Western media have totally failed to see the problems in India as religiously based, and apply the Western concept of a secular nation-state to India when in reality it is a confederation of religious groups with a history of religious conflicts. Secularization of the government in India has not occurred nearly to the extent it has in the United States, and to apply a North American view of government on India is a mistake.

As in India, conflicts are arising in many countries that have no state church but that contain major faith groups who historically are antagonistic to each other. Bala Musa outlines the great difficulties faced by what, on the surface, is a secular government ruling the nation of Nigeria (Kamalipour, p. 98). Though the national laws guarantee freedoms of religion and conscience, and push for peaceful coexistence, great conflicts arise in trying to govern a Muslim majority in the north and Christian majority in the south. The writer brings this tense situation into focus in discussing the restrictions on religion that arise in local governments, without regard for national laws. Of importance to journalists are those restrictions that have an impact on freedoms of the press, such as when the media is brought under government control in an effort to maintain peace in the volatile nation. For example, the decree establishing the National Broadcast Company in Nigeria forbids licensing of religious broadcasts (Kamalipour, p. 107).

I have highlighted just a few of the many essays in both tomes. It should be noted that religious conflicts and their effects on media issues are global, and that representational essays from other nations such as China, Iran, Japan, Indonesia, and Latin America are also found in the volumes. Although the majority deal with the press or news media, there is also an article on the impacts of religion-based values on advertising. Linda Fuller outlines the conflict that arises when modern secular cultures collide with traditional values in nations where the government still controls the media. Her discussion of the "Wonder Bra" advertisements' conflict with Confucius based values in Singapore is illustrative (Kamalipour, p. 141).

Taken in total, these essayists seem to cry with the hymnist, Henry Wadsworth Longfellow, at least with regard to many nations: "God is not dead nor doth he sleep." Though it may be that the writers, and their critiques of Western media, are in themselves biased, these books do point out what appears to be a general perception that there is a lack of understanding among the Western media of the importance that religion continues to play in both political and economic activities of many nations. As the good counselor knows, to simply dismiss something as a biased perception does nothing to resolve the issue. Wise media services will recognize the importance of dealing with perceptions, regardless of their own opinions as to whether the perception has a basis in truth. A careful reading of these volumes would be a great start toward dealing with those perceptions and acting to overcome them.

D. *Keith Shurtleff is currently a Chaplain in the U.S. Army. He was formerly a Judge Advocate General Officer in the U.S. Navy, having received his J.D. from Brigham Young University.*

Unplug the Simplicity Drug: A Review by Michael M. Monahan

Scheuer, Jeffrey. (1999). *The sound bite society: Television and the American mind.* New York: Four Walls Eight Windows. 230 pp., $19.16 (Hbk).

It was a painfully ironic twist of coincidence. I closed Jeffrey Scheuer's book, *The Sound Bite Society,* and flipped through the local newspaper sitting on my table and lit on a blandly written story announcing FCC approval of the megamerger of Time- Warner® and AOL®. The relentless growth of corporate mass media, marked by mergers such as this, seemed exactly what Scheuer's insightful work was heeding against. The alarm with which I took the news was certainly exacerbated by having just finished reading such a striking and profound critique of television and its mind-numbing influence in today's society.

In *The Sound Bite Society,* Scheuer proposes the rather obvious notion that television, by its very nature, embraces and elevates the simple, visceral, and immediate. Because it is tailor made to propagate simplistic messages, television systematically dumbs down the media, leaving us with infotainment and bumper-sticker logic rather than genuine news and complex thinking.

Scheuer broadens this argument, though, to also encompass political ideology. He claims that television's inherent preference for simplicity leaves it an ideal handmaiden for conservative politics. It is the combination of television's sheer ubiquity and simplifying nature, Scheuer argues, that has allowed American political culture to move steadily to the right, the simpler of political poles. Conservative politics, according to Scheuer, is defined primarily by its simplistic ideology of individualism and its propensity for vitriolic attacks. These are both traits that are easily transformed into televised pseudonews and sound bite messages such as "no new taxes" and "tax and spend liberalism." Generally speaking, the argument that forms the heart of *The Sound Bite Society* is bicameral. According to Scheuer

> The first [premise] is that television, in nearly all its forms and functions, and for both economic and structural reasons, acts as a simplifying lens,

filtering out complex ideas in favor of blunt emotional messages that appeal to the self and to narrower moral-political impulses. The second is that, for reasons that are inherent in the nature of ideology and do not impugn the politics of the left or right, simplification promotes, and epitomizes, political conservatism. (p. 10)

Television works best, according to Scheuer, when it portrays the simple and episodic, the immediate events of reality, rather than complex issues and whole social movements. In this sense television works as a "surrogate eye" with vast technical advantages, unrestrained by space and time, but with significant deficiencies in drawing complex connections and critically synthesizing its images. Television does not merely mediate images of reality, its mediation necessarily simplifies reality.

In sum, what is simple, fragmented, short-term or localized plays well on the tube; what is compound, integrated, long-term, or general, does not. Symptoms are telegenic; preventive measures and complex solutions involving the long view, the broad context, the underlying pattern or the root cause, are the bane of television and all electronic media—and the hallmarks of modern liberalism. (pp. 87–88)

On the road to establishing this claim, Scheuer delves briefly into some of the epistemological tensions between television and reality. His task is to illustrate that the effect television has on how we structure our notions of reality is a two-way street. He calls this the "phenomenology" of television and argues that "… television plays games with reality and appearance; and those games, while themselves complicated, render a picture of the world that is artificially simple and enslaved to appearance" (p. 93). Central to this thesis is the distinction between consciousness and "teleconsciousness." In the latter, "Television thus confers on its subjects a kind of 'hyper-reality': we exalt it beyond our own sense-experience" (p. 103). Without getting at the subtleties of his claim, this point seems well proven by the masses of people enthralled by the vicarious "adventure experience" of hit shows like "Survivor." Not only do we often mistake television's mediated reality for truth, much of the time we prefer it.

The book goes on, after much foreshadowing, to try and demonstrate the more difficult aspect of Scheuer's two-part thesis, that conservatism is essentially simple whereas liberalism is complex. In so doing, he makes clear the disclaimer that this is merely a theoretical difference and not to be thought of as carrying any set value. I do not attempt here to reproduce his argument, as it is subtle and complex, but I will say that I am convinced. Scheuer does a nice job in stripping away political trappings and uncovering the underlying, and equally valid, ideological basis for each. I am hesitant to call him successful in this piece of his writing, however, because as a reader I found him to be preaching to the choir. Regardless though, in a truly masterful treatment of some extremely difficult philosophical content, he discusses the cognitive functions that comprise human perception and how those functions find analogies in our political ideologies. I certainly cannot do him justice in this review, but suffice it to say that Scheuer makes it as plain as the nose on your face how we, as humans, perceive the nose on your face. His argument regarding complex versus simplex political concepts rises quite naturally out of the said philosophical groundwork. Moreover, after several promises of "a point to be clarified later on," Scheuer does indeed live up to his word. This chapter fits into place like a well-cut capstone for an otherwise incomplete argument.

> *We need to fight back against [television's] simplifying view of reality.*

After laying out, in quite pleasant form, all the important nuances of his argument, Scheuer concludes the book with some important, perhaps prophetic, advice for a televised society. We all must rethink the role television plays in our lives and our culture. If we are ever to reassert our own independent thinking into our political discourse, we must begin by realizing how vast and insidious the influence of television has been. To combat this influence, we need to fight back against its simplifying view of reality. This means a new emphasis on critical thinking, starting with our young. Through visual literacy programs and critical thinking education the younger generation will have the tools necessary to separate the televised from the felt experience. They will be able to understand the simplification that goes on when reality is mediated by television, and only then can they separate television's "good" from its "bad." As Scheuer says, "The purpose of critical viewing is not to shield people from television, but to enable them to use and enjoy it intelligently, while recognizing the legitimacy of its sedative and entertaining functions" (p. 171).

On a more critical note, though, there are some things I wish Scheuer had done differently. The first and foremost is to give more space to the commercial engine behind much of televised content. As our world is driven more and more by corporate interests, I think it valid to place more of the blame for television's skewed picture of reality on its corporate masters. Simplicity may well be natural "grammar" for television, but it is also what sells. Scheuer certainly does not ignore this aspect of television, but does not, in my opinion, discuss it enough. A second issue is with the obvious conflict between his own political views and his argument regarding simplex conservatism. His disclaimers are belied by an explicit liberal (he even says at one point "radical") personal bias, and I think that bias detracts from his attempt to paint the simplex conservative in neutral light.

Overall I found *The Sound Bite Society* to be excellent and well worth all the critical praise it has received. Scheuer has the rare ability to blend difficult analytic and theoretical content with an inspiring and rhythmic literary style. The result of such a blend is a book that is philosophically rich, culturally enlightening, necessarily critical, and a joy to read. He has chosen a topic that, as the aforementioned megamerger shows, is in desperate need of critical ink. In a culture and era on the verge of almost complete immersion in "hyper-reality," social criticism need not only explore the flaws in our culture, but the technological tools that facilitate or create those very flaws. In any case, this is a text anyone living in a world so confronted with mediated versions of reality should pay attention to. The only problem is getting those who need to read it most to unplug the drug long enough to accept the task.

Michael M. Monahan is the Assistant Book Review Editor for the Journal of Mass Media Ethics. He is currently working toward a Masters in Philosophy through the Practical Ethics Center at the University of Montana.

Ted Koppel: We Hardly Want to Know Ye: A Review by Paul Martin Lester

Koppel, T. (2000). *Off camera private thoughts made public.* New York: Knopf. 320 pp., $25.00 (Hbk), $20.76 (Audio Book).

Quick. Think of Ted Koppel, that no-nonsense, erudite host of ABC's *Nightline.* That should be easy. We've been able to see his face on television for almost 40 years.

If you need help, you can look at the cover of his new book, *Off Camera Private Thoughts Made Public.* Except for a change in clothing and location, he looks exactly as he does on television, although that might not have been the intent. The portrait by Michael Wilson is an obvious attempt to make him look friendly and engaging, in keeping with the title of the book, but the effort falls flat.

He leans against a huge, brown trunk of a tree in a black cotton shirt, leather jacket, and cargo pants—certainly an outfit you don't see on *Nightline.* But look closer. Although his eyes are directed right into the camera, they are dark and suspicious. His attempt at a smile looks forced. He looks tentative and shy as if he doesn't really want us to know him. In addition, a low camera angle gives the impression he's looking down on the reader. The picture reveals, as does his book, that Koppel is never really comfortable with being "off camera."

In the 20-plus years as head honcho of *Nightline*, the premier, long-form news interview show, he has always been a gently probing gentleman. Koppel is one of the most respected journalists, having won every significant television award. Unlike many, mostly cable questioners, Koppel doesn't interrupt a guest in the middle of a response. He doesn't attack someone personally. He never loses his temper. We never really know what he's thinking on any topic of conversation. He is the epitome of the formal, well-mannered, objective, and most strikingly, impersonal journalist. It's that last trait, I suspect, that inspired him to tell his "private thoughts" in his book.

For the entire year of 1999, he kept a day-by-day diary that "contains opinions I would never express on the air" (p. viii), and after reading his journal, I can objectively say that's a good thing.

Koppel is kind of a cranky guy with few friends and a yacht near his getaway home on Captiva Island, Florida. His book is filled with gripes for every day of the year. He complains about the price of Cap'n Crunch® cereal at his local market. He calls Valentine's Day cards "the cold-blooded commercialism of our most tender moments" (p. 50). He dismisses traveling in the Balkans with this direct quote: "The toughest thing about traveling in the Balkans is traveling in the Balkans" (p. 109). He calls ex-President Jimmy Carter's op-ed piece in the *New York Times* criticizing ex-President Bill Clinton's Kosovo strategy "tacky" (p. 125). He doesn't like the violence portrayed by the World Wrestling Federation. He calls 900 telephone sex operators "verbal prostitutes" (p. 235), and over several days he tediously describes and unnecessarily complains about his trouble in getting a caller ID feature installed on his home telephone. Who would have thought that Ted has the same troubles as you and me?

Naturally, with his vast experience as a top-tier newsperson, he rants about his own medium. Yet when his complaints are nestled between the high price of gas and playing with his grandson, his criticisms are, to say the least, diluted.

He spends parts of days complaining about all the media mergers, the underfunding of news departments, the general competitiveness of the media, the fact that television doesn't provoke thinking on serious issues, the overwhelming coverage of John F. Kennedy Jr.'s funeral compared with the death of King Hassan II of Morocco, the shrinking right of privacy of ordinary persons, the lack of appreciation for the work of a creative journalist Robert Krulwich, and computers—he hates computers.

Here's my rant. Simply identifying and describing a social condition is not helpful. I sometimes get and give bad reviews to research papers that usually use surveys or content analysis as their chief research methods. In the conclusions, the researchers simply restate the descriptive nature of the study without any attempt to address in a critical way the concerns expressed through the research. This objective retelling of facts doesn't move the profession to any higher plane. It is at best shortsided and at worse an academic magic act—a form of nonanalysis analysis.

Ted Koppel, with his years in the business and his ease in getting a publishing contract (yes, he wrote about that too), should know better. He wails against the media without offering a day's worth of thinking about possible remedies. For example, on July 7 he wrote, "If television isn't covering the story and Americans are reading less and less, I suppose it's inevitable that we will become dumber and dumber. And that's very dangerous indeed" (p. 162). Unfortunately, that's about as penetrating as his comments get in his book of days. It's one of several Koppel Kop-Outs.

But lucky for him, he can get away from all his Virginia manse and DC media frustrations and enjoy the sunshine on Captiva. In fact, I counted how many days out of the year his diary was written from that island resort—42. But even in paradise he wrote, "A Huey helicopter flew over the Gulf of Mexico" (p. 75). Hope it didn't block the sun.

This is an ill-conceived, egotistical, colossal waste of time—not because it lets us inside the life and mind of one of the nation's most respected journalists, but because that life and mind, as presented in this work, is so banal. Having to report his daily events and thoughts in which he admits "there have obviously been days when my only motive has been 'to get the damned thing done'" (p. 319) leaves him with little time for self-reflection. Yet perhaps that's a good thing. I want to like Ted Koppel the interviewer. I really don't need to know that he threw up behind a haystack after smoking for the first time as a child growing up in England.

By the way, the Web site for Captiva Island is: http://www.captivaisland.com/

Paul Martin Lester is a Professor of Communications at California State University, Fullerton on leave as a research fellow with the Practical Ethics Center at the University of Montana.

SUBSCRIPTION ORDER FORM

Please ❑ enter ❑ renew my subscription to:

JOURNAL OF MASS MEDIA ETHICS

Volume 16, 2001, Quarterly—ISSN 0890-0523

Subscription prices per volume:

Individual:
❑ $35.00 US/Canada
❑ $65.00 All Other Countries

Institution:
❑ $295.00 US/Canada
❑ $325.00 All Other Countries

Electronic Only:
❑ $31.50 Individual
❑ $265.50 Institution

Subscriptions are entered on a calendar-year basis only and must be paid in advance in U.S. currency—check, credit card, or money order. Prices for subscriptions include postage and handling. Journal prices expire 12/31/01. **NOTE:** Institutions must pay institutional rates. Individual subscription orders are welcome if prepaid by credit card or personal check. **Electronic access is available at no additional cost to full-price print subscribers. Electronic-only subscriptions are available at a reduced price.**

❑   **Check Enclosed** (U.S. Currency Only)   Total Amount Enclosed $_____

❑   **Charge My**: ❑ VISA   ❑ MasterCard   ❑ AMEX   ❑ Discover

Card Number _____Exp. Date_____/_____

Signature_____
(Credit card orders cannot be processed without your signature.)

PRINT CLEARLY for proper delivery. STREET ADDRESS/SUITE/ROOM # REQUIRED FOR DELIVERY.

Name_____

Address_____

City/State/Zip+4_____

Daytime Phone #_____E-mail address_____
Prices are subject to change without notice.

Please note: A $20.00 penalty will be charged against customers providing checks that must be returned for payment. This assessment will be made only in instances when problems in collecting funds are directly attributable to customer error.

For information about online subscriptions, visit our website at *www.erlbaum.com*

Lawrence Erlbaum Associates, Inc., Journal Subscription Department
10 Industrial Avenue, Mahwah, NJ 07430; (201) 236–9500; FAX (201) 760–3735

LIBRARY RECOMMENDATION FORM

Detach and forward to your librarian.

Please enter my subscription to:

JOURNAL OF MASS MEDIA ETHICS

Volume 16, 2001, Quarterly—ISSN 0890-0523

Institutional Rate: ❑ $295.00 (US & Canada)   ❑ $325.00 (All Other Countries)

Order from your subscription agent or directly from the publisher.

Name_____Title_____

Institution_____

Address_____

City/State/Zip+4_____

Lawrence Erlbaum Associates, Inc., Journal Subscription Department
10 Industrial Avenue, Mahwah, NJ 07430; (201) 236–9500; FAX (201) 760–3735

WITHDRAWN

The Panama Canal

GREAT STRUCTURES IN HISTORY

Other titles in the Great Structures in History
series include:

The Great Wall of China
A Medieval Castle
The Roman Colosseum
Stonehenge

The Panama Canal

GREAT STRUCTURES IN HISTORY

Rachel Lynette

KIDHAVEN PRESS

An imprint of Thomson Gale, a part of The Thomson Corporation

THOMSON

GALE

Detroit • New York • San Francisco • San Diego • New Haven, Conn.
Waterville, Maine • London • Munich

LIBRARY OF CONGRESS CATALOGING-IN-PUBLICATION DATA

Lynette, Rachel.
  The Panama Canal / by Rachel Lynette.
     p. cm. — (Great structures in history)
  ISBN 0-7377-1559-6 (hardback : alk. paper)
Summary: Discusses the Pamana Canal includng why it was built, how it was con-
structed, the life of the workers, and the operanton of the canal today.
  1. Panama Canal (Panama)—History. I. Title.
  F1569.C2L96 2004
  972.87'5—dc22   2004007491

CONTENTS

CHAPTER ONE 6
An Amazing Accomplishment

CHAPTER TWO 15
Life in the Canal Zone

CHAPTER THREE 23
Constructing the Canal

CHAPTER FOUR 32
The Panama Canal Today

Glossary 41

For Further Reading 43

Index 45

Picture Credits 47

About the Author 48

An Amazing Accomplishment

The Panama Canal is one of the most ambitious building projects ever undertaken in human history. The 50-mile-long (80.5 kilometer) canal was constructed 85 feet (26 meters) above sea level. Ships must be lifted far above the ocean to travel the canal and then lowered again at the other end to continue their journeys.

Building the canal above sea level was a major feat of engineering and an enormous amount of hard work. The canal was built above sea level because it crosses the mountains of the Continental Divide. The Continental Divide is the highest point in the Americas. The mountains of the divide in Panama are tall, often reaching heights of over 4,000 feet (1,219.2 meters). This mountainous land meant that building a canal at sea level would be a tremendous amount of work. Millions of tons of rocks and dirt would have to be excavated. In addition to the mountains, Panama's tropical climate presented other challenges.

Cargo ships make their way along a small section of the fifty-mile-long Panama Canal.

The country of Panama has only two seasons. The dry season lasts from January to April. During this time temperatures are hot and rain is scarce. The temperature at the hottest part of the day can reach 130 degrees Fahrenheit (54 degrees Celsius). The wet season lasts much longer, from early May all the way through December. During the long wet season heavy rain falls almost constantly. Rivers overrun their banks, flooding the land for miles around and turning the earth to slippery mud.

The heavy rain and the steep mountains made it impossible to dig the canal at sea level. Unfortunately, the first people to attempt the project did not know this. They came from Europe. They had never experienced the rainy season in Panama and did not understand the effect it would have on their efforts.

The French Attempt to Build the Canal

In 1869 the French successfully completed the Suez Canal in the Middle East. This canal was built at sea level through flat, sandy desert. It was a great accomplishment. The leader of the project, Ferdinand-Marie de Lesseps, was confident that a sea level canal across Panama could be built with equal success. He brought in thousands of workers and began construction in 1881. Things started to go wrong for Lesseps almost immediately.

Even though Lesseps had the best and most modern equipment available at the time, it was no match for the constant rain of the wet season in Panama. The rain turned the soil to heavy clay, which stuck to the steam shovels and made them ineffective. Machinery rusted within just a few days. Mudslides were a constant problem. Months of work could be undone by a single slide. Often excavated areas were so flooded with water that work became impossible. In addition, many workers were lost to disease.

In 1896 workers led by French engineer Ferdinand-Marie de Lesseps (inset) remove rock in an effort to build a canal in Panama.

Malaria, yellow fever, and other tropical diseases took thousands of lives during the French attempt to build the canal. In the late 1800s no one knew what caused these diseases, which meant that no one knew how to prevent them. In addition, Lesseps did not provide clean and healthy living conditions or adequate medical care for the workers. One in every five workers died from disease. By the time the French project ended in 1889, nearly twenty thousand workers and their family members had died from disease.

At this point many people believed that building a canal across Panama was impossible. But others refused to drop the idea. They knew that a canal would someday save huge amounts of time, money, and even lives.

Location

The reason the Panama Canal is so important is because of its location. The tiny country of Panama is located in Central America. Panama is a narrow stretch of land, or **isthmus**, connecting North and South America. At its narrowest point it is only 50 miles (80.5 kilometers) across. This meant that only fifty miles of land divided the Pacific and the Atlantic oceans. The canal was built to connect these oceans.

Before the canal was built, sailors were forced to take their ships all the way around South America. For a ship sailing from New York to San Francisco, this route added 8,000 miles (12,800 kilometers) to the voyage. This could mean as much as five extra months of travel. In addition, it was dangerous. The waters

around the tip of South America, sometimes called the Great Horn, were usually stormy. Many ships were lost on the journey. The canal made this long and dangerous trip unnecessary. In less than a day a ship could make the journey from one ocean to the other simply by crossing through the canal. Trade ships could get their goods to foreign ports in a fraction of the time it took before. Travelers could get to their destinations much sooner, and in wartime the advantage of using the canal for naval forces could be invaluable.

Despite the failed effort by the French to build the canal, the idea was not abandoned. The canal was too important, and many people, including American president Theodore Roosevelt, believed it could be

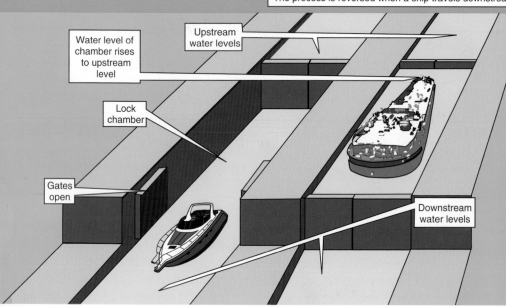

Traveling Through a Canal Lock

To travel upstream, a ship enters a lock in which the water level has been lowered, so it is even with the water directly downstream. The lock's gates are then closed, and the chamber is filled with water. Once the ship is lifted to the level of the water upstream, the gates again open, and the ship passes into the next lock or channel. The process is reversed when a ship travels downstream.

Water level of chamber rises to upstream level

Upstream water levels

Lock chamber

Gates open

Downstream water levels

built. The key to American success in Panama would be to build the canal above sea level.

The High Elevation Plan

Building the canal above sea level would require a series of **locks**. These would be used to raise ships 85 feet (26 meters) above sea level and then to lower them again. Locks are like giant stairs made of water. When the ship is secured inside the lock, the gate is closed and water is piped into the lock through hundreds of holes in the bottom. It takes just eight minutes for 28 million gallons (127 million liters) of water to fill the lock. As the water pours into the chamber, the level of the water rises. When the lock is full, the gate in front of the ship is opened and the ship moves forward into the next lock. The process is repeated two more times. When the last gate is opened the ship has been raised a total of 85 feet (26 meters) and is ready to cross the country of Panama.

It would take three locks to raise the ships when they first enter the canal and three more to lower them before they leave. The plan called for twelve locks all together, six for each end of the canal. By building the locks in pairs it would be possible for ships to travel in both directions at the same time.

Panama's Locks

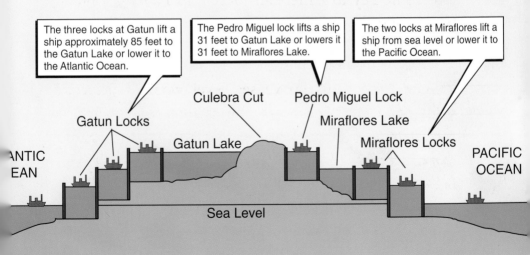

The three locks at Gatun lift a ship approximately 85 feet to the Gatun Lake or lower it to the Atlantic Ocean.

The Pedro Miguel lock lifts a ship 31 feet to Gatun Lake or lowers it 31 feet to Miraflores Lake.

The two locks at Miraflores lift a ship from sea level or lower it to the Pacific Ocean.

Culebra Cut
Pedro Miguel Lock
Gatun Locks
Miraflores Lake
Gatun Lake
Miraflores Locks
Gatun Lake
ATLANTIC OCEAN
PACIFIC OCEAN
Sea Level

But the locks alone would not solve the flooding problem in the rainy season. The problem was centered on the Chagres River. This mighty river flowed from high in the mountains to the Atlantic Ocean. During the rainy season the river overran its banks and flooded the surrounding land. The canal route was well within the river's **floodplain**. The canal could not be built unless the Chagres could be controlled. The solution was to dam the Chagres River. Damming the river would create a giant lake. This would not only solve the flooding problem but would also save a lot of digging. Twenty-three miles (thirty-seven kilometers) of the trip across Panama would be over this massive, man-made lake.

When the Americans began working on the canal in 1904 they were planning to build it at sea level. But after his first rainy season in Panama, John Stevens, the man in charge of the project, realized that a sea level canal would not be possible. He convinced the U.S. Congress to adopt the high elevation plan. This was just one of many challenges successfully overcome by Stevens in the early days of the canal.

CHAPTER TWO

Life in the Canal Zone

A mericans who came to work on the canal were promised clean quarters and decent living conditions. This was not what they found. The workers were expected to live in the barracks originally constructed by the French. Many of these buildings were poorly constructed and falling apart. Furniture was scarce and filth was everywhere due to a lack of proper sewage and running water. Overcrowding was common and many slept on the floor because there were not enough beds.

Tropical insects and other pests were a constant problem. At times the mosquitoes were so thick that they would put out the candles they swarmed around. At other times black ants completely covered the floors. Poisonous insects, including six-inch-long (fifteen centimeter) scorpions, were not uncommon. Everyone checked their shoes for unwelcome visitors before putting them on.

Food was an additional problem. There were not enough farms in Panama to produce the food needed

Workers blast out and haul off tons of rock during construction of the canal in the early 1900s.

by the canal workers. Meat, eggs, milk, and fresh produce were scarce and expensive. The food often made the workers ill because it was not refrigerated properly.

These poor living conditions, along with the growing fear of tropical disease, made it hard to keep people working on the canal. Most of the workers left Panama as soon as they could book a passage back to the United States. The morale of those who stayed was very low.

Improved Living Conditions for American Workers

All of this changed when John Stevens took over the project in 1905. Stevens stopped all work on the canal and put people to work building decent houses and barracks, hospitals, schools, hotels, and churches. He paved the roads and brought in running water and a sewage system. He also started clubs and organized baseball games, concerts, dances, and theater productions. He encouraged single workers to marry and those who were already married to bring their families to Panama. In addition, Stevens built a refrigeration plant and brought in food from the United States, including plenty of meat, milk, produce, and other fresh food. The food was inexpensive so that everyone could afford to buy as much as they needed.

The communities he built became pleasant places to live. American children attended schools in the Canal Zone and participated in sports, clubs, and other after-school activities. Salaries for the workers

Students and their teacher pose in front of one of the Canal Zone schools established by John Stevens (inset).

were higher than they were back home, and good-quality clothing and household goods were inexpensive. Many Americans enjoyed a higher standard of living in Panama than they had back in the United States.

Living Conditions for Other Workers

Unfortunately, workers from other countries did not share in these benefits. **Segregation** was the policy throughout the Zone. This meant that all nonwhite workers, most of whom were from the West Indies, the Caribbean, Barbados, and Jamaica, were housed separately from the Americans. These nonwhite workers lived in crowded slums or shacks. They had no running water or electricity. Their children attended overcrowded, undersupplied schools. They were not allowed to associate with the Americans or to enter the social halls, parks, schools, and other buildings built for the Americans.

Working conditions for nonwhites were no better than the living conditions. They were paid significantly less than the Americans. They were given the dirtiest

Hispanic workers, who were paid much less than American workers, shovel dirt on the canal job site in 1909.

and most dangerous jobs such as shoveling coal into sweltering boilers and loading dynamite. Promotion was not a possibility for these workers. Supervisors treated them unfairly and sometimes resorted to physical violence.

In addition, nonwhites were not given adequate medical care. Out of the fifty-six hundred people who died during the American construction of the canal, over forty-five hundred were nonwhites. Most of these people died from untreated tropical diseases. Hospitals were for white workers. The nonwhites were left to care for their own.

Malaria and Yellow Fever

Nearly twenty thousand people had died of tropical diseases during the French attempt to build the canal. Most of these people died of yellow fever and malaria. At that time no one knew that both of these diseases were spread by mosquitoes. Fortunately, this discovery was made just a few years before the Americans started building the canal.

President Roosevelt put Major William Gorgas in charge of the effort to make the Canal Zone safe from disease. Gorgas, who served in the Army Medical Corps as a surgeon, had previously worked in Havana, Cuba. Using new ideas about how tropical diseases were spread, Gorgas helped to rid Havana of disease-carrying mosquitoes. After seeing how well these methods worked, he was ready to fight the mosquitoes in Panama.

Gorgas knew that yellow fever and malaria were spread by two different types of mosquitoes. Panama was overrun with mosquitoes, including those that caused these two deadly diseases. Administration buildings, barracks, and even hospitals swarmed with mosquitoes. Few buildings had screens to keep them out.

Following the method of William Gorgas (inset), a worker spreads kerosene in a ditch to kill mosquito larvae.

Female mosquitoes lay their eggs in standing water, and there was plenty of that all over the Canal Zone. Some people even put the legs of their beds in buckets of water to keep other insects from crawling up onto them at night. This may have stopped the other insects, but it made an ideal breeding ground for the dangerous mosquitoes. Gorgas put an end to this practice. He had kerosene dumped on swamps, ponds, and puddles to kill the mosquitoes and their eggs. He had everyone cover pots, pitchers, and other containers where water was stored. He had houses fumigated and screens put in all the windows.

Fighting the mosquitoes was expensive and time-consuming, but in the end it was successful. It took a year and a half to rid the Canal Zone of the mosquitoes that spread yellow fever and malaria. Although a few thousand people died of these diseases, the death tolls were nowhere near that of the French.

Improving living conditions and making the Canal Zone safe from yellow fever and malaria were essential for the success of the canal. But it was only the beginning. The real work of building the canal was still ahead.

CHAPTER THREE

Constructing the Canal

The main work of building the canal consisted of three big projects. The first of these projects was building the three sets of locks on each end of the canal. The second project was damming the Chagres River to create Gatun Lake. The third was digging the nine-mile-long (14.5 kilometer) route through the mountains. This route was named Culebra Cut.

Although they were separate projects, they were all worked on at the same time. Each of these projects involved moving huge amounts of rocks and dirt, called **spoil**. Sometimes the spoil was simply dumped away from the canal, but at other times it was used in another part of construction. The Gatun Dam was built with large amounts of spoil from the Culebra Cut. All of this spoil was moved using a large and well-coordinated railroad system.

Before he came to the canal, John Stevens had built thousands of miles of railroad tracks in the western United States. He knew that the only way to move the massive

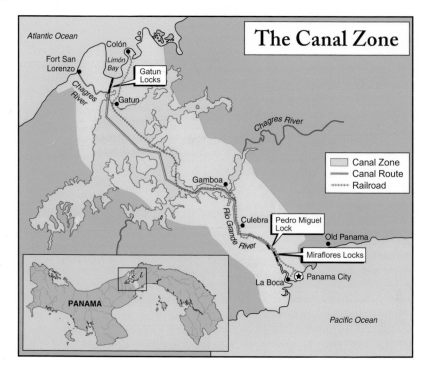

amounts of spoil would be to construct a new railroad system. The railroad built by the French years before was much too small and was also falling apart. Most of the engines did not even run. Stevens tore the old tracks down and had more than forty miles (sixty-four kilometers) of new tracks built. He brought in sixty large locomotives. Each locomotive pulled twenty to thirty flatcars. The railroads were always in use, hauling spoil to different parts of the project. The railroad was an essential part of the success of the canal. Without the railroad, it would have been impossible to move all of that spoil.

Digging the Culebra Cut

The most challenging job in the Canal Zone was digging the Culebra Cut. The cut was dug to a depth of

120 feet (36.5 meters). Much of the earth was solid rock and shale.

Landslides were a huge problem. There were two different types of slides. The first kind happened during the rainy season. The heavy rains loosened the mud along the sides of the canal, causing it to slide downward. Days, even weeks of work could be destroyed in a single slide. The most damaging of these slides occurred at Cucaracha. In October 1907 after days of heavy rain, tons of rocks and dirt tumbled into the cut. The problems did not end when the rain

Workers lay railroad tracks used to haul earth and rock during the digging of the Culebra Cut.

stopped. The landslides in the dry season were even more destructive.

The dry season slides took the canal planners and workers completely by surprise. Until they started digging, the canal planners did not know that the rocks at the top of the cut were heavier than those located near the bottom. As the workers dug the steep-sided cut, the heavier rocks along the upper edges of the cut could not be supported by the weaker rocks beneath them. Exposure to air and water further weakened these underlying rocks. Cracks formed in the sides of

Railcars loaded with rock sit stranded in the Culebra Cut during a flood in December 1906.

the cut and when the weight became too much, massive amounts of dirt and rocks came crashing down.

These slides were dangerous and frustrating. They could not be stopped. The only way to minimize them was to dig the canal much wider than was originally planned so that the steep sides sloped more gently. This required the workers to remove twice as much earth. In the end, the top edges of the canal were nearly a third of a mile (half a kilometer) apart.

All that extra work was made a little easier by new designs of steam shovels. Bucyrus steam shovels were huge. They were three times as big as the ones the French had used. Each one weighed ninety-five tons and could move eight tons of spoil with a single scoop. It took ten men to operate each of these giant machines. Working together, these ten men could remove an enormous amount of spoil. It took only eight minutes for one steam shovel to fill an entire flatcar.

Damming the Chagres River

Some of the spoil from the cut was used to dam the Chagres River. The dam was built at a point where the river flowed through a narrow valley. The valley was only a mile and a half (2.4 kilometers) wide and was bordered by rocky hills. The earthen dam was built across the valley.

The dam was constructed by building two parallel rock walls a quarter mile (402 meters) apart. A mixture of sand, clay, and mud was pumped between the walls. As this fill material dried, it became hard. Spoil from

Workers build Gatun Dam across the Chagres River. When completed, the dam created Gatun Lake.

the Culebra Cut was then dumped on top of the hardened fill. This resulted in an extremely durable wall that was as hard as cement. As the dam grew, the Chagres River began to form a lake. Water covered hundreds of acres of land that had once been forest. The higher hills became islands. When it was complete, Gatun Lake spread over 164 square miles (425 square kilometers). It became the largest man-made lake in the world at that time.

Building the Locks

Like the cut and the dam, building the locks was a huge job. Just digging out the space for the locks took two years. Once the site was ready it took more than four years to build all six sets of locks. The walls of the locks were constructed in thirty-six-foot-long (eleven meter) sections using giant steel forms or molds. Cranes were used to erect the forms, which were then filled with concrete to create the walls.

Large numbers of cranes were needed to place the huge steel forms used to construct the Upper Gatun Lock.

Two workers pose in front of the enormous concrete-filled steel walls of a lock in 1913.

The concrete was made from a mixture of sand, gravel, and cement. The sand and gravel were quarried in Panama, but the cement had to be shipped from the United States. Four and half million barrels of Portland cement went into the locks. Like nearly everything in the Zone, the materials needed for the locks were brought to the construction site by railroad.

The concrete was made at the construction site. The materials were mixed with water in giant concrete mixers, which were located inside the locks. The mixed concrete was loaded into huge buckets and then attached to hooks and lifted into the air on a cable. These six-ton buckets of concrete traveled by cable to the steel forms.

Then the concrete was dumped into the forms, where it was spread by workers. When the concrete was dry, the steel forms were removed and carried to the next section of the wall by giant cranes. Cranes were also used to carry the mixed concrete to the forms in places where it was not practical to build a cable system.

Building the Gates

The steel gates at the ends of the locks were made with special care. Each one had to withstand millions of pounds of water. The gates were 7 feet (2 meters) thick and their hinges weighed over 14 tons (12.7 metric tons) each. The gates were constructed by riveting steel plates to steel **girders**. Riveting was one of the most dangerous jobs in the Zone. Riveters worked on small platforms, which often dangled several stories from the ground. The rivets were red-hot and had to be loaded into a rivet gun before they could be used. Over 6 million rivets were used on the locks. Every one of these rivets was inspected to be sure it would hold.

It took over eleven years and one hundred thousand workers to build the canal. It cost $370 billion. At the time, this was by far the most expensive construction project the United States had ever funded. Despite the many challenges, the morale of the workers for most of the construction period was high. They believed the work they did was important and felt proud to be a part of the canal project. When it was completed in 1914, the Panama Canal became one of the most important waterways in the world.

CHAPTER FOUR

The Panama Canal Today

Despite the enormous scope of the job and the many challenges that had to be overcome, the Panama Canal was finished six months ahead of schedule and under budget. Most of the credit for this amazing achievement was given to Colonel George Washington Goethals. Goethals took over as chief engineer when Stevens resigned in 1907. Like Stevens, he was an excellent manager and well liked by the canal workers. He was highly praised for the completion of the canal and served as the first governor of the Canal Zone.

The Canal Completed

Construction on the canal was completed near the end of 1913, but the oceans were still not connected. A temporary dam had been built to hold back the Chagres River during construction. At 2:00 P.M. on October 13, U.S. president Woodrow Wilson pressed a button in the White House in Washington, D.C. A telegraph signal was sent across thousands of miles to Panama. At 2:01 P.M. the temporary dam was blown to pieces and water came rushing into the Culebra Cut. Thousands of onlookers cheered as the cut began to fill with water. It took several more months for the entire cut to fill.

The *Alexandre La Valley* makes a trial run through the Panama Canal in 1914 to test the lock system.

On January 7, 1914, an old crane boat called the *Alexandre La Valley* was sent through the canal as a test. The locks worked perfectly and the journey was a smooth one. This was the first boat to navigate the entire canal.

A grand celebration had been planned for the official opening of the canal, which was scheduled for August 15, 1914. One hundred decorated U.S. warships were to make the journey through the canal in an event that would be attended by thousands and make front-page headlines around the world. But the celebration never happened. World War I started just a few days earlier, and the eyes of the world were on Europe, not Panama. Instead of a grand procession of U.S. naval ships, an old cement boat called the SS *Ancon* became the first ship to make the voyage through the canal once it was officially open for business.

The Canal Today

Since the *Ancon* made that first voyage, nearly nine hundred thousand ships from countries throughout the world have passed through the canal. When the canal first opened it was used mostly by ships sailing from one coast of the United States to the other. Using the canal saved shipping companies time and money. Passenger ships also used the canal. Many people preferred to travel on a comfortable ship rather than take a long train or car trip across the country. But as time passed, companies began to ship cargo overland

A tugboat escorts a large cargo ship through one of the canal locks in 1996.

using railroads, trucks, and pipelines. Air travel became common and fewer people traveled by ship.

Although there are now other ways to ship cargo, the Panama Canal is still an important link in world trade. Between thirteen and fourteen thousand ships travel the canal each year carrying 5 percent of the world's trade. Over fifty countries from around the world use the canal. The busiest trade routes to pass through the canal are from the East Coast of the United States to Asia and the Middle East. If the canal had not been built, these ships would have to sail all the

A ship and sailboat wait until the water level in a lock rises enough to allow them to continue.

way around South America to reach their destinations. The canal operates twenty-four hours a day every day of the year and employs nine thousand workers.

The canal is self-supporting. This means that the cost of running the canal is paid for by the **tolls** charged to ships that cross through the canal. In an average day about thirty-two ships pass through. Tolls are determined by the size of the ship and the amount of cargo it is carrying. An average-size cargo ship would pay about $43,000 to use the canal. The tolls may seem high, but they are actually a bargain when compared with the cost of taking a ship all the way around South America.

Changes for the Canal

Many improvements have been made on the canal since its construction. Landslides have been a constant problem, especially at the Culebra Cut. (Culebra Cut is now called Gaillard Cut in honor of General David Gaillard who was in charge of construction at the cut.) Work has been done on the hills surrounding

A cargo ship passes through the canal, one of several thousand ships that make use of the waterway every year.

In 1961 this steel bridge was built across the canal's western entrance to connect the east and west sides of Panama.

the cut to minimize the slides, but there seems to be no way to stop them. In fact, the work often causes more slides to occur. During the 1960s three large slides occurred during excavation to widen the cut. Another large slide occurred in 1974 when tons of dirt and rocks came tumbling into the cut from Gold Hill, which borders the canal. These slides have stopped traffic in the canal for weeks at a time.

Other improvements have helped to modernize the canal. Another much smaller dam was built to control the flow of water into Gatun Lake. Parts of the Gaillard Cut have been widened to accommodate larger ships. Lights were installed in 1966 so that the canal can run twenty-four hours a day. Computers now run the traffic control system. In addition, in 1962 a large steel bridge was built across the western entrance to the canal to connect the east side of Panama to the west.

Panama's Canal

Although the Americans built the canal, it is run and owned by the country of Panama now. On September 12, 1977, U.S. president Jimmy Carter signed a **treaty** with the Panamanian chief of government. The treaty outlined a thirty-year period of change for the canal. The treaty required the United States to return most of the land and all of the buildings, utilities, and railroads in the Zone to Panama. In addition, Panama began to take responsibility for the huge task of running the canal. This treaty expired at noon on

December 31, 1999. On that day the canal was returned to Panama.

After nearly a century of use the canal is still one of the most important waterways in the world. It is also a wonderful place to visit. Thousands of people come to Panama every year to learn more about the canal at the recently constructed Miraflores Visitor Center and to watch as ships are raised and lowered in the locks.

Glossary

floodplain: An area of low-lying land through which a river flows. The land is covered with sediment as a result of frequent flooding.

girder: A long, thick piece of steel used to support a large structure.

isthmus: A narrow stretch of land that connects two larger areas of land.

lock: An enclosure of water, with gates at either end, where the level of water can be raised or lowered to allow ships to move from one level to another through a canal.

malaria: An infectious disease transmitted by mosquitoes. Common in hot countries, the disease causes recurring chills and fever.

segregation: Separating ethnic, racial, or gender groups by the use of separate schools, transportation, housing, and other facilities. Typically facilities for the minority group are inferior to that of the majority.

spoil: Refuse material, usually consisting of dirt, rocks, and sand removed from an excavation.

toll: A fee charged for a privilege such as crossing a bridge or using a road.

treaty: A formal contract or agreement negotiated between countries.

yellow fever: An infectious, often fatal disease spread by mosquitoes and common in hot countries. Symptoms include high fever, hemorrhaging, vomiting blood, liver damage, and jaundice.

For Further Reading

Books

Ann Graham Gaines, *The Panama Canal*. Berkeley Heights, NJ: Enslow, 1999. This informative book details the history of the canal from the first explorers through the transition. It also includes a time line of events.

Elizabeth Mann, *The Panama Canal*. New York: Mikaya, 1998. This beautifully illustrated book tells the story of how the canal was constructed. There is a foldout page depicting the locks as well as a collection of facts about the canal.

Patricia Maloney Markun, *It's Panama's Canal!* North Haven, CT: Linnet, 1999. This book offers a great deal of information about the canal with an emphasis on the transition period.

Carl R. Oliver, *Panama's Canal*. New York: Franklin Watts, 1990. This book about the history of the canal is filled with photographs taken during construction as well as quotes from people who worked on the canal.

Charles J. Shields, *Panama*. Philadelphia, PA: Mason Crest, 2003. This colorful book offers a wealth of information about the country of Panama. It includes cultural information as well as chapters about how the canal has affected Panama. Also included are a time line, glossary, and quick facts sections.

Web Sites

Ared Networks (www.ared.com/kora/java/pcc/javaani. html). This site features a fifty-five-second animation showing how a ship makes the voyage across the canal. There are also photos and information about the canal.

CZ Brats (www.czbrats.com/cz_brats.htm). This amazing Web site was created for kids by Americans who live in the Canal Zone. It features a wealth of information about the canal as well as two live webcams and many photographs. There are also sections about what it is like to live in the Canal Zone.

The Panama Canal Authority (www.pancanal.com/ eng/index.html). This is the official Web site of the Panama Canal. It features information about how the canal operates today. There are also many photographs of the canal and information about its history.

Index

Alexandre La Valley (crane boat), 34

bridge, 39

Carter, Jimmy, 39
Chagres River, 14, 23, 27–28
computers, 39
concrete, 30–31
Continental Divide, 6
costs
    deaths, 10, 20
    money, 31
    time, 32
cranes, 29, 31
Cucaracha, 25
Culebra Cut
    landslides at, 37, 39
    making, 23, 24–28

deaths
    during American construction, 20
    during French construction, 10
diseases, 9–10, 20–22
dry season landslides, 26–27

floodplain, 13–14
food, 15, 17

France, 8–10

Gaillard Cut, 37, 39
Gatun Lake
    created, 23, 24–28
    water flow into, 39
Goethals, George Washington, 32
Gorgas, William, 20–22
Great Horn, 11

Havana (Cuba), 20
height (above sea level), 6
high elevation plan, 12–14
hospitals, 20

insects, 15

landslides
    during construction, 9, 25–27
    at Culebra Cut, 37, 39
length, 6
Lesseps, Ferdinand-Marie de, 8–10
living conditions, 15, 17–19
location, 10
locks, 12–13, 29–31

machinery
    cranes, 29, 31

problems, 9
steam shovels, 27
malaria, 10, 20–22
materials
    for locks, 29, 30–31
    for Chagres River dam,
        27–28
Miraflores Visitor Center, 40
mosquitoes, 15, 20–22
mudslides, 9, 25

Panama Canal
    completed, 32–34
    currently, 35–37, 39–40
    improvements, 37, 39
    passage through, 34–35

railroad system, 24
rainy season, 8
    flooding during, 14
    mudslides during, 9, 25
Roosevelt, Theodore, 11, 20
route, 23, 24–28

seasons, 8
segregation, 18–19
South America, trip around,

10–11
spoil, 23
SS *Ancon* (ship), 34
steam shovels, 27
Stevens, John
    background of, 23
    high elevation plan and,
        14
    living conditions for
        American workers and,
        17–18
    railroad built by, 24
Suez Canal, 8

temperatures, 8
tolls, 36–37

wet season. *See* rainy season
Wilson, Woodrow, 32
workers
    conditions for nonwhite,
        18–20
    conditions for white, 15,
        17–18, 19
    number of, 31

yellow fever, 10, 20–22

Picture Credits

Cover image: © Bettmann/CORBIS

© Paul Almasy/CORBIS, 7, 38

© Morton Beebe/CORBIS, 36

© Bettmann/CORBIS, 9 (inset), 28

© CORBIS, 9, 26

© Keith Dannemiller/CORBIS Saba, 37

© Danny Lehman/CORBIS, 35

Library of Congress, 18 (inset), 19, 21 (inset), 25, 29, 30

National Archives, 18, 33

© National Archives/CORBIS, 21

© Underwood & Underwood/CORBIS, 16

About the Author

Rachel Lynette has written several books for KidHaven Press as well as dozens of articles on children and family life. She has taught children of all ages and is currently working as a technology teacher in Seattle, Washington. She lives in the Songaia Cohousing Community with her husband Scott, her two children David and Lucy, a cat named Cookie, and two playful rats. When she is not teaching or writing, she enjoys spending time with her family and friends, traveling, reading, drawing, and rollerblading.